Study Guide

for use with

The Micro Economy Today

Ninth Edition

Bradley R. Schiller
American University

Prepared by
Linda Wilson
University of Texas – Arlington

Kevin Klein
Illinois College

McGraw-Hill Irwin

Boston Burr Ridge, IL Dubuque, IA Madison, WI New York San Francisco St. Louis
Bangkok Bogotá Caracas Kuala Lumpur Lisbon London Madrid Mexico City
Milan Montreal New Delhi Santiago Seoul Singapore Sydney Taipei Toronto

McGraw-Hill Irwin

Study Guide for use with
THE MICRO ECONOMY TODAY
Bradley R. Schiller

Published by McGraw-Hill/Irwin, an imprint of The McGraw-Hill Companies, Inc., 1221 Avenue of the Americas, New York, NY 10020.

4 5 6 7 8 9 0 QPD/QPD 0 9 8 7 6 5 4 3

ISBN 0-07-247203-0

www.mhhe.com

The McGraw-Hill Companies

STUDY GUIDE

Table of Contents

STUDY GUIDE

Preface

This study guide is written to accompany *The Micro Economy Today*, 9th edition, by Bradley R. Schiller. The overall focus of the Study Guide is to reinforce the economic principles and concepts presented in the textbook. Each section of each chapter has a particular objective.

The *Quick Review* and *Learning Objectives* sections provide brief summaries of the basic contents of the corresponding text chapters.

The *Using Key Terms* section allows students to practice using the words defined in each chapter in a crossword puzzle format.

The *True or False* and *Multiple Choice* sections help students apply economic principles in a familiar problem-solving setting. This will help greatly in the preparation for exams.

The *Problems and Applications* section lets students discover economic principles for themselves. Students not only learn the techniques that economists use, but they also discover the basis for the economic concepts they have learned.

Semester after semester, students have difficulty with the same concepts and make the same mistakes. The section called *Common Errors* addresses some of these problems, and provides an explanation using appropriate economic principles.

STUDY GUIDE

Online Learning Center

The Online Learning Center is an exciting feature of the *The Micro Economy Today*'s 9th edition. The Student Center provides a number of ways to supplement your study efforts including Chapter Summaries, Key Terms, Multiple Choice Quizzes, Web-Based Projects, News Flashes, *New York Times* articles, DiscoverEcon, and PowerPoint slides.

A summary of each feature is provided below along with instructions on how to use it.

Chapter Summary – This is a simple summary of the material covered in the text for each chapter. To access this feature, choose the chapter number you want to work on and then click on the *Chapter Summary* link in the left-hand column.

Key Terms – This section lists the chapter's key terms, and provides a definition for each term. To access this feature, choose the chapter number you want to work on and then click on the *Key Terms* link.

Multiple Choice Quiz – This is a 15 question multiple choice quiz that tests how well you learned the concepts covered in the chapter. After answering the questions, you can submit the quiz for grading and send the results of the quiz to your professor by e-mail. To access this feature, choose the chapter number you want to work on and then click on the *Multiple Choice Quiz* link in the left-hand column. After answering the quiz questions, click the "Submit Answers" button to have the quiz automatically graded.

Web-based Activities – There are two interactive activities provided for each chapter. These activities allow you to explore each chapter's content through a series of questions that are tied to specific World Wide Web links. To access this feature, choose the chapter number you want to work on and then click on the *Web-based Activities* link.

Web-based Projects – These projects are designed to help you use the World Wide Web to explore economic questions. In these projects, you are asked a series of questions relevant to the content you are exploring in class. To find the answers, you must explore specific content located on the World Wide Web by following the links provided. These projects also have a collaborative feature that may be assigned by your professor. With this feature you collaborate with other students in your class to develop answers to specific questions together. To access this feature, simply click on the *Web-based projects* link and choose the topic relevant to the material being covered in class or the material assigned by your professor.

NewsFlashes – As up-to-date as *The Economy Today* is, it can't foretell the future. As the future becomes the present, however, Brad Schiller writes 2 page *News Flashes* describing major economic events in the news and relating them to specific text references. To access this feature, simply click on the *NewsFlashes* link and choose the topic relevant to the material being covered in class or the *NewsFlash* assigned by your professor.

***New York Times* news articles** – This section contains news articles from the New York Times that are relevant to the course. To access this feature, simply click on the *New York Times News* link and choose the chapter number you want to work on.

DiscoverEcon – Software specifically designed to supplement Brad Schiller's *The Economy Today,* 9e was developed by Gerald Nelson at the University of Illinois, Urbana-Champaign. This software is designed to be an interactive textbook that parallels the paper textbook. DiscoverEcon is available with the textbook either on the web or on CD-ROM. When you purchased your new textbook, you should have found either an online code card or a CD folder inside the package. If you received a code card, follow the instructions on the back of the code card to access the online version of DiscoverEcon and enter your unique code. If you received a CD folder, follow the instructions for installation in the User's Manual inside the folder.

PowerPoints – Developed using Microsoft PowerPoint software, these slides are a great step-by-step review of the key points and graphs in each of the book's 36 chapters. To access this feature, choose the chapter number you want to work on and then click on the *PowerPoints* link in the left-hand column. Click on the chapter file that appears on the screen. It will take a few seconds for your computer to launch PowerPoint, but once you see the first slide, you can begin using the arrow keys to move from slide to slide within the chapter.

If you need additional help, you can click on Help Center to scroll through a list of help topics, or send your question to the webmaster via e-mail by selecting the Feedback option.

PART 1 Basic Concepts

CHAPTER 1

Economics: The Core Issues

Quick Review

- Resources (land, labor, capital, and entrepreneurship) are considered scarce, even when they seem abundant, because there are not enough resources to satisfy all of society's wants.

- Because resources are limited, society must make choices about what to produce. Choosing to produce one thing means giving up the opportunity to produce something else. Economists refer to the best forgone alternative as opportunity cost.

- Economists illustrate these choices by drawing a production-possibilities curve. This curve shows the combinations of goods and services a society could produce if it were operating efficiently and all of its resources were fully employed.

- The production-possibilities curve appears bowed out from the origin because of the law of increasing opportunity costs, which occurs because resources are not equally well suited to the production of all goods.

- If society uses its resources inefficiently, it will produce inside the production-possibilities curve. Additional resources and technological advances result in an outward shift of the production-possibilities curve. This is known as economic growth.

- Every society confronts the problem of scarcity and must somehow answer these basic questions: WHAT is to be produced?
HOW should it be produced?
FOR WHOM should the output be produced?

- In the United States, our choices are largely accomplished through the market mechanism. The "invisible hand" of the market mechanism coordinates the production and consumption decisions of millions of individuals and directly affects the allocation of the economy's resources. In some economies the market mechanism has not been allowed to work. Planned (or command) economies, like that of the old Soviet Union, are good examples of this.

- When the market mechanism fails to provide goods and services efficiently and equitably – a situation called "market failure" – the public sector must provide assistance. However, it is possible that government intervention will make the situation even worse, which is referred to as "government failure."

- It is useful to break economics into two categories: microeconomics and macroeconomics. Microeconomics focuses on a specific individual, firm, industry, or government agency; macroeconomics focuses on the entire economy.

Learning Objectives

After reading Chapter 1 and doing the following exercises, you should:

1. Understand the debate concerning market allocation vs. government allocation of resources.
2. Understand that economics is the study of how to allocate society's scarce resources – land, labor, capital, and entrepreneurship.
3. Know that scarcity occurs because resources are not sufficient to satisfy all of society's wants.
4. Be able to define and illustrate opportunity costs using a production-possibilities curve.
5. Understand the law of increasing opportunity costs.
6. Be able to demonstrate efficiency, growth, unemployment, and underemployment using a production-possibilities curve.
7. Know why every economy must answer the same basic questions – WHAT, HOW, FOR WHOM.
8. Be able to distinguish macroeconomic issues from microeconomic issues.
9. Be able to describe how the market mechanism seeks to allocate society's resources to their most valued use.
10. Be aware that there is serious debate and controversy over how the economy works.
11. Be able to discuss the tradeoffs inherent in the "peace dividend."
12. Be able to describe the mixed economy and distinguish market failure from government failure.

Using Key Terms

Fill in the puzzle on the opposite page with the appropriate terms from the list of Key Terms at the end of the chapter in the text.

Across

1. The reason there is no such thing as a "free lunch."
3. Occurs when government intervention fails to improve economic outcomes.
6. Represented by land, labor, capital, and entrepreneurship.
7. Economic study concerned with the behavior of individuals, firms, and government agencies.
11. The study of how best to allocate society's scarce resources.
14. Referred to as the "invisible hand" by Adam Smith.
16. Latin term meaning "other things remaining equal."
17. Economic policy supported by Adam Smith.

Down

2. The curve represented in Figure 1.1 in the text.
4. The assembling of resources to produce new or better products.
5. The study of the economy as a whole.
8. The use of both market signals and government directives to select the mix of output.
9. Illustrated in Figure 1.5 in the text by the outward shift of the production-possibilities curve.
10. Occurs when the market mechanism results in the wrong mix of output.
12. Final goods used to produce other goods.
13. The idea that there are not enough resources available to satisfy all desires.
15. Every point on the production-possibilities curve represents a situation of ___________.

Puzzle 1.1

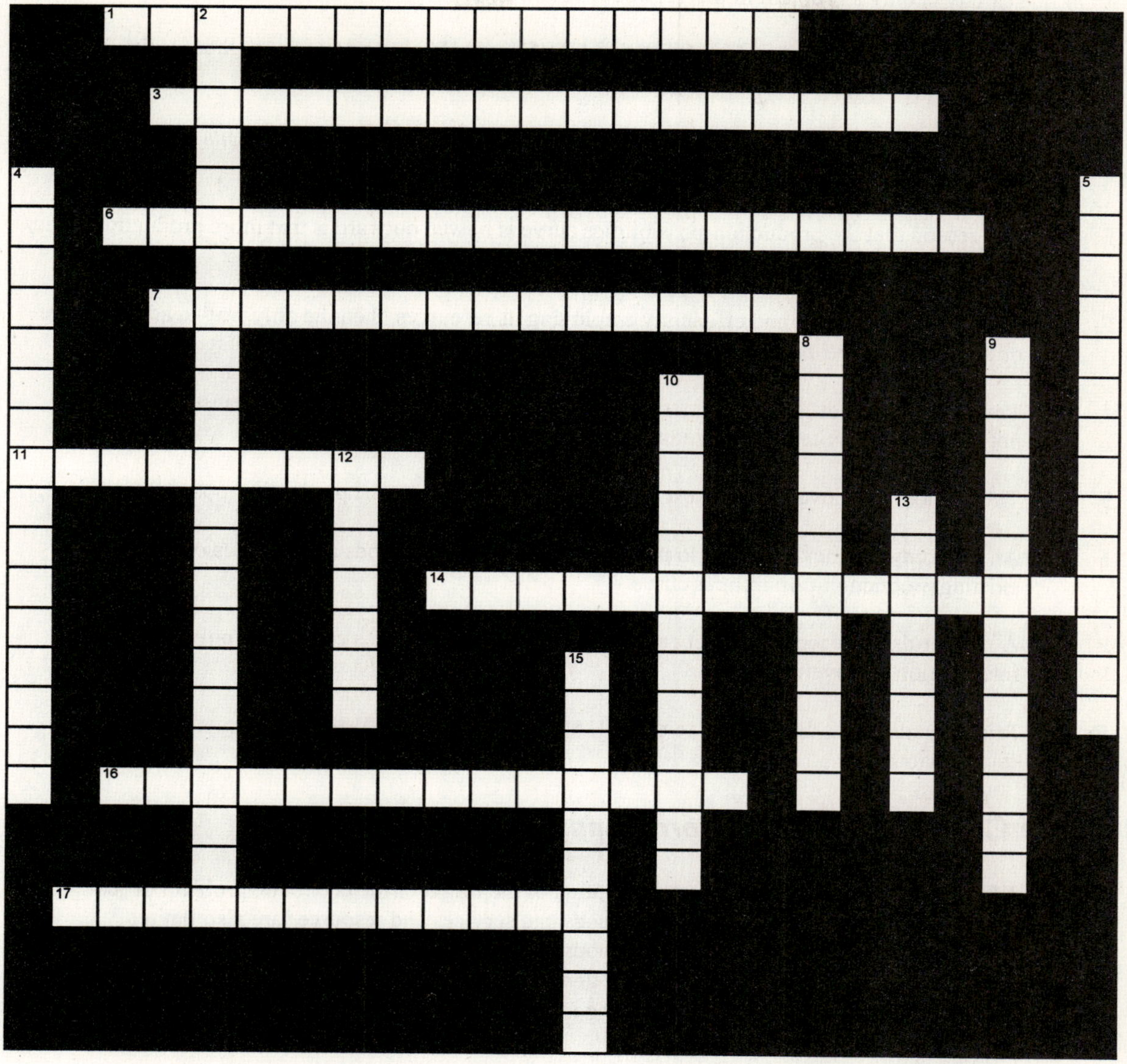

True or False: *Circle your choice and explain why any false statements are incorrect.*

T F 1. Scarcity is only a problem in the very poor countries of the world.

T F 2. Students do not pay tuition in public school, so from society's point of view, there is no opportunity cost involved in their education.

T F 3. A production-possibilities curve can be drawn only if a scarce resource prevents unlimited production of a product.

T F 4. One reason that the production-possibilities curve is bowed outward is that more production means the economy is less efficient in producing output.

T F 5. If the economy is fully and efficiently employing its resources, then the only way to acquire more of one good, *ceteris paribus*, is to accept less of something else.

T F 6. The opportunity cost of a good increases as more of the good is produced because resources are not equally well-suited to the production of all goods.

T F 7. The economy achieves the greatest efficiency when it is inside the production-possibilities curve.

T F 8. An economy will never be able to produce a combination of goods and services outside of its existing production-possibilities curve.

T F 9. A market-driven economy is not capable of solving the problems created by pollution without intervention by government.

T F 10. Price signals direct the answers to the WHAT, HOW, and FOR WHOM decisions in a laissez-faire economy.

Multiple Choice: *Select the correct answer.*

_____ 1. Which of the following is the best description of the origin of the economic problem of scarcity?
(a) Humans have limited wants for goods and services and resources are also limited.
(b) Humans have limited wants for goods and services and resources are unlimited.
(c) Humans have unlimited wants for goods and services but resources are limited.
(d) Humans have unlimited wants for goods and services and resources are also unlimited.

_____ 2. Which of the following best describes the term "resource allocation"?
(a) Which goods and services society will produce with available factors of production.
(b) How society spends the income of individuals based on resource availability.
(c) How society purchases resources, given its macroeconomic goals.
(d) How individual market participants decide what to produce given fixed resource constraints.

_____ 3. A consequence of the economic problem of scarcity is that:
(a) Choices have to be made about how resources are used.
(b) There is never too much of any good or service produced.
(c) The production of goods and services has to be controlled by the government.
(d) The production-possibilities curve is bowed outward.

_____ 4. Which of the following is *not* a factor of production?
(a) A college professor.
(b) A chalkboard used in an economics classroom.
(c) The $10 million donated to the college by wealthy alumni.
(d) The land on which a college is located.

_____ 5. Centrally planned economies are most likely to underestimate the value of:
(a) Land.
(b) Labor.
(c) Capital.
(d) Entrepreneurship.

_____ 6. Which of the following describes how resources are typically allocated in the U.S. economy?
(a) By tradition.
(b) By democratic vote.
(c) By markets.
(d) By government.

_____ 7. I plan on going to a $5 movie this evening instead of studying for an exam. The total opportunity cost of the movie:
(a) Depends on how I score on the exam.
(b) Is $5.
(c) Is what I could have purchased with the $5 plus the study time I forgo.
(d) Is the forgone studying I could have done in the same time.

_____ 8. The opportunity cost of installing a traffic light at a dangerous intersection is:
(a) Negative, since it will reduce accidents.
(b) The best possible alternative bundle of other goods or services that must be forgone in order to build and install the traffic light.
(c) The time lost by drivers who approach the intersection when the light is red.
(d) The cost of the stoplight plus the cost savings from a reduction in the number of accidents.

_____ 9. Which of the following events would cause the production-possibilities curve to shift inward?
(a) Immigration into a country increases.
(b) New factories are built.
(c) A technological breakthrough occurs.
(d) A terrorist attack destroys roads, bridges, and factories.

_____ 10. Which of the following events would cause the production-possibilities curve to shift outward?
(a) The economy's capital stock increases.
(b) A new, strong plastic is developed for use in building houses.
(c) More women enter the labor force.
(d) All of the above.

_____ 11. The slope of the production-possibilities curve provides information about:
(a) The growth of the economy.
(b) Technological change in the economy.
(c) Opportunity costs in the economy.
(d) All of the above.

_____ 12. The law of increasing opportunity cost explains:
(a) How everything becomes more expensive as the economy grows.
(b) The shape of the production-possibilities curve.
(c) Inflation.
(d) All of the above.

_____ 13. When an economy is producing efficiently it is:
- (a) Producing a combination of goods and services outside the production-possibilities curve.
- (b) Getting the most goods and services from the available resources.
- (c) Experiencing decreasing opportunity costs.
- (d) All of the above are correct.

_____ 14. In a market economy, the answer to the WHAT to produce question is determined by:
- (a) Direct negotiations between consumers and producers.
- (b) Producer profits and sales.
- (c) Government directives.
- (d) A democratic vote of all producers.

_____ 15. In a market economy, the answer to the HOW to produce question is determined by:
- (a) Government planners.
- (b) The production possibilities curve.
- (c) The least-cost method of production.
- (d) The method of production that uses the least amount of labor.

_____ 16. The trend toward greater reliance on the market mechanism by former communist societies is evidence of:
- (a) Government failure.
- (b) Market failure.
- (c) The failure of a mixed economy.
- (d) *Ceteris paribus.*

_____ 17. Which of the following are major macroeconomic goals of the economy?
- (a) Full employment.
- (b) Control of inflation.
- (c) Economic growth.
- (d) All of the above.

_____ 18. Microeconomics focuses on the performance of:
- (a) Individual consumers, firms and government agencies.
- (b) Firms only.
- (c) Government agencies only.
- (d) The economy as a whole.

_____ 19. Reread the *In the News* article "Bush Seeking Defense Increase." The article illustrates that increased military spending causes:
- (a) The production-possibilities curve to shift outward, *ceteris paribus.*
- (b) The production-possibilities curve to shift inward, *ceteris paribus.*
- (c) The production-possibilities curve to bow outward from the origin, *ceteris paribus.*
- (d) Society to give up the production of civilian goods, *ceteris paribus.*

_____ 20. Reread the *World View* article "North Korea Says It Is Running Out of Food." Implicitly, the article is suggesting that the maintenance of an army results in:
- (a) An opportunity cost in terms of consumer goods.
- (b) An opportunity cost in terms of investment goods only.
- (c) No opportunity cost because the army keeps the country safe.
- (d) No opportunity cost because the soldiers are being paid.

[CHAPTER 1 APPENDIX QUESTIONS]

_____ 21. The slope of a curve at any point is given by the formula:
(a) The change in y coordinates between two points divided by the change in their x coordinates.
(b) The change in x coordinates between two points divided by the change in their y coordinates.
(c) The percentage change in y coordinates between two points divided by the percentage change in their x coordinates.
(d) The percentage change in x coordinates between two points divided by the percentage change in their y coordinates.

_____ 22. When the relationship between two variables changes:
(a) There is movement from one point on a linear curve to another point on the same curve.
(b) The entire curve shifts.
(c) The labels on the axes must be changed.
(d) The curve becomes linear.

_____ 23. A linear curve can be distinguished by:
(a) The continuous change in its slope.
(b) The same slope throughout the curve.
(c) The changing relationship between the two variables.
(d) A shift in the curve.

Problems and Applications

Exercise 1

Suppose you have only 20 hours per week to allocate to study or leisure. The following table indicates the tradeoff between leisure time (not studying) and the grade-point average achieved as a result of studying.

Table 1.1

	(a)	*(b)*	*(c)*	*(d)*	*(e)*
Leisure time (hours / week)	20	18	14.5	10	0
Grade-point average	0	1.0	2.0	3.0	4.0

1. In Figure 1.1, draw the production-possibilities curve that represents the possible combinations from Table 1.1.

Figure 1.1

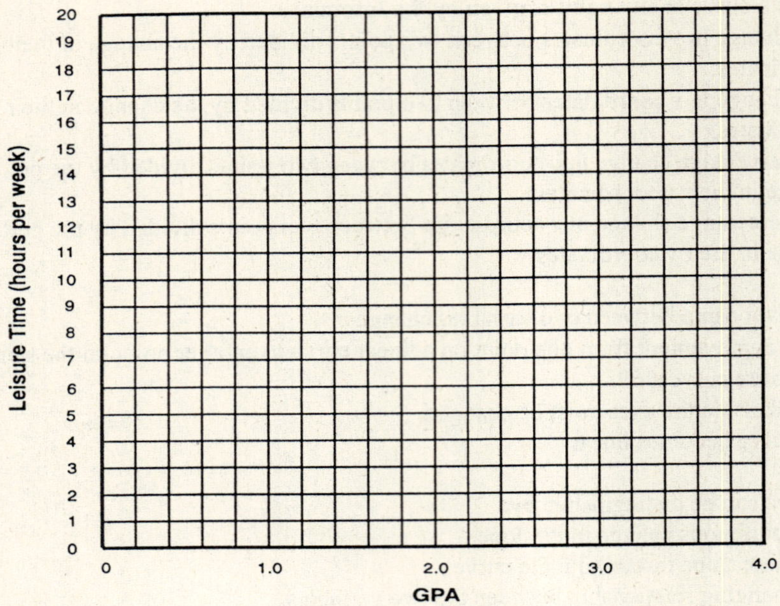

2. Using the information above, what is the opportunity cost of raising your grade-point average from 2.0 to 3.0? ____________________

3. What is the opportunity cost of raising your grade-point average from 3.0 to 4.0?
____

4. Why does the opportunity cost of improving your grade-point average increase?
____

Exercise 2

This exercise is similar to the problem at the end of Chapter 1 in the text. It provides practice in drawing and interpreting a production-possibilities curve and demonstrating shifts of such a curve.

1. A production-possibilities schedule showing the production alternatives between corn and lumber is presented in Table 1.2. Plot combination *A* in Figure 1.2 and label it. Do the same for combination *B*. In going from combination *A* to combination *B*, the economy has sacrificed _____ billion board feet of lumber production per year and has transferred the land to production of _____ billion bushels of corn per year. The opportunity cost of corn in terms of lumber is _____ board feet per bushel.

Table 1.2

Combination	*Quantity of corn (billions of bushels per year)*	*Quantity of lumber (billions of board feet per year)*
A	0	50
B	1	48
C	2	44
D	3	38
E	4	30
F	5	20
G	6	0

2. In answering Question 1 you determined the opportunity cost of corn when the economy is initially producing only lumber (combination *A*). Using the information in Table 1.2, plot the rest of the production-possibilities combinations in Figure 1.2 and label each of the points with the appropriate letter. Connect the points to form the production-possibilities curve.

Figure 1.2

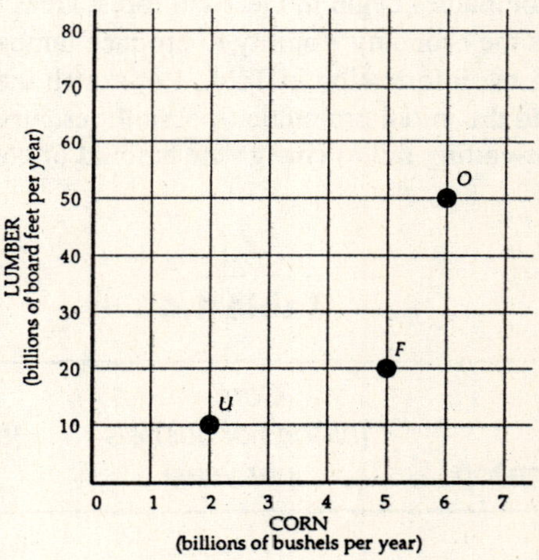

3. When Table 1.3 is completed, it should show the opportunity cost of corn at each possible combination of lumber and corn production in the economy. Opposite "1st billion bushels" insert the number of board feet per year of lumber sacrificed when the economy shifts from combination *A* to combination *B*. Complete the table for each of the remaining combinations.

Table 1.3

Corn production (billions of bushels per year)	*Opportunity cost of corn in terms of lumber (billions of board feet per year)*
1st billion bushels	______________
2nd billion bushels	______________
3rd billion bushels	______________
4th billion bushels	______________
5th billion bushels	______________
6th billion bushels	______________

4. In Table 1.3, as more corn is produced (as the economy moves from combination *A* toward combination *G*), the opportunity cost of corn (falls, rises, remains the same), which illustrates the law of ____.

5. Suppose that lumber companies begin to clear-cut forest areas instead of cutting them selectively. Clear-cutting improves the economy's ability to produce lumber but not corn. Table 1.4 describes such a situation. Using the information in Table 1.4, sketch the new production-possibilities curve in Figure 1.2 as you did the initial production-possibilities curve based on Table 1.3. For which combination does clear-cutting fail to change the amount of corn and lumber produced?

____

Table 1.4

Combination	*Corn (billions of bushels per year)*	*Lumber (billions of board feet per year)*
A'	0	75
B'	1	72
C'	2	66
D'	3	57
E'	4	45
F'	5	30
G'	6	0

6. After the introduction of clear-cutting most of the new production-possibilities curve is (outside, inside, the same as) the earlier curve. The opportunity cost of corn has (increased, decreased) as a result of clear-cutting.

7. Study your original production-possibilities curve in Figure 1.2 and decide which of the combinations shown (*U, F, O*) demonstrates each of the following. (*Hint:* Check the answers at the end of the chapter to make sure you have diagrammed the production-possibilities curve in Figure 1.2 correctly.)
   (a) Society is producing at its maximum potential. Combination ______.
   (b) Society has some unemployed or underemployed resources. Combination ______.
   (c) Society cannot produce this combination at this time. Combination ______.
   (d) Society might be able to produce this combination if new resources were found or technology improved, but it cannot produce this combination currently. Combination ______.
   (e) If society produces this combination, some of society's wants will go unsatisfied unnecessarily. Combination ______.

Exercise 3

This exercise requires the understanding of scarcity, opportunity cost and production possibilities. Answer the following questions based on the information on pages 6 through 11 in the text.

_______ 1. In the U.S., the share of total output devoted to military goods:
   (a) Has remained fairly constant since 1940.
   (b) Is currently about 25 percent.
   (c) Is fairly low and results in no opportunity cost.
   (d) Is less than the share of total output devoted to military goods in China.

_______ 2. According to Figure 1.1 in the text, as the mix of output moves from point *C* to point *D*:
   (a) There is an increase in the production of televisions.
   (b) There is no opportunity cost because point *D* represents the optimal mix of output.
   (c) More factors of production are available for both shoes and televisions.
   (d) All of the above are true.

_______ 3. According to the text, the North Korean army:
   (a) Is the largest in the world in terms of number of personnel.
   (b) Absorbs a large share of output because North Korea is such a large country.
   (c) Absorbs approximately 14 percent of the country's resources.
   (d) All of the above are true.

_______ 4. Which of the following is the opportunity cost of maintaining an army in North Korea?
   (a) There is no opportunity cost because North Korea needs a large army to protect its citizens.
   (b) There is no opportunity cost because North Korea is producing the optimal mix of output.
   (c) Only the money spent on military equipment and salaries.
   (d) The food and other consumer goods that must be given up.

_______ 5. According to the text, Russia made the decision to reduce the size of its army, which released "... over 300,000 workers to produce civilian goods and services." This represents:
   (a) A market economy at work.
   (b) The concept of opportunity cost.
   (c) The tradeoff between consumption and investment.
   (d) The tradeoff between food and civilian goods.

Exercise 4

This exercise provides practice in the use of graphs.

Use Figure 1.3 below to answer the following questions.

Figure 1.3

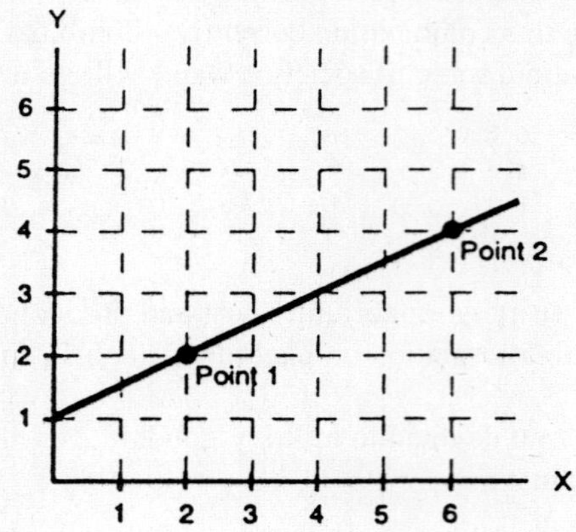

The slope of a line is the rate of change between two points or the vertical change divided by the horizontal change.

1. The vertical distance between the two points equals ________ .

2. The horizontal distance between the two points equals ________ .

3. The slope of the line equals ________ .

4. The slope of the line is (positive, negative) because as one variable increases the other variable (increases, decreases).

5. The line has the same slope at every point implying a (constant, changing) relationship between the two variables.

6. When the slope of a line is the same at every point, the curve is (linear, nonlinear).

Common Errors

The first statement in each "common error" below is incorrect. Each incorrect statement is followed by a corrected version and an explanation.

1. Words mean the same thing in economics that they do in our everyday conversation. WRONG!

   Words used in everyday conversation *very often* have different meanings when they are used in economics. RIGHT!

   You'll have to be very careful here. Words are used with precision in economics. You'll have difficulty if you confuse their everyday meanings with their economic meanings. For example, the term "capital" in economics means simply "man-made instruments of production." In everyday usage it may mean money, machines, a loan, or even the British response to the question "How are you feeling?"

2. Economic models are abstractions from the real world and are therefore useless in predicting and explaining economic behavior. WRONG!

   Economic models are abstractions from the real world and *as a result* are useful in predicting and explaining economic behavior. RIGHT!

   You have to be willing to deal with abstractions if you want to get anything accomplished in economics. By using economic models based on specific assumptions, we can make reasonable judgments about what's going on around us. We try not to disregard any useful information. However, to try to include everything (such as what cereal we like for breakfast) would be fruitless. For example, the production-possibilities frontier is an abstraction. No economist would argue that it is an economy! But it certainly is useful in focusing on public-policy choices, such as the choice between guns and butter.

3. Because economics is a "science," all economists should come up with the same answer to any given question. WRONG!

   Economics is a science, but there is often room for disagreement in trying to answer a given question. RIGHT!

   Economics is a social science, and the entire society and economy represent the economist's laboratory. Economists cannot run the kind of experiments that are done by physical scientists. As a result, two economists may attack a given problem or question in different ways using different models. They may come up with different answers, but since there is no answer book, you cannot say which is right. The solution is, then, to do more testing, refine our models, compare results, and so on. By the way, the recent space probes have given physicists cause to reevaluate much of their theory concerning the solar system, and there is much controversy concerning what the new evidence means. But physics is still a science, as is economics!

4. Increasing opportunity cost results from increasing inefficiency. WRONG!

   Increasing opportunity cost occurs even when resources are being used at their peak efficiency. RIGHT!

   Increasing opportunity cost and inefficiency are confused because both result in a lower amount of output per unit of input. However, inefficiency results from poor utilization or underemployment of resources, while increasing opportunity cost results from the increasing difficulty of adapting resources to production as more of a good is produced. Inefficiency can be represented as a movement inward from the production-possibilities curve, while increasing opportunity cost can be measured in movements along the production-possibilities curve. As the slope becomes steeper because of a movement down the production-possibilities curve, the good on the *x*-axis experiences increasing opportunity cost (a steeper slope). Similarly, a movement up along the production-possibilities curve represents a higher opportunity cost for the good on the *y*-axis – this time in the form of a flatter slope as more of the good on the *y*-axis is produced.

•ANSWERS•

Using Key Terms

Across

1. opportunity cost
3. government failure
6. factors of production
7. microeconomics
11. economics
14. market mechanism
16. ceteris paribus
17. laissez faire

Down

2. production possibilities
4. entrepreneurship
5. macroeconomics
8. mixed economy
9. economic growth
10. market failure
12. capital
13. scarcity
15. efficiency

True or False

1. F All societies experience the problem of scarcity because human wants for goods and services will always exceed society's ability to produce goods and services.
2. F Factors of production are required to produce education. These factors could have been used to produce other goods and services. The opportunity cost of education is the value of the best goods and services given up to get education.
3. T
4. F Efficiency is maximized along a given production-possibilities curve. The production-possibilities curve bows outward because of the law of increasing opportunity costs, i.e., resources are not perfectly transferable from the production of one good to the production of another. Efficiency means "getting the most from what you have."
5. T
6. T
7. F The economy achieves the greatest efficiency when it is on the curve.
8. F An economy could produce a combination of goods and services outside its existing curve in the future if technology improves and/or the quantity of resources increase sufficiently.
9. T
10. T

Multiple Choice

1. c	5. d	9. d	13. b	17. d	21. a
2. a	6. c	10. d	14. b	18. a	22. b
3. a	7. c	11. c	15. c	19. d	23. b
4. c	8. b	12. b	16. a	20. a	

Problems and Applications

Exercise 1

1. **Figure 1.1 Answer**

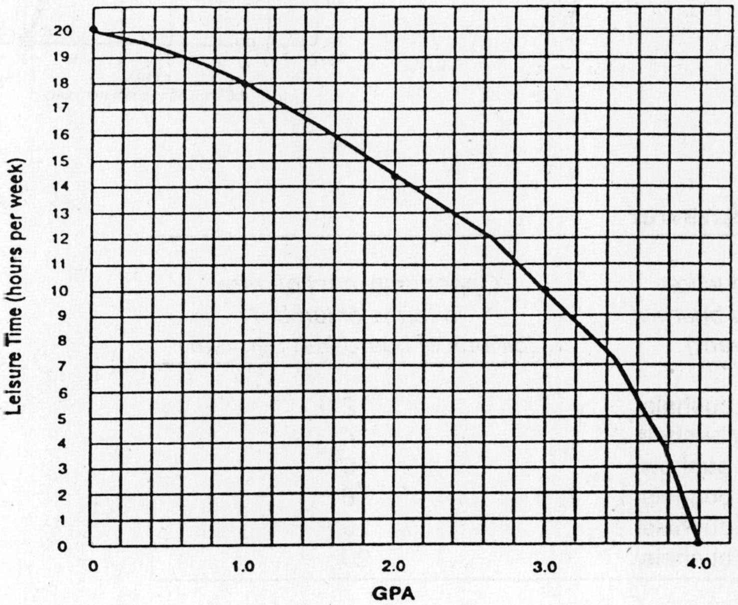

2. **4.5 hours of leisure time.**

3. **10 hours of leisure time.**

4. **Higher grades are harder to get, particularly if the class is graded on a curve, with higher grades being received by a decreasing number of students. The "law" of increasing opportunity cost is evident in the economy and in the classroom.**

Exercise 2

1. 2, 1, 2

2. **Figure 1.2 Answer**

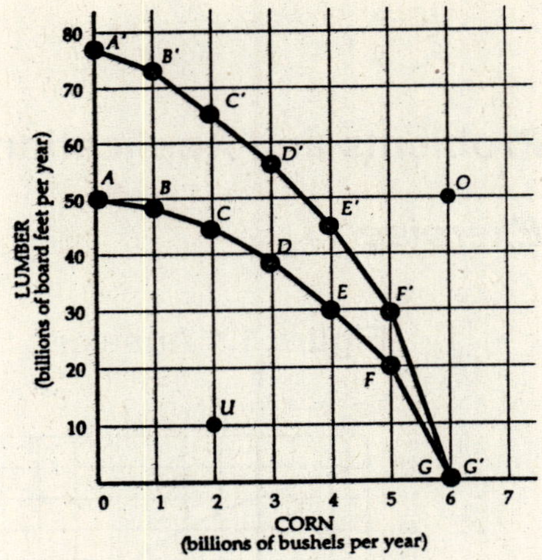

3. **Table 1.3 Answer**

Corn production (billions of bushels per year)	*Opportunity cost of corn in terms of lumber (billions of board feet per year)*
1st billion bushels	2
2nd billion bushels	4
3rd billion bushels	6
4th billion bushels	8
5th billion bushels	10
6th billion bushels	20

4. Rises, increasing opportunity costs
5. See Figure 1.2 answer; combination *G.*
6. Outside, increased
7. a. *F;* b. *U;* c. *O;* d. *O;* e. *U*

Exercise 3

1. d
2. a
3. c
4. d
5. b

Exercise 4

1. 2
2. 4
3. Slope = vertical change/horizontal change = 2/4 = 1/2 or 0.5
4. Positive, increases
5. Constant
6. Linear

CHAPTER 2

The U.S. Economy: A Global View

Quick Review

- The answers to the WHAT, HOW, and FOR WHOM questions in the U.S. economy are a product of both market activity and government intervention. Economic activity is assessed using economic statistics.

- The most frequently used measure of an economy's production is gross domestic product (GDP), which is the monetary value of a nation's output. Real GDP is the measure of output adjusted for inflation. GDP for the United States, at over $10 trillion, is approximately one-fourth of the world's total output.

- The pattern of production in the United States has changed over the last century. At the beginning of the century farming was the dominant sector, then manufacturing, and now services. Service industries currently produce over 70 percent of total output.

- GDP can be classified as consumer goods, investment goods, goods purchased by the government (federal, state, and local levels) and net exports. Consumer goods represent the largest portion of U.S. output.

- Per capita GDP for the United States is more than five times the world's average. Abundant resources, skilled management, an educated work force, and advanced technology have contributed to the high level of output. Factor mobility and capital-intensive production have resulted in high productivity. Economic freedom has also played a significant role in growth for the U.S. economy.

- Government establishes the legal rules of the game under which economic activity takes place. Government provides protection to consumers, labor and the environment through laws and regulations. Sometimes the answers to the WHAT, HOW, and FOR WHOM questions are made worse by government intervention, which is referred to as "government failure."

- GDP can be classified as consumer goods, investment goods, goods purchased by the government (federal, state, and local levels) and net exports. Consumer goods represent the largest portion of U.S. output.

- Income is not distributed equally in the United States. Those in the highest income quintile receive almost half of the total U.S. income.

- In the future, society will demand different answers to the WHAT, HOW, and FOR WHOM questions as new concerns cause us to revise our priorities.

Learning Objectives

After reading Chapter 2 and doing the following exercises, you should:

1. Be able explain why GDP and its components are an answer to the WHAT question.
2. Understand that factors of production differ in quantity, quality, and mobility in the United States and elsewhere.
3. Be able to trace the broad changes in industry structure in the United States from 1900 to the present.
4. Understand the role of government intervention as the economy answers the HOW question.
5. Understand that the economy's answer to the FOR WHOM question lies in the income distribution.
6. Expect that new market signals and government directives will change the answers to the WHAT, HOW, and FOR WHOM questions.

Using Key Terms

Fill in the puzzle on the opposite page with the appropriate term from the list of Key Terms at the end of the chapter in the text.

Across

1. Account for nearly half of all federal government spending but are not part of GDP.
6. Used in Figure 2.6 in the text to divide the population and then rank by income level.
9. The ability of a country to produce a good at a lower opportunity cost than another country.
10. The high level of ____________ in the U.S. is explained to some extent by the level of education according to the article in the text titled "The Education Gap Between Rich and Poor Nations."
12. Goods and services bought from other countries.
13. A market situation in which the government intervenes to protect consumers from exploitation.
14. The costs or benefits of a market activity that affect a third party.
15. The resources used to produce goods and services.
16. A high ratio of capital to labor in the production process.

Down

2. Goods and services sold to other countries.
3. The sum of consumption, investment, government expenditure, and net exports.
4. The knowledge and skills possessed by the labor force.
5. An expansion of production possibilities.
7. Used to compare the average living standards in one country versus another according to the text.
8. The value of exports minus imports.
11. Expenditures for plant, machinery, and equipment.

Puzzle 2.1

True or False: *Circle your choice and explain why any false statements are incorrect.*

T F 1. The top 20 percent of U.S. households get nearly 20 percent of all U.S. income.

T F 2. If the economic growth rate exceeds the population growth rate, per capita GDP will increase.

T F 3. Federal government purchases of goods and services make up approximately 20 percent of GDP.

T F 4. Food stamps, medicare, and veterans' benefits are counted as government expenditures in the GDP.

T F 5. Whenever technology improves, an economy can produce more output with existing resources.

T F 6. As a percentage of GDP, output by the U.S. manufacturing sector has declined since World War II.

T F 7. If a business installs outdoor lighting that makes it difficult for you to sleep, this is an externality.

T F 8. The corporation is the dominant form of business organization in the United States in terms of numbers, assets, and sales.

T F 9. In developed countries, the richest quintile of the population gets a smaller proportion of total income than that quintile receives in poor, developing nations.

T F 10. Income transfers are intended to alter the market's answer to the HOW question.

Multiple Choice: *Select the correct answer.*

_____ 1. The economic growth rate of the economy is best measured by:
- (a) The percentage change in the GDP between two points in time.
- (b) The percentage change in per capita GDP between two points in time.
- (c) The sum of the value of the factors of production used to produce output in a country.
- (d) A measure of output divided by a measure of population.

_____ 2. GDP per capita will decline:
- (a) Whenever the GDP falls.
- (b) If the percentage change in per capita GDP rises.
- (c) If the rate of population growth exceeds the rate of economic growth.
- (d) If factor growth exceeds economic growth.

_____ 3. Suppose that during the course of a year, an economy produces $4.8 trillion consumer goods, $1.2 trillion investment goods, $1.4 trillion government services, $0.6 trillion exports, and $0.8 trillion imports. For that economy, GDP would be:
- (a) $8,000 trillion.
- (b) $7,000 trillion.
- (c) $8,800 trillion.
- (d) $7,200 trillion.

_____ 4. Which of the following countries (or regions) annually produces the most output?
- (a) Japan.
- (b) United States.
- (c) China.
- (d) The combined European Union.

_____ 5. Since 1900 the change in the relative importance of different sectors in the U.S. economy is best characterized as:

(a) Relative growth in farm output share.
(b) Relative growth in manufacturing output share.
(c) Relative growth in service output share.
(d) Relative decrease in service output share.

_____ 6. As the United States economy relies more and more heavily on the production of services rather than goods:

(a) GDP will decrease since there will be less "real" production.
(b) International trade will become more difficult.
(c) Mass unemployment will result.
(d) None of the above are likely to occur.

_____ 7. Which of the following has contributed to the increase in international trade in the United States since the 1920s?

(a) Reduced trade barriers.
(b) Improved communication systems.
(c) The growing share of services in U.S. production.
(d) All of the above.

_____ 8. Most of the United States GDP is used by:

(a) Consumers.
(b) Federal, state and local governments.
(c) Businesses.
(d) Foreign individuals and businesses.

_____ 9. Investment goods:

(a) Both maintain and expand production possibilities.
(b) Maintain production possibilities but do not expand them.
(c) Expand production possibilities but do not maintain them.
(d) Include consumption goods.

_____ 10. Which of the following are included in the GDP?

(a) Social security benefits.
(b) Net exports.
(c) Imports.
(d) Welfare checks.

_____ 11. Which of the following explains the low productivity of workers in poor, developing countries?

(a) Labor intensity of their production processes.
(b) The low factor mobility.
(c) The low quality of labor as a result of poor education.
(d) All of the above.

_____ 12. An increase in the level of human capital in an economy, *ceteris paribus*, will have the following effect on the economy's production possibilities curve.

(a) Shift the curve inward.
(b) Result in a movement from inside the curve to a point on the curve.
(c) Shift the curve outward.
(d) Result in a movement along the curve.

_____ 13. The primary way to distinguish among corporations, partnerships, and proprietorships is through:
(a) Their ownership characteristics.
(b) The size of firms.
(c) The market share of leading firms.
(d) The number of firms in each classification.

_____ 14. Which of the following would *not* be a common government activity in the U.S. economy?
(a) The distribution of goods and services.
(b) The regulation of water pollution.
(c) Enforcing child labor laws.
(d) Requiring producers to label the contents of baby food.

_____ 15. When the production of a good creates external costs:
(a) Profits for the producer of the good will be lower.
(b) Production of the good will be lower.
(c) Society's collective well-being will be lower.
(d) The level of environment pollution will be lower.

_____ 16. When monopolies exist:
(a) Prices tend to be lower than in a competitive market.
(b) Production tends to be higher than in a competitive market.
(c) Quality tends to be lower than in a competitive market.
(d) All of the above can occur.

_____ 17. The result of government intervention in the market in the case of market failure is that:
(a) Society is always better off.
(b) The production-possibilities curve will always shift outward.
(c) Society may be worse off.
(d) Society will always be worse off.

_____ 18. Which of the following statements about the way markets allocate resources is most accurate from society's perspective?
(a) The market always allocates resources in the best way.
(b) The market may allocate resources in a way that is not in society's best interest.
(c) Resource allocation by markets may not be perfect, but it is always better than when the government allocates resources.
(d) Markets often fail to allocate resources properly, so we must rely on governments to determine the proper use of our resources.

_____ 19. Inequalities in income caused by market forces:
(a) Are always undesirable.
(b) Can provide incentives and rewards for achievements.
(c) Cannot be addressed by government action.
(d) Do not exist.

_____ 20. According to The Heritage Foundation and Figure 2.5 in the text, highly regulated and taxed economies have:
(a) Lower per capita GDPs than relatively unregulated, low-taxed economies.
(b) Higher per capita GDPs than relatively unregulated, low-taxed economies.
(c) Lower birth rates than relatively unregulated, low-taxed economies.
(d) Higher birth rates than relatively unregulated, low-taxed economies.

Problems and Applications

Exercise 1

Each year an economic report on the state of the U.S. economy is prepared, called *The Economic Report of the President.* It summarizes the essential features of the economy's performance and describes the policy initiatives that are likely to be undertaken. This exercise uses the kind of information that is developed in this publication. Data was chosen from a specific period of time in order to show particular economic occurrences.

1. Table 2.1 shows the real GDP and the nominal GDP for the years 1990-97.

Table 2.1
Real GDP and nominal GDP, 1990-97

Year	*Real GDP (in billions of dollars per year)*	*Nominal GDP (in billions of dollars per year)*	*Percentage growth in real GDP*	*Percentage growth in nominal GDP*	*U.S. population (in millions)*	*Real GDP per capita*
1990	6,136.3	5,743.8	------------	-----------	249.9	______
1991	6,079.4	5,916.7	______	______	252.6	______
1992	6,244.4	6,244.4	______	______	255.4	______
1993	6,389.6	6,558.1	______	______	258.1	______
1994	6,610.7	6,947.0	______	______	260.6	______
1995	6,742.1	7,265.4	______	______	263.0	______
1996	6,928.4	7,636.0	______	______	265.5	______
1997	7,191.4	8,083.4	______	______	267.9	______

2. From the information in Table 2.1, calculate the percentage growth in nominal and real GDP for each of the years 1991-97 and insert your answers in the appropriate columns.
Use the following formula:

$$\text{Percentage growth in real GDP} = \frac{\text{real GDP}_t - \text{real GDP}_{t-1}}{\text{real GDP}_{t-1}} \times 100\%$$

where: t = current year

$t - 1$ = previous year

For example, for 1994 real GDP grew by the following percentage:

$$\frac{\text{real GDP}_t - \text{real GDP}_{t-1}}{\text{real GDP}_{t-1}} = \frac{\$6{,}610.7 - \$6{,}389.6}{\$6{,}389.6} \times 100\% = 3.46\% \text{ or } 3.5\%$$

3. T F When nominal GDP grows, real GDP must also grow.

4. By what nominal-dollar amount did nominal GDP grow from 1990 to 1997? $________

5. By what constant-dollar amount did real GDP grow from 1990 to 1997? $________

6. The U.S. population for the years 1990–97 is presented in column 6 of Table 2.1. Calculate the real GDP per capita in column 7.

7. T F When real GDP rises, real GDP per capita must also rise.

Exercise 2

This problem is designed to help you understand the mix of output in the United States.

1. Calculate the percentage of total output accounted for by each of the expenditure categories in Table 2.2 for 1997. (Your answers may not be exactly the same as the answers in this book due to rounding.) Now compare your answers to Figure 2.3 in the text, and notice the differences in various categories.

Table 2.2
U.S. national-income aggregates, 1997 (billions of dollars per year)

Expenditure categories		*Percentage of total output*
Consumption goods and services	$5,489	________
Investment goods	1,238	________
Exports	959	________
Imports	1,056	________
Federal government purchases	525	________
State and local government purchases	929	________

2. Which of the categories is the largest percentage of total output? ______________________________

3. Which of the categories is the second largest percentage of total output? ________________________

4. Are net exports positive or negative in Table 2.2 above? ________________

5. T F When net exports are negative, an economy uses more goods and services than it produces.

Exercise 3

This exercise focuses on the growth rates for GDP, population, and per capita GDP.

Refer to Table 2.1 in the text to answer questions 1-5.

1. Which country had the highest growth rate of per capita GDP during this time period? ______________

2. Which country had the lowest growth rate of per capita GDP during this time period? ______________

3. In Nigeria, the growth rate of GDP during this time period was ________ percent and the growth rate of population was ________ percent. When the population growth rate is greater than the GDP growth rate, then per capita GDP must (increase, decrease).

4. In general, the population of high-income countries grew more (rapidly, slowly), which made it easier to raise living standards.

5. T F Since the GDP growth rate for Kenya was greater than the GDP growth rate for Venezuela, during this time period, then Kenya experienced a greater increase in per capita GDP than did Venezuela.

Common Errors

The first statement in each "common error" below is incorrect. Each incorrect statement is followed by a corrected version and an explanation.

1. A higher GDP means an increase in the standard of living. WRONG!

   A high per capita GDP is an imperfect measure of the standard of living. RIGHT!

   Many developing countries experience a rise in GDP, but their population grows faster. This means that there is actually less income per person and the standard of living falls! The growth in population must be taken into account in measuring the standard of living, which is the reason that the per capita GDP, not just the GDP, is used. However, even the per capita GDP measure fails to take into account the distribution of income.

2. Investors make an economic investment when they invest in the stock market. WRONG!

   Economic investment occurs only with the *tangible* creation or maintenance of capital goods. RIGHT!

   A distinction must be made between financial investment and economic investment. Common usage usually refers to financial investment, in which individuals purchase a financial security backed by a financial institution. Such an activity is called saving, which is the alternative to immediate consumption. Such saving may eventually be used by financial corporations to make loans that will eventually lead to economic investment. But economists have found that there are a lot of things that can happen to saving before it turns into tangible production of capital goods. Therefore economists analyze saving and investment separately.

3. As the United States imports more, consumption rises and therefore so does the GDP. WRONG!

   Imports replace consumption of goods produced in the United States and lower the GDP. RIGHT!

   The GDP is the sum of consumption, investment, government purchases, and *net exports*. Net exports are computed by *subtracting* imports from exports. So, let's look at the GDP as an equation:

   GDP = consumption + investment + government purchases + exports - imports

   Greater imports mean a lower GDP, *ceteris paribus*! Consumption of foreign goods is not the concept of U.S. consumption used by economists. Economists focus on the output that is actually produced *in the United States* to satisfy U.S. consumers, not all of the expenditures that consumers make.

4. Export goods are not included in the GDP because they are not consumed by Americans. WRONG!

   Export goods are produced in the United States and therefore are included in the GDP. RIGHT!

   The GDP is the sum of consumption, investment, government purchases, and *net exports*. Once again the equation appears as follows:

   GDP = consumption + investment + government purchases + exports - imports

   Larger exports mean a higher GDP! The GDP focuses on the output of the economy and our use of resources to produce that output, regardless of who consumes it.

•ANSWERS•

Using Key Terms

Across

1. income transfers
6. income quintile
9. comparative advantage
10. productivity
12. imports
13. monopoly
14. externalities
15. factors of production
16. capital intensive

Down

2. exports
3. gross domestic product
4. human capital
5. economic growth
7. per capita GDP
8. net exports
11. investment

True or False

1. F The top 20 percent of U.S. households receive nearly 50 percent of all U.S. income.
2. T
3. F Federal government purchases of goods and services only make up approximately 8 percent of GDP.
4. F These are income transfers and are not included in GDP. No good or service is directly provided in exchange for these payments.
5. T
6. T
7. T
8. F The corporation is dominant in sales and assets, but the single proprietorship is the most common form of business structure in the U.S.
9. T
10. F Income transfers alter the market's answer to the FOR WHOM question.

Multiple Choice

1. a	5. c	9. a	13. a	17. c
2. c	6. d	10. b	14. a	18. b
3. d	7. d	11. d	15. c	19. b
4. b	8. a	12. c	16. d	20. d

Problems and Applications

Exercise 1

1. **Table 2.1 Answer**

Year	Real GDP (in billions of dollars per year)	Nominal GDP (in billions of dollars per year)	Percentage growth in real GDP	Percentage growth in nominal GDP	U.S. population (in millions)	Real GDP per capita
1990	6,136.3	5,743.8	----	----	249.9	24,555
1991	6,079.4	5,916.7	-0.9	3.0	252.6	24,067
1992	6,244.4	6,244.4	2.7	5.5	255.4	24,449
1993	6,389.6	6,558.1	2.3	5.0	258.1	24,756
1994	6,610.7	6,947.0	3.5	5.9	260.6	25,367
1995	6,742.1	7,265.4	2.0	4.6	263.0	25,635
1996	6,928.4	7,636.0	2.8	5.1	265.5	26,096
1997	7,191.4	8,083.4	3.8	5.9	267.9	26,844

2. See Table 2.1 answer, columns 4, 5
3. F
4. $2,339.6 billion
5. $1,055.1 billion
6. See Table 2.1 answer, column 7
7. F

Exercise 2

1. **Table 2.2 Answer**

Expenditure categories		Percentage of total output
Consumption goods and services	$5,489	67.9
Investment goods	1,238	15.3
Exports	959	11.9
Imports	1,056	13.1
Federal government purchases	525	6.5
State and local government purchases	929	11.5

2. Consumer goods and services
3. Investment goods
4. Negative
5. T

Exercise 3

1. China
2. Ethiopia
3. 2.4, 2.8, decrease
4. Slowly
5. F

CHAPTER 3

Supply and Demand

Quick Review

- Participation in the market by consumers, businesses, and government is motivated by the desire to maximize something: utility for consumers, profits for businesses, and general welfare for the government.

- Interactions in the marketplace involve either the factor market, where factors of production are bought and sold, or the product market, where goods and services are bought and sold.

- The demand curve represents buyer behavior. It slopes downward and to the right, showing that buyers are willing and able to purchase greater quantities at lower prices, *ceteris paribus*. The supply curve represents producer behavior. It slopes upward and to the right, indicating that producers are willing and able to produce greater quantities at higher prices, *ceteris paribus*.

- Movements along a demand curve result from a change in price. Shifts in a demand curve result from a change in a nonprice determinant—tastes, income, other goods, expectations, the number of buyers.

- Movements along a supply curve result from a change in price. Shifts in a supply curve result from a change in a nonprice determinant—technology, factor costs, other goods, taxes and subsidies, expectations, the number of sellers.

- Market demand and market supply summarize the intentions of all those participating on one side of the market or the other.

- Equilibrium price and quantity are established at the intersection of the supply and demand curves. At any price other than the equilibrium price, disequilibrium will occur.

- Price ceilings are set below the equilibrium price and result in shortages; price floors are set above the equilibrium price and result in surpluses. In either case, the market does not clear.

- The market mechanism relies on the forces of demand and supply to establish market outcomes (prices and quantities) in both product and factor markets. The market mechanism thus can be used to answer the WHAT, HOW, and FOR WHOM questions.

Learning Objectives

After reading Chapter 3 and doing the following exercises, you should:

1. Know the basic questions in economics and how the U.S. economy answers the questions.
2. Be able to describe the motivations of participants in the product and resource markets.
3. Understand how a demand schedule represents demand and how a supply schedule represents supply.
4. Be able to define, graph, and interpret supply and demand curves.
5. Know the nonprice determinants of both supply and demand and the direction they shift the curves.
6. Know what causes movements along demand and supply curves.
7. Understand how market-demand and market-supply curves are derived from individual demand and supply curves.
8. Know how equilibrium is established and why markets move toward equilibrium.
9. Understand the consequences of price ceilings and price floors.
10. Understand how the market mechanism provides the answer to the WHAT, HOW, and FOR WHOM questions.

Using Key Terms

Fill in the puzzle on the opposite page with the appropriate term from the list of Key Terms at the end of the chapter in the text.

Across

3. The result of the price ceiling on electricity set by the California legislature according to the text.
6. Changes from $20 to $30 in Figure 3.7 in the text.
7. The willingness and ability to sell various quantities of a good at alternative prices.
10. The willingness and ability to buy a particular good at some price.
12. The assumption by economists that nothing else changes.
15. Where businesses purchase the factors of production.
16. The use of market price and sales to signal desired output.
17. Refers to the inverse relationship between price and quantity.

Down

1. The result of an income change in Figure 3.3 in the text.
2. According to the webnote on page 53 in the text, consumers reveal their ______ ______ to Priceline.
3. The sum of all producers' sales intentions.
4. The name of the table from which Figure 3.2 in the text is drawn.
5. Where goods and services are exchanged.
8. According to Figure 3.6 in the text, at a price of $25 per hour, a ________ exists.
9. Put in place by the California legislature to control the retail price of electricity according to the text.
11. Explains why the curve in Figure 3.5 in the text is upward sloping.
13. The value of the most desired forgone alternative.
14. The name for the final curve drawn in Figure 3.4 in the text.

Puzzle 3.1

True or False: *Circle your choice and explain why any false statements are incorrect.*

T F 1. The demand curve shows how much of a good a buyer will actually buy at a given price.

T F 2. A change in one of the determinants of demand causes a movement along the demand curve for the good.

T F 3. An increase in the price of one good can cause the demand for another good to increase if the goods are substitutes.

T F 4. Supply curves reflect the potential behavior of the sellers or producers of a good or service, not of the buyers.

T F 5. The "law of supply" has nothing to do with opportunity costs.

T F 6. When the number of suppliers in a market changes, the market supply curve also changes, even if the individual supply curves of original suppliers do not shift.

T F 7. The equilibrium price can be determined through the process of trial and error by both the buyers and the sellers in a market.

T F 8. There are never shortages or surpluses when the price in a market is equal to the equilibrium price for the market.

T F 9. When economists say that the market mechanism provides an "optimal" allocation of resources they mean that all consumer desires are satisfied and business profits are maximized.

T F 10. In a market economy, producers earn profits by producing the goods and services that consumers want the most.

Multiple Choice: *Select the correct answer.*

_____ 1. The goals of the principal actors in the economy are:
- (a) Income for consumers, profits for businesses, and taxes for government.
- (b) Goods and services for consumers, scarce resources for businesses, and resources not used by businesses for government.
- (c) Satisfaction from purchases for consumers, profits for businesses, and general welfare for government.
- (d) Available goods and services for consumers, scarce resources for businesses, and general welfare for government.

_____ 2. Which of the following helps to explain why economic interaction occurs?
- (a) Limited ability to produce what we need.
- (b) Constraints on time, energy, and resources.
- (c) The gains possible from specialization.
- (d) All of the above.

_____ 3. Consumers:
- (a) Provide dollars to the product market.
- (b) Receive dollars from the product market.
- (c) Provide dollars to the factor market.
- (d) Receive goods and services from the factor market.

_____ 4. The law of demand states that:

(a) As price falls, quantity demanded falls, *ceteris paribus*.
(b) As price falls, quantity demanded increases, *ceteris paribus*.
(c) As price falls, demand falls, *ceteris paribus*.
(d) As price falls, demand increases, *ceteris paribus*.

_____ 5. Which of the following must be held constant according to the *ceteris paribus* assumption in defining a demand schedule?

(a) The price of the good itself.
(b) Expectations of sellers.
(c) Income.
(d) Technology.

_____ 6. The quantity of a good that a consumer is willing to buy depends on:

(a) The price of the good.
(b) The consumer's income.
(c) The opportunity cost of purchasing that good.
d) All of the above.

_____ 7. Jon's demand schedule for donuts indicates:

(a) How much he likes donuts.
(b) His opportunity cost of buying donuts.
(c) Why he likes donuts.
(d) How many donuts he will actually buy.

_____ 8. According to the law of supply, a supply curve:

(a) Has a negative slope.
(b) Has a positive slope.
(c) Is a horizontal, or flat, line.
(d) Will always be less than the demand curve.

_____ 9. When a seller sells a good, *ceteris paribus*:

(a) There is no change in supply or the quantity supplied.
(b) The supply curve shifts to the left, but quantity supplied remains the same.
(c) The quantity supplied of the good falls, but supply remains unchanged.
(d) The supply curve shifts to the left, and the quantity supplied falls.

_____ 10. If corn and wheat are alternative pursuits for a farmer, a change in the supply of corn will take place:

(a) When the price of corn changes.
(b) When the price of wheat changes.
(c) When the demand for corn changes.
(d) When consumers want to buy more corn at the same price.

_____ 11. Suppose the MC Birdhouse Co. announces that they need higher prices than last year to sell the same quantity of birdhouses. We can conclude that there has been:

(a) An increase in demand.
(b) A decrease in demand.
(c) A decrease in the company's supply.
(d) An increase in the company's supply.

_____ 12. To calculate market supply we:

(a) Add the quantities supplied for each individual supply schedule horizontally.
(b) Add the quantities supplied for each individual supply schedule vertically.
(c) Find the average quantity supplied at each price.
(d) Find the difference between the quantity supplied and the quantity demanded at each price.

_____ 13. In the market for web design services, an increase in the number of people with web designing skills will cause:

(a) An increase in the equilibrium price and a decrease in the equilibrium quantity.
(b) A decrease in the equilibrium price and an increase in the equilibrium quantity.
(c) An increase in the equilibrium price and an increase in the equilibrium quantity.
(d) A decrease in the equilibrium price and a decrease in the equilibrium quantity.

_____ 14. In a market, the equilibrium price is determined by:

(a) What buyers are willing and able to purchase.
(b) What sellers are willing and able to offer for sale.
(c) Both demand and supply.
(d) The government.

_____ 15. A leftward shift in a demand curve and a leftward shift in a supply curve both result in a:

(a) Lower equilibrium quantity.
(b) Higher equilibrium quantity.
(c) Lower equilibrium price.
(d) Higher equilibrium price.

_____ 16. If the number of consumers in a market decreases, this will cause:

(a) An increase in the equilibrium price and a decrease in the equilibrium quantity.
(b) A decrease in the equilibrium price and an increase in the equilibrium quantity.
(c) An increase in the equilibrium price and an increase in the equilibrium quantity.
(d) A decrease in the equilibrium price and a decrease in the equilibrium quantity.

_____ 17. In a market economy, the people who receive the goods and services produced are the people who:

(a) Need the goods and services.
(b) Want the goods and services the most.
(c) Have the most political power.
(d) Are willing and able to pay the market price.

_____ 18. When economists talk about "optimal outcomes" in the marketplace, they mean that:

(a) The allocation of resources by the market is perfect.
(b) All consumer desires are satisfied and business profits are maximized.
(c) The allocation of resources by the market is likely to be the best possible, given scarce resources and income constraints.
(d) Everyone who wants a good or service can get it.

_____ 19. When effective price ceilings are set for a market:

(a) Quantity supplied will be less than the equilibrium quantity, and price will be less than the equilibrium price.
(b) Quantity supplied will be less than the equilibrium quantity, and price will be greater than the equilibrium price.
(c) Quantity supplied will be greater than the equilibrium quantity, and price will be less than the equilibrium price.
(d) Quantity supplied will be greater than the equilibrium quantity, and price will be greater than the equilibrium price.

_____ 20. One *In the News* article in the text is titled "Californians Pinched by Power Prices." This article best illustrates the concept that:

(a) An increase in the price of electricity causes the supply of water to decrease.
(b) A decrease in the supply of electricity causes the price of electricity to increase.
(c) A decrease in the quantity supplied of electricity causes the price of electricity to increase.
(d) An increase in the demand for electricity causes the price of electricity to decrease.

Problems and Applications

Exercise 1

This exercise provides practice in graphing demand and supply curves for individual buyers and sellers as well as graphing market demand and market supply curves.

1. Suppose you are willing and able to buy 20 gallons of gasoline per week if the price is $1 per gallon, but if the price is $3 per gallon you are willing and able to buy only the bare minimum of 10 gallons. Complete the demand schedule in Table 3.1.

Table 3.1
Your demand schedule for gasoline

Price (dollars per gallon)	*Quantity (gallons per week)*
$1	______
3	______

2. Use the demand schedule in Table 3.1 to draw the demand curve in Figure 3.1. Assume the demand curve is a straight line.

Figure 3.1
Your demand curve for gasoline.

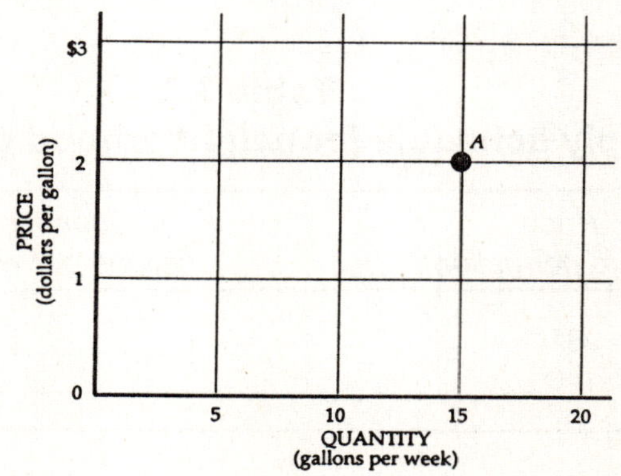

If you have drawn your demand curve correctly, it should go through point *A*.

3. Suppose that 999 other people in your town have demand curves for gasoline that are just like yours in Figure 3.1. Fill out the town's market-demand schedule in Table 3.2 at each price. (Remember to include your own quantity demanded along with everyone else's at each price.)

Table 3.2
Market-demand schedule for gasoline in your town

Price (dollars per gallon)	*Quantity (gallons per week)*
$1	________
3	________

4. Using the market-demand schedule in Table 3.2, draw the market-demand curve for gasoline for your town in Figure 3.2. Assume that the curve is a straight line, and label it *D*.

Figure 3.2
Market supply and demand curves for gasoline in your town

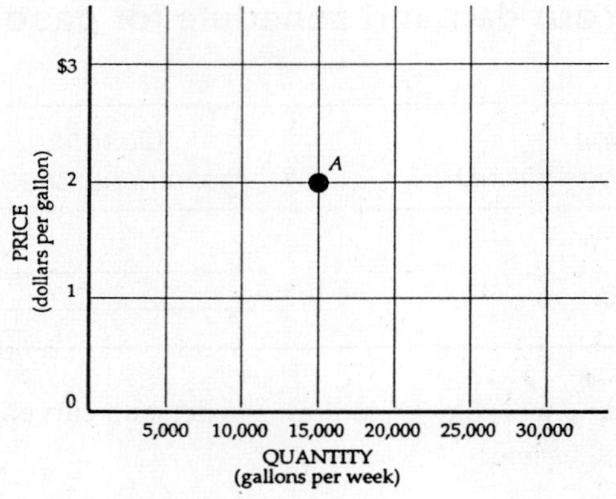

If you have drawn the demand curve correctly, it should pass through point *A*.

5. Suppose the friendly neighborhood gas station is willing to sell 250 gallons of gasoline per week at $1 per gallon and 1,250 gallons per week at $3 per gallon. Fill in the supply schedule for this gas station in Table 3.3.

Table 3.3
Supply schedule for neighborhood gas station

Price (dollars per gallon)	*Quantity (gallons per week)*
$1	________
3	________

6. Graph the supply curve for the gas station in Figure 3.3 using the information in Table 3.3. Assume that the supply curve is a straight line.

Figure 3.3
Supply curve for neighborhood gas station

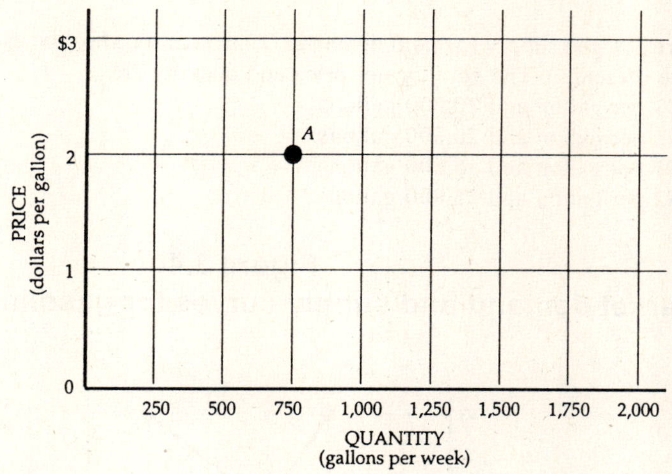

If you have drawn the supply curve correctly, it should pass through point *A*.

7. Suppose that 19 other gas stations in your town have the same supply schedule as your neighborhood gas station (Table 3.3). Fill out the market-supply schedule for gasoline of the 20 gas stations in your town in Table 3.4.

Table 3.4
Market supply schedule for gasoline in your town

Price (dollars per gallon)	*Quantity (gallons per week)*
$1	________
3	________

8. Using the market supply schedule in Table 3.4, draw the market supply curve for gasoline for your town in Figure 3.2. Assume that the market supply curve is a straight line. If you have drawn the curve correctly, it should pass through point *A*. Label the supply curve *S*.

9. The equilibrium price for gasoline for your town's 20 gas stations and 1,000 buyers of gasoline (see Figure 3.2) is:
   (a) Above $2.
   (b) Exactly $2.
   (c) Below $2.

10. At the equilibrium price:
   (a) The quantity demanded equals the quantity supplied.
   (b) There is a surplus.
   (c) There is a shortage.
   (d) There is an excess of inventory.

Exercise 2

This exercise shows the market mechanics at work in shifting market-demand curves.

1. In Figure 3.4, the supply (S_1) and demand (D_1) curves for gasoline as they might appear in your town are presented. The equilibrium price and quantity are:
   (a) $3 per gallon and 20,000 gallons.
   (b) $2 per gallon and 20,000 gallons.
   (c) $1 per gallon and 15,000 gallons.
   (d) $2 per gallon and 15,000 gallons.

Figure 3.4
Market demand and supply curves for gasoline in your town

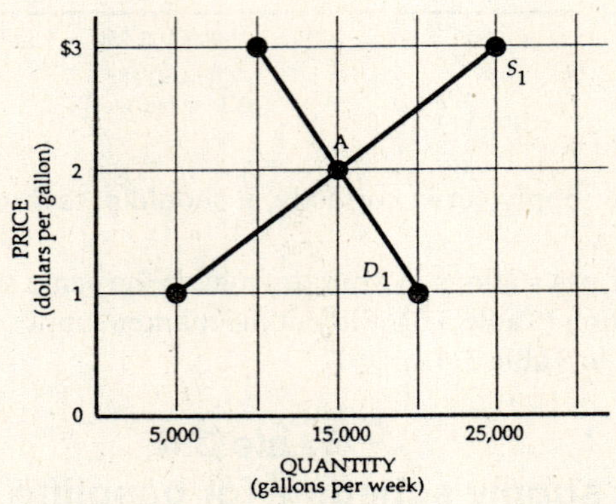

2. Assume that one-half of the people in your town move away. Because of this, suppose that the remaining buyers are willing and able to buy only half as much gasoline at each price as was bought before. Draw the new demand curve in Figure 3.4 and label it D_2.

3. When the number of buyers in a market changes, the market demand curve for goods and services shifts and there is a change in (demand, quantity demanded).

4. When half of the buyers move from your town and the demand curve shifts, the new equilibrium price:
   (a) Is above the old equilibrium price.
   (b) Is below the old equilibrium price.
   (c) Remains the same as the old equilibrium price.
   (*Hint:* See the second demand curve, D_2, in Figure 3.4.)

5. Given the new demand curve, if the market price remains at the old equilibrium price of $2 then:
   (a) The quantity demanded will equal the quantity supplied.
   (b) A shortage of gasoline will occur.
   (c) A surplus of gasoline will occur.

6. When there is a surplus in a market:
   (a) Buyers do not wish to buy as much as sellers want to sell.
   (b) Sellers are likely to offer discounts to eliminate expensive excess inventories.
   (c) Buyers who cannot buy commodities at the current market price are likely to make offers to buy at lower prices that sellers will now accept.
   (d) All the above.

7. When there is a leftward shift of the market-demand curve, market forces should push:
   (a) Market prices upward and market quantity downward.
   (b) Market prices upward and market quantity upward.
   (c) Market prices downward and market quantity downward.
   (d) Market prices downward and market quantity upward.

8. Whenever there is a rightward shift of the market demand curve, market forces should push:
   (a) Market prices upward and market quantity upward.
   (b) Market prices upward and market quantity downward.
   (c) Market prices downward and market quantity upward.
   (d) Market prices downward and market quantity downward.

Exercise 3

This exercise gives practice in computing market demand and market supply curves using the demand and supply curves of individuals in a market. It is similar to a problem for chapter 3 in the text.

1. Table 3.5 shows the weekly demand and supply schedules for various individuals. Fill in the total market quantity that these individuals demand and supply.

Table 3.5
Individual demand and supply schedules

Price	*$4*	*$3*	*$2*	*$1*
Buyers				
Al's quantity demanded	1	3	4	6
Betsy's quantity demanded	2	2	3	3
Casey's quantity demanded	2	2.5	3	3.5
Total market quantity demanded	____	____	____	____
Sellers				
Alice's quantity supplied	5	3	2	0
Butch's quantity supplied	6	5	4	3
Connie's quantity supplied	5	4	3	2
Ellen's quantity supplied	4	3	1	0
Total market quantity supplied	____	____	____	____

Use the data in Table 3.5 to answer questions 2-4.

2. Construct and label market-supply and market-demand curves in Figure 3.5.

3. Identify the equilibrium point and label it *EQ* in Figure 3.5.

4. What is true about the relationship between quantity demanded and quantity supplied at a price of $3 in Figure 3.5? ____________________

Figure 3.5
Market-supply and market-demand curves for buyers and sellers

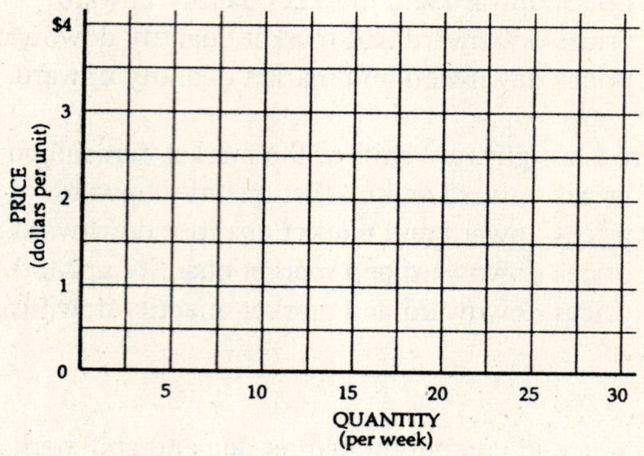

Exercise 4

This exercise provides examples of events that would shift demand or supply curves. It is similar to a problem at the end of the chapter in the text.

Figure 3.6
Shifts of curves

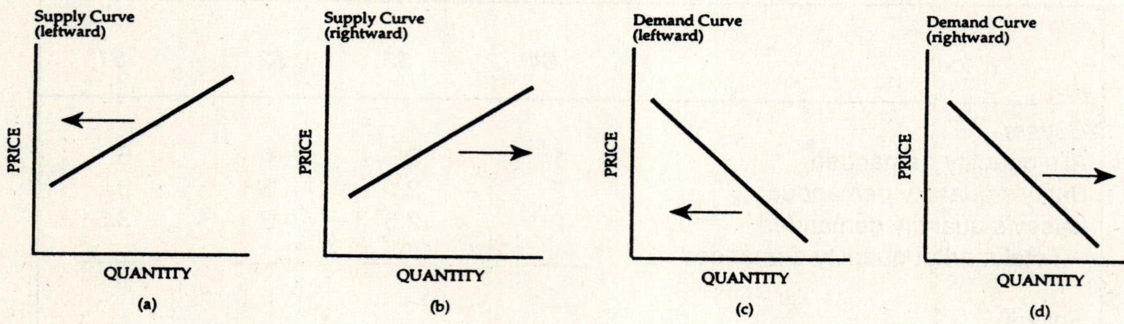

Choose the letter of the appropriate diagram in Figure 3.6 that best describes the shift that would occur in each of the following situations. The shifts are occurring in the market for U.S. defense goods. (*Hint:* Ask yourself if the change first affects buyers or the sellers. Refer to the nonprice determinants for demand and supply listed in the text if necessary.)

_____ 1. Because of increased protectionism for steel, steel producers are able to raise the price of specialty steel, which is a key resource in the production of defense goods.

_____ 2. A new process for creating microchips is developed that reduces the cost of materials needed to produce nuclear submarines.

_____ 3. As a result of worldwide terrorist threats, new buyers enter the market to purchase defense goods.

_____ 4. A country that previously bought U.S. defense goods enters into a peace agreement.

_____ 5. A large firm in the defense industry closes down when it loses a defense contract.

Exercise 5

The media often provide information about supply and demand shifts. This exercise uses one of the articles in the text to show the kind of information to look for.

Reread the *In the News* article entitled "Californians Pinched by Power Prices." Then answer the following questions:

1. Which of the four diagrams in Figure 3.6 in the previous exercise best represents the shift in the market for electricity? a b c d (circle one)

2. The change in the electricity market is referred to as a:
   (a) Change in quantity supplied.
   (b) Change in supply.
   (c) Change in quantity demanded.
   (d) Change in demand.

3. What is the expected change in equilibrium price and quantity in the electricity market?

   ____

Common Errors

The first statement in each "common error" below is incorrect. Each incorrect statement is followed by a corrected version and an explanation.

1. If a large number of people petition the government in order to get something, then there is a large demand for that item. WRONG!

   If a large number of people desire a commodity *and have the ability to pay for it,* then there is a large demand for that item. RIGHT!

   People want something, but there is no "demand" for it unless they are able to pay for it. Economists use the word "demand" in a way that is quite different from normal usage. People who want (desire; have preferences, a taste, or liking for) a commodity are seen as going to a market to purchase the commodity with money. "Demand" does not mean claiming the right to something when a person does not have the ability to buy it.

2. Market price is the same thing as equilibrium price. WRONG!

The market price moves by trial and error (via the market mechanism) toward the equilibrium price. RIGHT!

When demand and supply curves shift, the market is temporarily out of equilibrium. The price may move along a demand or supply curve toward the new equilibrium.

3. Since the quantity bought must equal the quantity sold, every market is always in equilibrium by definition. WRONG!

Although the quantity bought equals the quantity sold, there may be shortages or surpluses. RIGHT!

Although the quantity actually bought does equal the quantity actually sold, there may still be buyers who are willing and able to buy more of the good at the market price (market shortages exist) or sellers who are willing and able to sell more of the good at the market price (market surpluses exist). If the market price is above the equilibrium price, there will be queues of goods (inventories). Prices will be lowered by sellers toward the equilibrium price. If the market price is below the equilibrium price, there will be queues of buyers (shortages). Prices will be bid up by buyers toward the equilibrium price.

4. The intersection of supply and demand curves determines how much of a good or service will actually be exchanged and the actual price of the exchange. WRONG!

The intersection of supply and demand curves shows only where buyers and sellers intend and have the ability to exchange the same amount of a commodity. RIGHT!

Many institutional interferences may prevent the market from ever reaching the equilibrium point, where supply and demand curves intersect. All that can be said is that, given a free market, prices and production will tend to move toward equilibrium levels.

5. A change in price changes the demand for goods by consumers. WRONG!

A change in price changes the quantity demanded by consumers in a given time period. RIGHT!

Economists differentiate the terms "quantity demanded" and "demand." A change in the quantity demanded usually refers to a movement along the demand curve as a result of a change in price. A change in demand refers to a shift of the demand curve as a result of a change in incomes, tastes, prices or availability of other goods, or expectations.

6. A change in price changes the supply of goods produced by a firm. WRONG!

A change in price changes the quantity supplied of a good by a firm in a given time period. RIGHT!

Economists differentiate the terms "quantity supplied" and "supply." A change in the quantity supplied usually refers to a movement along a supply curve as a result of a change in price or production rate. A change in supply refers to a shift of the supply curve as a result of a change in technology, prices of resources, number of sellers, other goods, expectations, or taxes.

•ANSWERS•

Using Key Terms

Across

3. market shortage
6. equilibrium price
7. supply
10. demand
12. ceteris paribus
15. factor market
16. market mechanism
17. law of demand

Down

1. shift in demand
2. demand curve
3. market supply
4. demand schedule
5. product market
8. market surplus
9. price ceiling
11. law of supply
13. opportunity cost
14. market demand

True or False

1. F The demand curve indicates how much a buyer would like to buy and is able to pay for. How much is actually bought also depends on supply.
2. F A change in one of the determinants of demand results in a shift in the demand curve.
3. T
4. T
5. F The quantity of a good that a producer is willing and able to produce and offer for sale at any price depends on the value of the alternative goods that could have been produced with those same resources, i.e., the opportunity costs.
6. T
7. T
8. T
9. F An optimal outcome does not mean that all consumer desires are satisfied and business profits are maximized. It simply means that the market outcome is likely to be the best possible given scarce resources and income constraints.
10. F In a market economy, producers earn profits by producing the goods and services that consumers demand, i.e., are willing and able to pay for.

Multiple Choice

1. c	5. c	9. a	13. b	17. d
2. d	6. d	10. b	14. c	18. c
3. a	7. b	11. c	15. a	19. a
4. b	8. b	12. a	16. d	20. b

Problems and Applications

Exercise 1

1. **Table 3.1 Answer**

p	*q*
$1	20
3	10

2. **Figure 3.1 Answer**

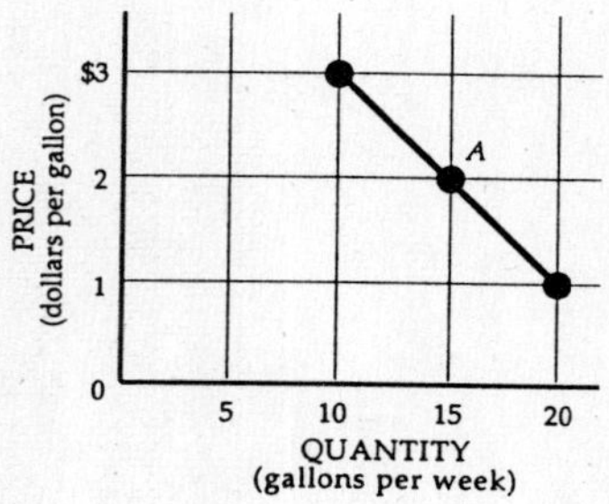

3. **Table 3.2 Answer**

p	*q*
$1	20,000
3	10,000

4. See Figure 3.2 Answer, curve D.

Figure 3.2 Answer

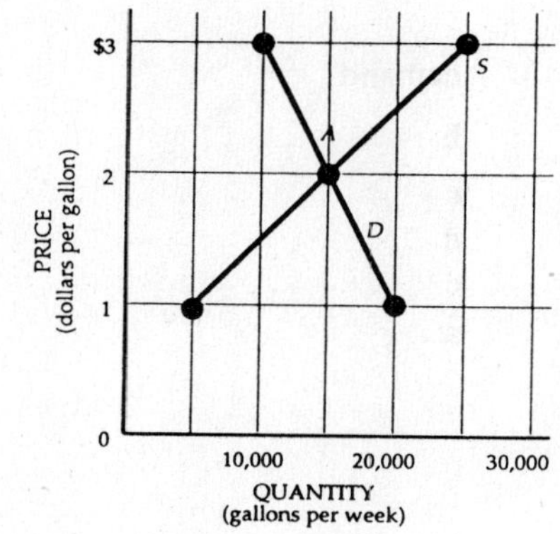

5. **Table 3.3 Answer**

p	*q*
$1	250
3	1,250

6. **Figure 3.3 Answer**

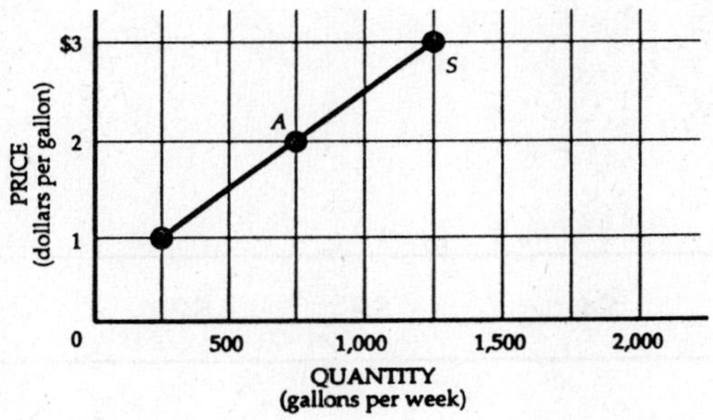

7. **Table 3.4 Answer**

p	*q*
$1	5,000
3	25,000

8. See Figure 3.2 Answer, curve S.

9. c
10. a

Exercise 2

1. d
2. **Figure 3.4 Answer**

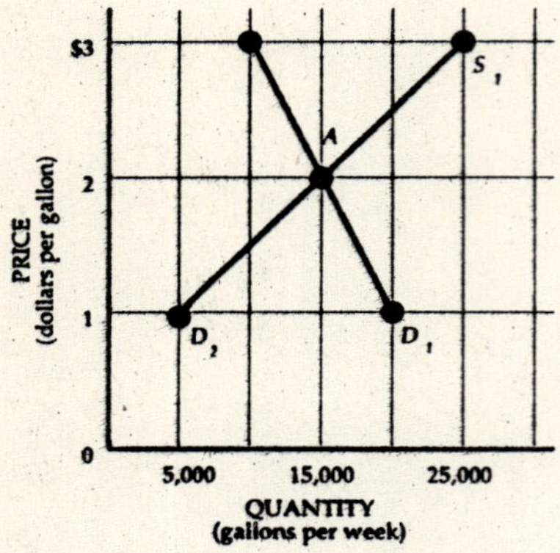

3. demand
4. b
5. c
6. d
7. c
8. a

Exercise 3

1. **Table 3.5 Answer**

Price	*$4*	*$3*	*$2*	*$1*
Buyers Total market quantity demanded	5	7.5	10	12.5
Sellers Total market quantity supplied	20	15	10	5

2. **Figure 3.5 Answer**

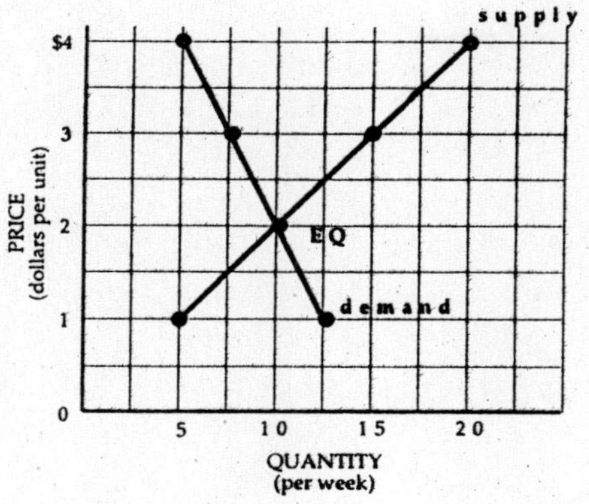

3. See point *EQ* in Figure 3.5.
4. The quantity supplied is greater than the quantity demanded or there is a surplus of 7.5 units (15 minus 7.5.)

Exercise 4

1. a
2. b
3. d
4. c
5. a

Exercise 5

1. a
2. b
3. An increase in equilibrium price and a decrease in equilibrium quantity.

CHAPTER 4

The Public Sector

Quick Review

- Market failure occurs when the market mechanism causes the economy to produce a combination of goods different from the optimal mix of output or results in an inequitable distribution of income. Market failure may prompt the government to intervene.

- There are four specific sources of market failure at the micro level: public goods, externalities, market power, and equity.

- Private goods can be consumed exclusively by those who pay for the goods, but public goods cannot. Public goods, such as national defense, can be consumed jointly by everyone no matter who pays. Because the link between paying and receiving is broken, everyone seeks to be a "free rider" and benefit from purchases made by others. As a result, the market underproduces public goods, and government intervention is necessary to provide these goods.

- Externalities are costs (or benefits) of a market transaction borne by a third party. Externalities cause a divergence between social costs and private costs and lead to suboptimal market outcomes. In the case of externalities such as pollution, which impose costs on society, too much of the polluting good is produced. If the externality produces benefits, too little of the good will be produced by the market alone. Regulations and emission fees are used to reduce the external costs associated with externalities.

- Market power allows producers to ignore the signals generated in the marketplace and produce a suboptimal mix of output. Antitrust policy and laws seek to prevent or restrict concentrations of market power.

- The market mechanism tends to allocate output to those with the most income. The government responds with a system of taxes and transfer payments to ensure a more equitable distribution of income and output.

- Markets may also fail at the macro level. In this case, the problems include unacceptable levels of unemployment, inflation, and economic growth. Government intervention is then necessary to achieve society's goals.

- State and local government activity exceeds that of the federal government and has grown much more rapidly in recent decades. Federal expenditures are supported mainly by personal income taxes and Social Security taxes. State and local governments rely most heavily on sales taxes and property taxes, respectively.

- Government intervention that does not improve economic outcomes is referred to as government failure.

Learning Objectives

After reading Chapter 4 and doing the following exercises, you should:

1. Understand that market failure can occur and as a result the government may decide to intervene.
2. Be able to describe the communal nature of public goods and the free-rider dilemma.
3. Know the nature of externalities and how they influence the decisions of producers and consumers.
4. Use the concepts of social cost and private cost to explain the problems associated with externalities.
5. Understand the policy options that can be used to address the problems associated with externalities.
6. Understand how antitrust activity attempts to combat monopoly power.
7. Be familiar with some fundamental antitrust laws.
8. Understand that inequity in income distribution is an example of market failure with respect to the FOR WHOM question.
9. Understand the concept of macro failure.
10. Understand the recent trend in terms of spending at the federal level vs. the state and local levels.
11. Know where government revenues come from and the difference between the different tax structures.
12. Understand that government failure can occur.

Using Key Terms

Fill in the puzzle on the opposite page with the appropriate term from the list of Key Terms at the end of the chapter in the text.

Across

1. The most desired goods and services that are given up in order to obtain something else.
5. An increase in the average level of prices.
8. Referred to as the "invisible hand."
10. The likely outcome of government intervention according to the survey titled "Persistent Doubts about Government Waste" in the text.
14. An industry in which a single firm achieves economies of scale over the entire range of output.
17. State lotteries are categorized in this way according to the article titled "Big Lotteries' Real Losers" in the text.
19. A form of government intervention to address the FOR WHOM question.
20. Theory that emphasizes the role of self-interest in public decision making.
21. The ability to alter the market price of a good or service.
22. The fee paid for the use of a public-sector good or service.
23. A tax system in which the tax rate stays the same as income rises.

Down

2. Labeled as point X in Figure 4.1 in the text.
3. Occurs when people are willing to work but are unable to find jobs.
4. The market failure discussed in the article "The Human Cost of Secondhand Smoke" in the text.
6. A tax system in which tax rates rise as incomes rise.
7. For a ______ ______, consumption by one person excludes consumption by others.
9. Federal grants to state and local governments for specific purposes.
11. Represented by point M in Figure 4.1 in the text.
12. Only one producer in an industry.
13. A good or service that society believes everyone is entitled to a minimal quantity of, such as food.
15. Can be consumed jointly.
16. One who does not pay but still enjoys the benefits.
18. The legislation used to prevent or break up concentrations of market power such as Microsoft.

Puzzle 4.1

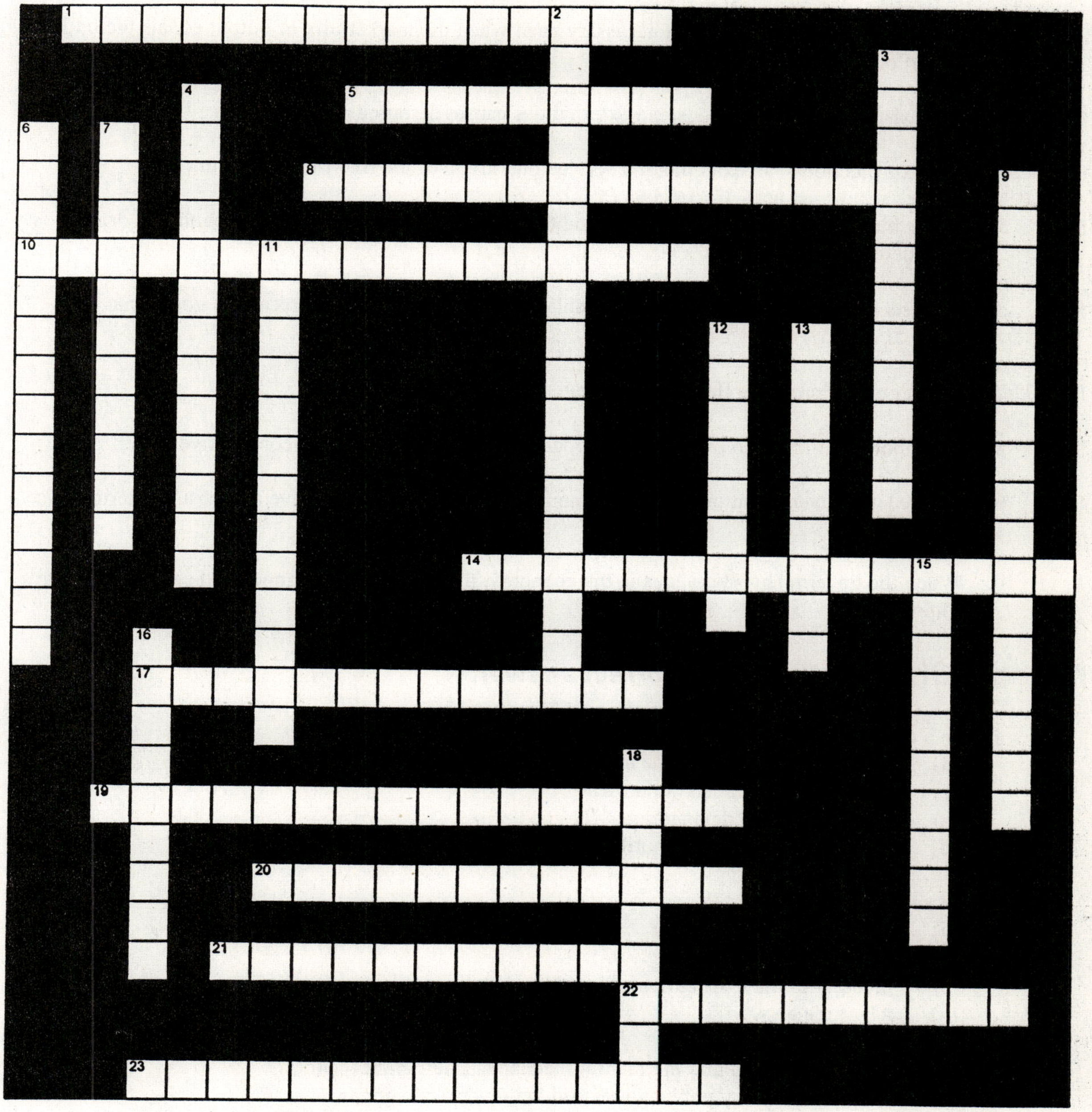

True or False: *Circle your choice and explain why any false statements are incorrect.*

T F 1. Market failure implies that the forces of supply and demand have not led to the best point on the production-possibilities curve.

T F 2. Government intervention is not necessary even when the market mix of output equals the optimal mix of output.

T F 3. The existence of public goods and externalities causes resource misallocations.

T F 4. Police protection is an example of a service that involves the free-rider problem.

T F 5. If you burn garbage in your backyard and the smoke damages a neighbor's health, the damage is considered an externality.

T F 6. Markets will overproduce goods that yield external benefits and underproduce goods that yield external costs.

T F 7. Market power creates a flawed response to an accurate price signal.

T F 8. Monopolies will tend to overproduce goods and charge a higher than competitive price.

T F 9. The federal government in the U.S. economy has grown in both relative and absolute terms since the 1950s.

T F 10. When the government intervenes in the economy, the market mix of goods and services is always improved.

Multiple Choice: *Select the correct answer.*

_____ 1. In a market economy, producers will produce the goods and services:
- (a) That consumers desire the most.
- (b) That consumers need the most.
- (c) That consumers demand.
- (d) That optimize consumer utility.

_____ 2. Market failure includes:
- (a) Externalities.
- (b) Market power.
- (c) Inequity in the distribution of goods and services.
- (d) All of the above.

_____ 3. Market failure suggests that the market mechanism, left alone, will:
- (a) Produce too many public goods and too few private goods.
- (b) Produce too many private goods and too few public goods.
- (c) Produce the optimal mix of output.
- (d) Result in too few resources being allocated to private goods.

_____ 4. The market will sometimes fail to produce society's optimum output because:
(a) Producers do not always measure the same benefits and costs as society.
(b) Producers will not produce certain types of important goods and services that cannot be kept from consumers who do not pay.
(c) When producers have market power, they will tend to underproduce goods and services.
(d) All of the above are correct.

_____ 5. When the market fails, which of the following is true?
(a) The mix of goods and services is inside the production-possibilities curve.
(b) Government intervention will improve the mix of goods and services.
(c) The mix of goods and services is at the wrong point on the production-possibilities curve.
(d) All of the above could be true.

_____ 6. Which of the following is most likely a public good?
(a) Roads.
(b) A hamburger.
(c) An automobile.
(d) Vegetables from a Farmer's market.

_____ 7. When public goods are marketed like private goods:
(a) Public goods are underproduced.
(b) Many consumers want to buy the goods.
(c) Public goods are overproduced.
(d) Government failure results.

_____ 8. For which of the following goods and services is the government likely to encourage production because of the existence of external benefits?
(a) Education.
(b) Health services for the poor.
(c) A neighborhood renovation project.
(d) All of the above.

_____ 9. The federal government's role in antitrust enforcement is justified by considerations of:
(a) Equity in the distribution of goods and services.
(b) Public goods and externalities.
(c) Underproduction by firms with market power.
(d) Macro failure.

_____ 10. The development of market power by a firm is considered to be a market failure because firms with market power:
(a) Produce more and charge a lower price than what is socially optimal.
(b) Tend to ignore external costs.
(c) Produce less and charge a higher price than what is socially optimal.
(d) Do not respond to consumer demand.

_____ 11. Transfer payments are an appropriate mechanism for correcting:
(a) Market power.
(b) Government failure.
(c) Inflation.
(d) Inequity in the distribution of goods and services.

_____ 12. Social demand is equal to
- (a) Private demand plus market demand.
- (b) Market demand plus external benefits.
- (c) Private demand.
- (d) Market demand minus external benefits.

_____ 13. The primary function of taxes is to:
- (a) Transfer command over resources from the private sector to the public sector.
- (b) Increase the purchasing power of the private sector.
- (c) Increase private saving.
- (d) Make it possible to sell bonds to finance the U.S. budget deficit.

_____ 14. Government intervention in the market:
- (a) Involves an opportunity cost.
- (b) Never involves an opportunity cost because only market activities result in other goods and services being given up.
- (c) Does not involve an opportunity cost if market outcomes are improved.
- (d) Results in the "free-rider dilemma."

_____ 15. The largest single source of revenue for the federal government is:
- (a) Borrowing (selling government bonds).
- (b) Social security taxes.
- (c) The corporate profits tax.
- (d) The personal income tax.

_____ 16. Which of the following can be classified as a regressive tax?
- (a) The federal corporate income tax.
- (b) The federal personal income tax.
- (c) The state sales tax.
- (d) All of the above.

_____ 17. Which of the following is an example of a progressive tax?
- (a) The excise tax on distilled spirits.
- (b) The federal tax on gasoline.
- (c) The federal personal income tax.
- (d) All of the above.

_____ 18. States receive most of their tax revenues from:
- (a) Sales taxes.
- (b) State income taxes.
- (c) Property taxes.
- (d) User charges.

_____ 19. Reread the article in the text titled "Napster Gets Napped." According to the article an item is a public good if:
- (a) The government produces the good.
- (b) Consumers can be excluded from consumption.
- (c) Consumers must meet certain criteria to consume the good.
- (d) Consumers cannot be excluded from consumption.

_____ 20. Which of the following would *not* support the theory of public choice?

(a) The governor of the state vetoes a highway bill even though the highway would enhance the value of property he owns.

(b) The local mayor campaigns in favor of a bond issue for the construction of sewer lines that will raise the value of his property.

(c) The local police chief fails to give the mayor a speeding ticket because the mayor might fire him.

(d) A college president asks the board of regents to allow her to remain in office so she can bolster her retirement income, even though she has reached the mandatory retirement age.

Problems and Applications

Exercise 1

Assume point *A* represents the optimal mix of output in Figure 4.1. Determine which letter best represents the following situations. Then answer questions 4-7.

Figure 4.1

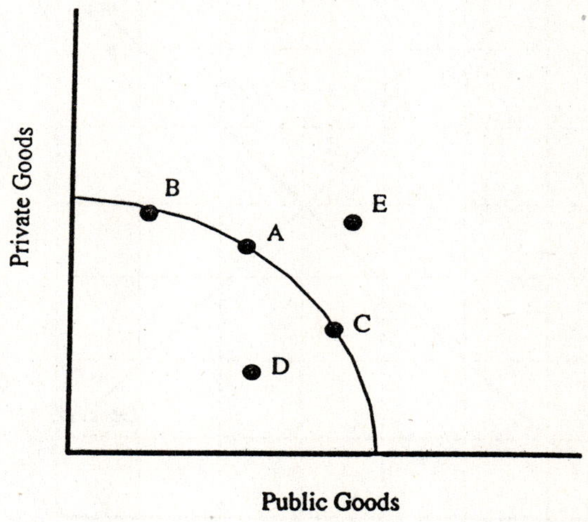

_____ 1. Government failure at the micro level that results in an overproduction of public goods.

_____ 2. Macro failure in the marketplace.

_____ 3. The free-rider dilemma.

4. The market mechanism tends to __________________ public goods and __________________ private goods.

5. In terms of the production-possibilities curve, ________________ failures imply that society is at the wrong point on the curve and __________________ failures imply that society is inside the curve.

6. Market failures justify government _______________.

7. If government involvement fails to improve market outcomes then there is _______________ _______________.

Exercise 2

This exercise examines the difference between internal and external costs and the impact on the demand curve.

The market-demand and market-supply curves for a particular good are drawn in Figure 4.2. Assume that the consumption of the good generates external costs equal to $2 per unit.

1. Draw the social demand curve in Figure 4.2 and label it.

Figure 4.2

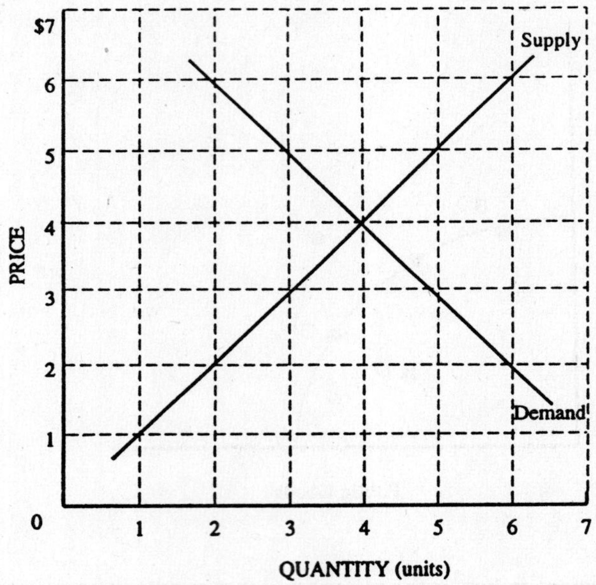

2. Market equilibrium occurs at a price of ______ and a quantity of _______ in Figure 4.3.

3. The socially optimal level of production occurs at a price of _______ and a quantity of _______.

4. External costs cause the market to produce (more, less) of a good than is optimal.

5. T F The social demand curve will always be less than the market demand curve if external costs are generated.

Exercise 3

This exercise focuses on the changes in public-sector spending in the U.S.

Refer to figure 4.4 in the text titled "Government Growth" to answer questions 1-4.

1. The large increase in total government purchases between 1940 and 1945 was the result of an increase in (only federal, both state and local and federal) government spending.

2. Compared to the level of federal spending in 1960, the level of federal spending for 2000 is (greater, less, the same).

3. Compared to the level of state and local spending in 1960, the level of state and local spending for 2000 is (greater, less, the same).

4. The decrease in total government purchases during the 1990s was primarily due to the decrease in (federal, state and local) purchases.

Exercise 4

This exercise examines progressive, regressive, and proportional tax structures.

Suppose Table 4.1 describes the incomes and taxes for individuals in the countries of Zebot and Dobler.

1. Calculate the following in Table 4.1:
(a) The percentage of income paid in taxes at each income level for the people of Zebot (column 3).
(b) The percentage of income paid in taxes at each income level for the people of Dobler (column 5).

Table 4.1 Taxes on income in the countries of Zebot and Dobler

(1) Income	(2) Taxes paid in Zebot	(3) Tax rate	(4) Taxes paid in Dobler	(5) Tax rate
$10,000	$2,000	________%	$1,000	________%
40,000	6,400	________	6,000	________
75,000	10,500	________	15,000	________
125,000	12,500	________	27,500	________

2. In Zebot, is the income tax progressive, regressive, or proportional? ____________________

3. In Dobler, is the income tax progressive, regressive, or proportional? ____________________

4. Which of the following is the most logical approach if a society wishes to redistribute income to the poor?
(a) A regressive tax structure.
(b) A progressive tax structure.
(c) A proportional tax structure.

5. T F A proportional tax structure means that the tax rate is constant regardless of income level.

Common Errors

The first statement in the "common error" below is incorrect. The incorrect statement is followed by a corrected version and an explanation.

1. Fire protection, police protection, education, and other services can be produced more efficiently by the private sector than by the public sector. WRONG!

   The public sector can produce many services more efficiently than the private sector. RIGHT!

   The existence of externalities and the free-rider problem force society to produce some goods and services through public-sector expenditures. Many of the goods and services we take for granted (such as education) would not be produced in sufficient quantities if left to the private sector. And can you imagine trying to provide for your own defense against foreign countries?

2. A public good is only produced by the government sector. WRONG!

   A public good is one whose consumption by one person does not prevent consumption by others. RIGHT!

   A public good can be produced by the private sector or the public sector. The source of production is not what makes it a public good. It is a public good because consumption is not exclusive. The government does provide many of the public goods such as national defense.

•ANSWERS•

Using Key Terms

Across

1. opportunity cost
5. inflation
8. market mechanism
10. government failure
14. natural monopoly
17. regressive tax
19. transfer payments
20. public choice
21. market power
22. user charge
23. proportional tax

Down

2. optimal mix of output
3. unemployment
4. externalities
6. progressive tax
7. private good
9. categorical grants
11. market failure
12. monopoly
13. merit good
15. public good
16. free rider
18. antitrust

True or False

1. T
2. F Equity considerations may necessitate government intervention.
3. T
4. T
5. T
6. F Markets will underproduce goods that yield external benefits and overproduce goods that yield external costs.
7. T
8. F Monopolies will tend to underproduce goods and are therefore able to charge a higher price.
9. F The federal government has grown in absolute terms since the 1950s but its relative share of production has declined, i.e., it has grown more slowly than the private sector.
10. F Sometimes government intervention worsens the market mix of goods and services. This is an example of "government failure."

Multiple Choice

1. c
2. d
3. b
4. d
5. d
6. a
7. a
8. d
9. c
10. c
11. d
12. b
13. a
14. a
15. d
16. c
17. c
18. a
19. d
20. a

Problems and Applications

Exercise 1

1. c
2. d
3. b
4. Underproduce, overproduce
5. Micro, macro
6. Intervention
7. Government failure

Exercise 2

1. See Figure 4.2 answer.

Figure 4.2 Answer

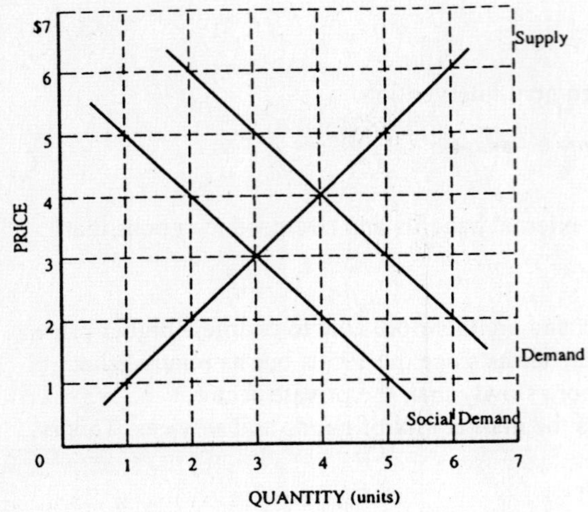

2. $4.00, 4 units
3. $3.00, 3 units
4. More
5. T

Exercise 3

1. Only federal
2. Less
3. Greater
4. Federal

Exercise 4

1. See Table 4.1 Answer.

Table 4.1 Answer

(1) Income	*(2)* Taxes paid in Zebot	*(3)* Tax rate	*(4)* Taxes paid in Dobler	*(5)* Tax rate
$10,000	$2,000	20.0 %	$1,000	10.0 %
40,000	6,400	16.0	6,000	15.0
75,000	10,500	14.0	15,000	20.0
125,000	12,500	10.0	27,500	22.0

2. Regressive. With greater income, a lower percentage of income goes to taxes (from 20% to 10% in column 3).
3. Progressive. With greater income, a higher percentage of income goes to taxes (from 10% to 22% in column 5).
4. b (A progressive tax is the most logical choice if society wants to redistribute income to the poor.)
5. T

PART 2 Product Markets: The Basics

CHAPTER 5

The Demand for Goods

Quick Review

- Economic theory focuses on demand—our willingness and ability to buy specific quantities of a good at various prices—and does not try to explain why people want the things they do.
- Utility is the satisfaction obtained from a particular good. Total utility is the total amount of satisfaction from consuming a particular quantity of a good; marginal utility is the satisfaction from consuming an additional unit of a good.
- The law of diminishing marginal utility says that the satisfaction from additional units of a good or service decreases as more of the good or service is consumed. This provides the basis for the law of demand. Marginal utility must be related to price in order to derive the law of demand.
- According to the law of demand, consumers will buy more of a good at a lower price, *ceteris paribus.* The nonprice determinants of demand—tastes, income, expectations, and the price and availability of other goods—are held constant when the demand curve is drawn. If any of these determinants change, the demand curve will shift.
- Price elasticity of demand measures the response of demand to a change in price. It is calculated as the percentage change in quantity demanded divided by the percentage change in price.
- The coefficient (E) that results from the elasticity calculation is always negative because of the law of demand, so its absolute value is used. If $|E| > 1$, demand is elastic; $|E| < 1$, demand is inelastic; and $|E| = 1$, demand is unitary elastic.
- Price elasticity determines the impact of a price change on total revenue ($P \times Q$). If price falls and demand is elastic, total revenue will increase; if price falls and demand is inelastic, total revenue will decrease. The opposite is true for a price increase.
- The determinants of price elasticity include the price of the good relative to income, the availability of substitutes, and the designation of the good as a necessity or a luxury.
- Income elasticity measures the response of demand to a change in income. Cross-price elasticity measures the response of demand for one good to a change in price of a related good.
- Optimal consumption occurs when utility is maximized. This is determined by comparing the marginal utility per dollar spent for each opportunity.

- Advertising is intended to increase the willingness of consumers to purchase a good. If advertising is successful, the demand curve will shift to the right.

Learning Objectives

After reading Chapter 5 and doing the following exercises, you should:

1. Be able to distinguish the demand for a good from the desire for it.
2. Be able to show how any change in the price of a good, in the price of a substitute, in the price of a complement, in incomes, in tastes, or in expectations will affect the demand curve.
3. Know how the law of diminishing marginal utility and the law of demand relate to each other.
4. Be able to draw a demand curve from a demand schedule and create a demand schedule by looking at a demand curve.
5. Be able to distinguish between a change in demand (a shift of the curve) and a change in quantity demanded (a movement along the demand curve).
6. Know the determinants of elasticity.
7. Be able to compute the price elasticity of demand between two points on the demand curve.
8. Be able to determine on the basis of the elasticity of demand what will happen to total revenue when price changes.
9. Understand income elasticity, cross-price elasticity and their role in demand theory.
10. Know how a consumer makes the optimal consumption decision.
11. Understand the role of advertising in the theory of demand.

Using Key Terms

Fill in the puzzle on the opposite page with the appropriate term from the list of Key Terms at the end of the chapter in the text.

Across

1. Items for which an increase in the price of good X causes a decrease in the demand for good Y.
6. In the cartoon in the text, the fourth hamburger does not provide as much satisfaction as the first hamburger because of the law of ______ ______ ______.
12. Explains why the curve in Figure 5.3 in the text is downward sloping.
13. The satisfaction obtained from the entire consumption of a good.
14. The quantity of a product sold times the price at which it is sold.
15. According to Figure 5.8 in the text, candy and popcorn are ______ ______.
17. Equal to the percentage change in quantity demanded divided by the percentage change in income.
18. Equal to the percentage change in quantity demanded of good X divided by the percentage change in the price of good Y.
19. The best forgone alternative.

Down

2. Influenced by tastes, income, expectations, and other goods.
3. Measures the response of consumers to a change in price.
4. The combination of goods which maximizes the total utility attainable from available income.
5. Positive but diminishing for the first five boxes of popcorn in Figure 5.2 in the text.
7. The result of a successful advertising campaign in Figure 5.9 in the text.
8. An item for which quantity demanded falls when income rises.
9. Affected by advertising in Figure 5.9 in the text.
10. Consumers buy more of such an item when their incomes rise.
11. The assumption that everything else is constant.
16. Satisfaction obtained from goods and services.

Puzzle 5.1

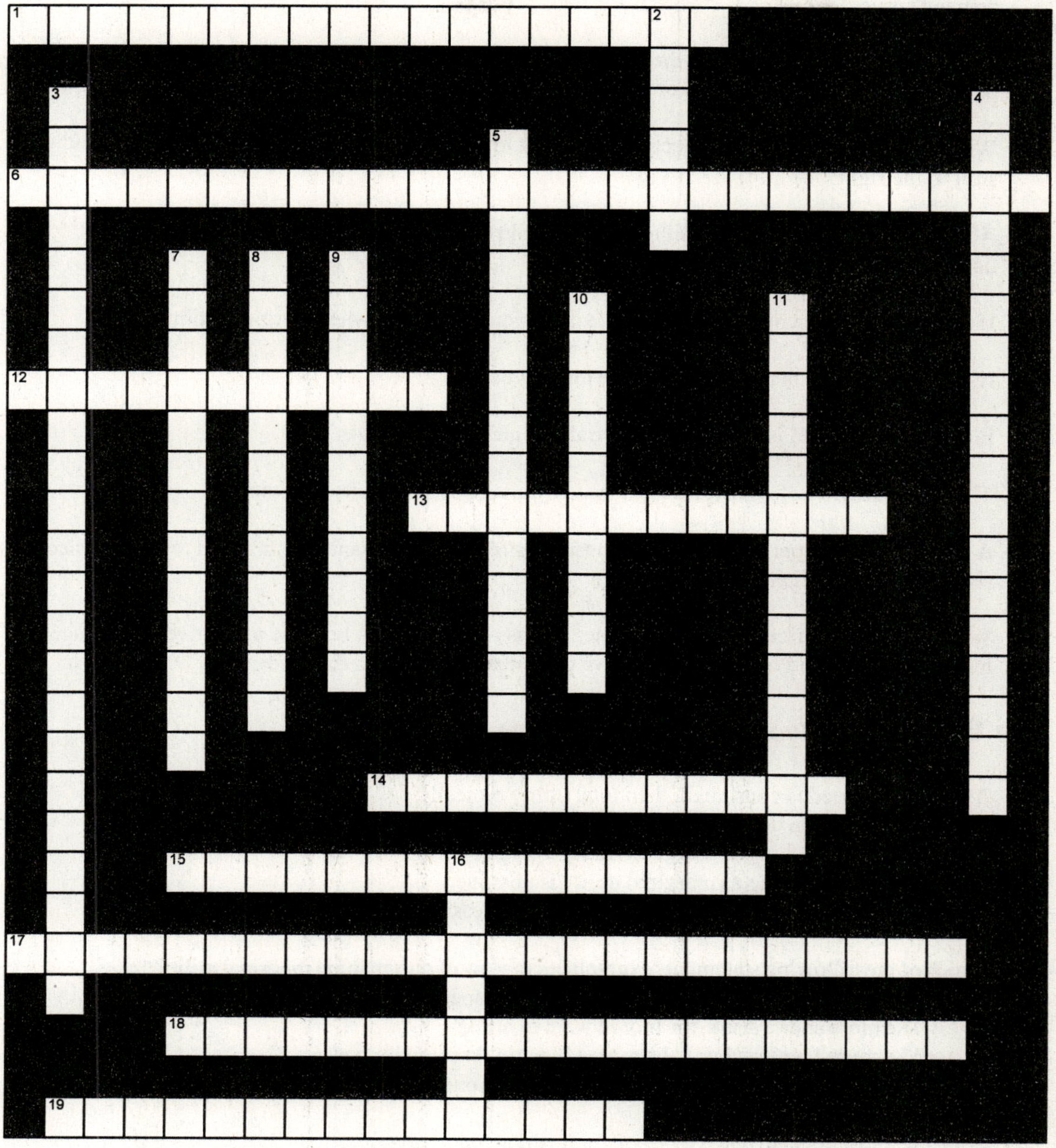

True or False: *Circle your choice and explain why any false statements are incorrect.*

T F 1. Sellers use advertising to change the consumer's utilities, thus causing a shift in the consumer's demand curve.

T F 2. The law of demand differs from the law of diminishing marginal utility in that it considers what a person is able to pay for a good or service, not just the person's desire for a good or service.

T F 3. When the price of a good is expected to fall next month, then the current demand curve should shift to the right.

T F 4. According to the law of diminishing marginal utility, the total utility we obtain from a product declines as we consume more of it.

T F 5. If there is no budget constraint, utility maximization is achieved when marginal utility is zero.

T F 6. If demand is elastic, a rise in price raises total revenue.

T F 7. Elasticity of demand is constant along straight-line demand curves.

T F 8. The price elasticity of demand is influenced by all the determinants of demand.

T F 9. A demand curve is perfectly elastic if consumers reduce their quantity demanded to zero if price rises by even the slightest amount.

T F 10. A negative cross-price elasticity indicates goods are substitutes because a positive percentage increase in one good results in a negative percentage increase in the other.

Multiple Choice: *Select the correct answer.*

_____ 1. As more of a good is consumed, then total utility typically:
- (a) Increases at a decreasing rate.
- (b) Decreases as long as marginal utility is negative.
- (c) Decreases as long as marginal utility is positive.
- (d) Is negative as long as marginal utility is decreasing.

_____ 2. Which of the following statements exemplifies the law of diminishing marginal utility?
- (a) Spinach gives me no satisfaction, so I won't spend my income for any of it.
- (b) The more soda I drink, the more I want to drink.
- (c) The more I go to school, the more I want to do something else.
- (d) Since we need water more than we need diamonds, water is more valuable.

_____ 3. Both the law of demand and the law of diminishing marginal utility:
- (a) State that quantity and price are inversely related.
- (b) Reflect declining increments of satisfaction from consuming additional units of product.
- (c) Reflect both the willingness and the ability of buyers to buy goods and services.
- (d) Can be illustrated by means of demand curves.

_____ 4. Which of the following is a reason why a demand curve is typically downward sloping?
(a) The law of diminishing marginal utility.
(b) Consumers are not willing to pay as much for a good with low marginal utility than for a good with a high marginal utility.
(c) Consumers have limited budgets.
(d) All of the above are reasons.

_____ 5. *Ceteris paribus*, as the number of substitutes for a good increase, the:
(a) Price elasticity of demand will become smaller.
(b) Price elasticity of demand will become larger.
(c) Cross-price elasticity of demand will become negative.
(d) Income elasticity of demand will become negative.

_____ 6. Which of the following causes demand to be more elastic with respect to price?
(a) Shorter periods of time to adjust to a change in price.
(b) A steeper demand curve for a given price and quantity.
(c) More substitutes.
(d) If the good takes up a larger portion of the consumer's budget.

_____ 7. Which of the following is likely to have a price elasticity coefficient greater than 1.0?
(a) Cigarettes.
(b) Coffee.
(c) An addictive drug.
(d) Meals at a restaurant.

_____ 8. Suppose your college or university raises tuition by 4 percent and as a result 2 percent fewer students enroll next semester. What is the value of the price elasticity of demand?
(a) -0.50.
(b) -2.0.
(c) -8.0.
(d) -6.0.

_____ 9. A demand curve is described as perfectly elastic if:
(a) The same quantity is purchased regardless of price.
(b) The same price is charged regardless of quantity sold.
(c) Only price can change.
(d) It is vertical.

_____ 10. Total revenue declines when demand is:
(a) Elastic and price rises, causing a demand shift.
(b) Elastic and price rises, causing a movement along the demand curve.
(c) Inelastic and price rises, causing a demand shift.
(d) Inelastic and price rises, causing a movement along the demand curve.

_____ 11. One of the airline industry's arguments against deregulation of airfares was that the resulting fall in prices would lower airline total revenue. Instead, total revenue rose. Assuming the increase in total revenue was due solely to the lower fares, it can be concluded that:
(a) Airline representatives thought demand for plane trips was elastic.
(b) Quantity demanded of airline service increased by a greater percentage than the percentage fall in price.
(c) Demand for airline service increased with the fall in prices.
(d) Airlines were more profitable after deregulation.

_____ 12. If a state legislature wishes to raise revenue by increasing certain sales taxes, it would increase sales taxes on goods that:
(a) Have inelastic demand.
(b) Are bought by those with high incomes.
(c) Are illegal.
(d) Have elastic demand.

_____ 13. Assume that a good has a downward sloping, linear demand curve. As the price of this good increases, total revenues:
(a) Increase indefinitely.
(b) Decrease indefinitely because the quantity sold will decrease.
(c) Remain constant.
(d) Increase then decrease.

_____ 14. Assume that the price elasticity of demand for Great Fit Shoe Co. shoes is -1.5. If the company decreases the price of each pair of shoes, total revenues will:
(a) Increase because more shoes will be sold.
(b) Decrease because the company will be receiving less revenue per pair of shoes.
(c) Increase because the percentage increase in the number sold is greater than the percentage decrease in the price.
(d) Impossible to predict because we do not know the percentage change in price.

_____ 15. When the price of postage stamps increases, the demand for long-distance telephone service increases, *ceteris paribus*. Postage stamps and long-distance service are therefore:
(a) Elastic.
(b) Inelastic.
(c) Complements.
(d) Substitutes.

_____ 16. Which of the following elasticities would be most useful in determining the impact of a recession on the demand for airline travel?
(a) The income elasticity of air travel.
(b) The price elasticity of demand for air travel.
(c) The cross-price elasticity of demand for air travel with respect to income.
(d) The cross-price elasticity of income with respect to air travel.

_____ 17. Suppose the cross-price elasticity of demand for automobiles with respect to the gasoline price is -0.20. If gasoline prices rise 20 percent, then automobile sales should, *ceteris paribus*:
(a) Fall 4 percent.
(b) Fall 100 percent.
(c) Rise 4 percent.
(d) Rise 100 percent.

_____ 18. If the price elasticity of demand is -2.0 and a firm raises its price by 8 percent, the quantity sold by the firm will:
(a) Increase by 16 percent.
(b) Decrease by 16 percent.
(c) Increase by 4 percent.
(d) Decrease by 4 percent.

_____ 19. To maximize utility when purchasing two or more goods, the consumer should choose that good which:
(a) Is priced the lowest.
(b) Has the highest price elasticity.
(c) Delivers the most marginal utility per dollar.
(d) Provides the most satisfaction.

_____ 20. The objective of advertising is to:
(a) Increase demand and increase the price elasticity of demand.
(b) Increase demand and decrease the price elasticity of demand.
(c) Increase demand only.
(d) Decrease demand and make the price elasticity of demand unitary.

[CHAPTER 20 APPENDIX QUESTIONS]

_____ 21. An indifference curve shows:
(a) The maximum utility that can be achieved for a given consumer budget.
(b) The maximum utility that can be achieved for different amounts of a good.
(c) The combinations of goods giving equal utility to a consumer.
(d) The optimal consumption combinations between two goods.

_____ 22. A budget line represents:
(a) Consumption possibilities.
(b) The combinations of goods giving equal utility to a consumer.
(c) The combinations of goods a consumer can afford.
(d) The amount of income that is required to purchase a given amount of a good.

_____ 23. Where the budget line and an indifference curve are tangent, there is:
(a) An optimal consumption point.
(b) A point indicating the quantity and price that would appear on a demand curve.
(c) A point where the ratio of marginal utility to price is equal for two goods.
(d) All of the above.

Problems and Applications

Exercise 1

This exercise will help you draw demand curves using demand schedules. It should also give you practice in constructing market demand curves.

1. Market demand is:
(a) The total quantity of a good or service that people are willing and able to buy at alternative prices in a given period of time, *ceteris paribus*.
(b) The sum of individual demands.
(c) Represented as the horizontal sum of individual demand curves.
(d) All of the above.

2. Table 5.1 presents a hypothetical demand schedule for cars manufactured in the United States.

Table 5.1 Demand for U.S. cars

Price	*Number of new U.S. cars (millions per year)*
$10,000	9.0
9,000	10.0

Graph this demand curve in Figure 5.1.

Figure 5.1

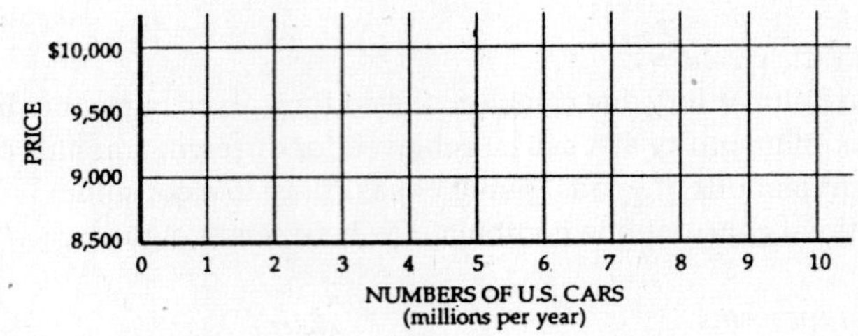

3. Table 5.2 presents a similar demand schedule for imported cars.

Table 5.2
Demand for foreign cars

Price	*Number of new foreign cars (millions per year)*
$10,000	1.0
9,000	2.0

Graph this demand curve in Figure 5.2.

Figure 5.2

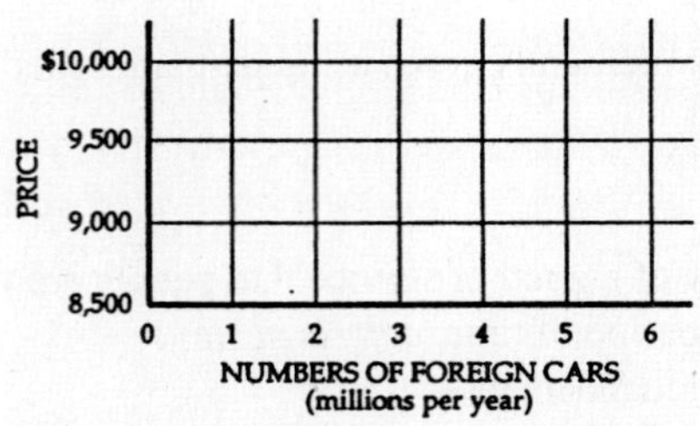

4. In Table 5.3 calculate the demand schedule for cars (both foreign and domestically produced) at the two prices shown.

Table 5.3
Market demand for new cars

Price	Number of new cars (millions per year)
$10,000	______
9,000	______

5. In Figure 5.3 draw the domestic market demand curve for both foreign and domestic cars.

Figure 5.3

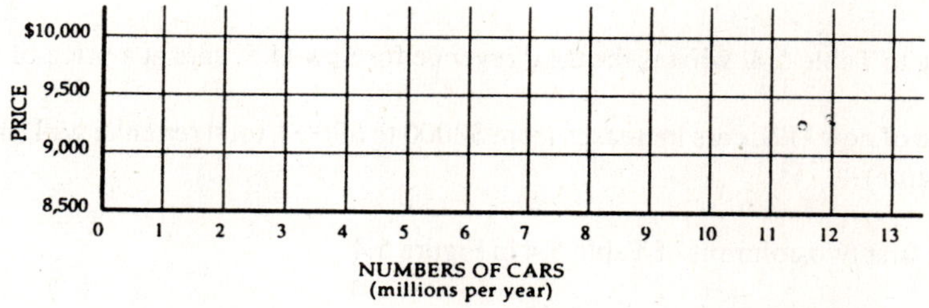

Exercise 2

This exercise should give you practice in computing and interpreting the price elasticity of demand. This exercise is similar to a problem in the text.

1. T F The midpoint formula for the price elasticity of demand is

$$\frac{(p_2-p_1)/[1/2(p_1+p_2)]}{(q_2-q_1)/[1/2(q_1+q_2)]}$$

2. If you answered "true" to problem 1, you goofed. The percentage change in quantity, $(q_2 - q_1) \div [1/2(q_1 + q_2)]$, should be on the top, not the bottom. The correct formula is

$$\frac{(q_2-q_1)/[1/2(q_1+q_2)]}{(p_2-p_1)/[1/2(p_1+p_2)]}$$

Apply this formula to the information in Table 5.4, which represents a hypothetical demand schedule for cars. Remember to use the absolute value of this expression, which makes the coefficient always positive. (When calculating elasticities, answers will vary depending on the number of decimal places used. To achieve the book answer you will need to round each calculation to 2 decimal places.)

Table 5.4
Market demand schedule for cars

Price	*Number of new U.S. cars (millions per year)*	*Elasticity of demand*
$10,000	10.0	—
9,000	12.0	______
8,000	14.0	______
7,000	16.0	______

3. According to Table 5.4, the price elasticity of demand for U.S. cars is (elastic, inelastic) between $9000 and $8000.

4. According to Table 5.4, what is the total revenue for new U.S. cars at a price of $8000?

5. If the price of new U.S. cars increases from $8000 to $9000, total revenue will (increase, decrease, stay the same).

6. Graph the first two columns of Table 5.4 in Figure 5.4.

Figure 5.4
Market demand curve

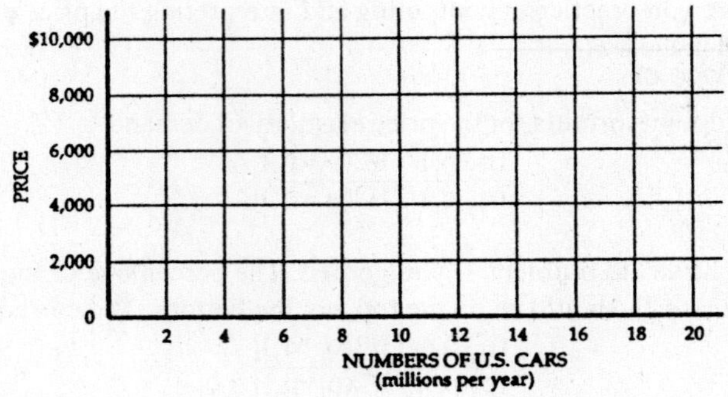

7. T F The curve is a linear demand curve.

8. What is the slope of the demand curve? __________

9. Moving down a linear demand curve results in:
   (a) More inelastic demand and a changing slope.
   (b) More inelastic demand but a constant slope.
   (c) More elastic demand and a changing slope.
   (d) More elastic demand and a constant slope.

10. T F While elasticity reflects a ratio of percentage changes in two variables, the slope reflects only changes in the variables, not percentage changes.

Exercise 3

This exercise focuses on calculating income elasticity and cross-price elasticity. It is similar to a problem in the text.

1. Use Table 5.5 to calculate the income elasticity of demand for peanut butter. Refer to the formula in the text. (Remember to round to 2 decimal places.)

Table 5.5

	Income (per year)	*Demand for peanut butter (jars per year)*		*Income elasticity of demand*
a	$10,000	12		
b	$20,000	7	a to b	______
c	$40,000	3	b to c	______
d	$80,000	1	c to d	______

2. Based on Table 5.5, peanut butter is a (normal, inferior) good because as income rises, the quantity demanded of peanut butter (rises, falls), and the income elasticity of demand is (negative, positive).

3. Use Table 5.6 to calculate the cross-price elasticity of demand for jelly when the price of peanut butter changes. Refer to the formula in the text. (Remember to round to 2 decimal places.)

Table 5.6

	Price of peanut butter (per jar)	*Demand for jelly (jars per year)*		*Cross-price elasticity of demand*
a	$2.00	12		
b	$3.00	10	a to b	______
c	$4.00	7	b to c	______
d	$5.00	2	c to d	______

4. Based upon Table 5.6, peanut butter and jelly are (substitute, complementary) goods because as the price of peanut butter rises, the demand for jelly (falls, rises) and the cross-price elasticity of demand is (negative, positive).

Exercise 4

This exercise shows the relationship between total and marginal utility. It also gives practice in identifying the law of diminishing marginal utility.

Suppose there are two types of entertainment you enjoy: an evening at home with friends, and an "event" entertainment, such as a sports event or a rock concert. The number of times that you experience each type of entertainment during a month determines the total utility of each type of entertainment for that month. Suppose Table 5.7 represents the total utility you achieve from consuming various quantities of the two types of entertainment.

Table 5.7
Total and marginal utility of two types of entertainment per month

Days of entertainment per month	Evening at home: Total utility	Evening at home: Marginal utility	Event: Total utility	Event: Marginal utility
0	0	________	0	________
1	170	________	600	________
2	360	________	1,250	________
3	540	________	1,680	________
4	690	________	2,040	________
5	820	________	2,350	________
6	930	________	2,550	________
7	1,030	________	2,720	________
8	1,110	________	2,820	________
9	1,170	________	2,820	________
10	1,170	________	2,760	________
11	1,120	________	2,660	________
12	1,020	________	2,460	________

1. Complete Table 5.7 by computing the marginal utility of each type of entertainment.

2. The law of diminishing marginal utility means:
   (a) The total utility of a good declines as more of it is consumed in a given time period.
   (b) The marginal utility of a good declines as more of it is consumed in a given time period.
   (c) The price of a good declines as more of it is consumed in a given period of time.
   (d) All of the above.

3. The law of diminishing marginal utility is in evidence in Table 5.7 for:
   (a) Both types of entertainment.
   (b) Home entertainment only.
   (c) Event entertainment only.
   (d) Neither type of entertainment.

(Hint: You should be able to tell by looking at the marginal utility columns in Table 5.7. Does the marginal utility become smaller as you go down the column?)

4. In Figure 5.5 graph the total utility curve for evenings at home.

Figure 5.5

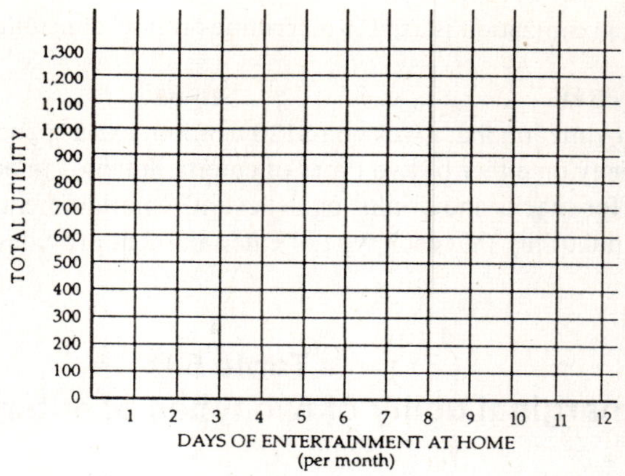

5. In Figure 5.6 graph the marginal utility curve for evenings at home.

Figure 5.6

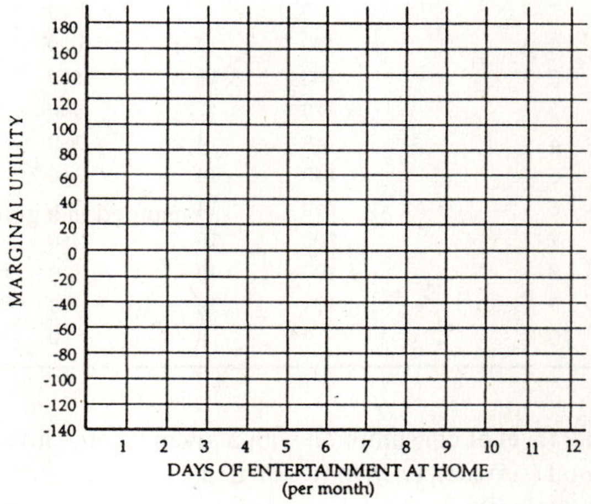

6. On the basis of the two graphs above, marginal utility becomes zero only when:
   (a) Total utility is zero.
   (b) Total utility reaches a maximum.
   (c) Total utility is rising.
   (d) Total utility is falling.

7. When total utility is rising, it is certain that:
   (a) Marginal utility is rising.
   (b) Marginal utility is negative.
   (c) Marginal utility is positive.
   (d) Marginal utility is zero.

Exercise 5

The principle of utility maximization is used to determine optimal consumption. This exercise builds on the previous exercise.

Suppose you hold a part-time job that gives you $120 a month extra spending money. On any day of the month you can spend that money on either of two types of entertainment—an evening at home with friends, for which you usually spend $10 for snacks and drinks, or an "event" entertainment, which costs $30. Table 5.8 shows the hypothetical marginal utility that each type of entertainment provides for you during the month.

Table 5.8
Total and marginal utility of two types of entertainment per month

	Evening at home (price = $10)		*Event entertainment (price = $30)*	
Days of entertainment per month	*Marginal utility*	*MU/price*	*Marginal utility*	*MU/price*
0	0	0	0	—
1	180	18	600	___
2	180	18	600	___
3	170	17	480	___
4	140	14	360	___
5	140	14	360	___
6	140	14	360	___
7	100	10	360	___
8	100	10	0	___
9	100	10	0	___
10	0	0	0	___

1. Finding the optimal level of consumption with a given income involves choosing successive *increments* of a good (service), *each of which* yields:
   (a) The largest total utility.
   (b) The largest marginal utility per unit of product or activity purchased.
   (c) The largest marginal utility for each dollar spent.
   (d) All of the above.

2. Divide marginal utility by the price of the event entertainment to complete Table 5.8.

Before you spend any money on any activity:

3. Which activity has the highest MU/*p* ratio? ____________________

4. Judging by the MU/*p* ratio, how many days of event entertainment should you buy before spending anything on at-home entertainment? __________

5. If you had $120 to spend on entertainment, how much money would you have left after buying two days of event entertainment? __________

6. Should you spend the entire balance from question 5 on at-home entertainment? __________

7. After you have bought three at-home nights and two events, how much income is left from the original $120? __________

8. Based on MU/*p*, which activity should you purchase with the income remaining in question 7?

    ____

9. T F When your income is $120, optimal consumption occurs with three evenings of each type of entertainment.

Appendix Exercise 6

This exercise provides practice in interpreting an indifference map and total utility.

For questions 1-7 refer to Figure 5A.2 in the appendix for Chapter 5.

1. At point E, the consumption combination includes _____ cokes and _____ video games.

2. At point D, the consumption combination includes _____ cokes and _____ video games.

3. Based on the indifference map, the consumer receives:
    (a) Greater satisfaction at point E than at point D.
    (b) Greater satisfaction at point D than at point E.
    (c) Equal satisfaction at point D and at point E.
    (d) Satisfaction cannot be determined from an indifference map.

4. At point B, the consumption combination includes _____ cokes and _____ video games.

5. At point C, the consumption combination includes _____ cokes and _____ video games.

6. Compare combinations B and C to point E. In each case, point E provides (greater, lesser) satisfaction than point B or point C.

7. For the given indifference map, the level of total utility is greatest at any point along curve __________.

Common Errors

The first statement in each "common error" below is incorrect. Each incorrect statement is followed by a corrected version and an explanation.

1. The law of demand and the law of diminishing marginal utility are the same. WRONG!

    The law of demand and the law of diminishing marginal utility are not the same. RIGHT!

    Do not confuse utility and demand. Utility refers only to expected satisfaction. Demand refers to both preferences and ability to pay. This distinction should help you to keep the law of diminishing marginal utility separate from the law of demand.

2. Figures 20.8a and 20.8b represent simple graphs drawn from a demand schedule.

Figure 5.8a

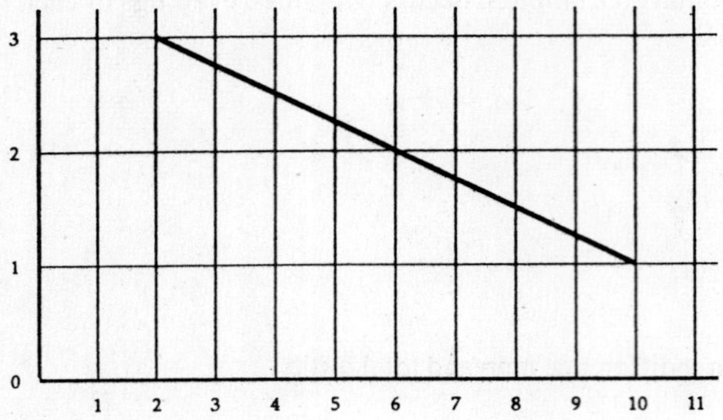

Price (dollars per unit)	*Output quantity per unit of time*
10	1
2	3

WRONG!

Figure 5.8b

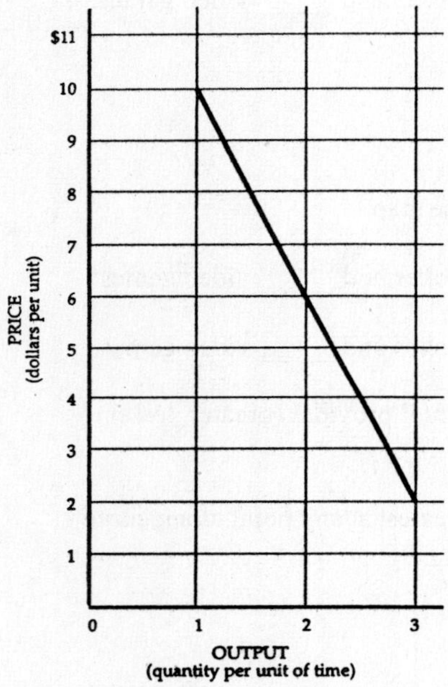

Price (dollars per unit)	*Output quantity per unit of time*
10	1
2	3

RIGHT!

The first graph has been drawn without any units indicated. It is something of an accidental tradition in economics to show price on the *y*-axis and quantity on the *x*-axis. This convention is sometimes confusing to mathematicians, who want to treat quantity as a function of price, according to the definition in the text. In Figure 5.8a the axes have been reversed and incorrect points have been chosen.

Be careful! When you are drawing a new graph, make a special effort to understand the units that are placed on the axes. Also, make sure you know the kinds of units in which each axis is measured. If you are drawing a graph from a table (or schedule), you can usually determine what should be on the axes by looking at the heading above the column from which you are reading the numbers.

Make sure price is shown on the *y*-axis (vertical) and quantity on the *x*-axis (horizontal). If you mix up the two, you may confuse a graph showing perfectly elastic demand with one showing perfectly inelastic demand.

3. The formula for the price elasticity of demand is

$$\frac{\text{Change in price}}{\text{Change in quantity}} \qquad \text{WRONG!}$$

The formula for the price elasticity of demand is

$$\frac{\text{Percentage change in quantity demanded}}{\text{Percentage change in price}} \qquad \text{RIGHT!}$$

The concept of elasticity allows us to compare relative changes in quantity and price without having to worry about the units in which they are measured. In order to do this, we compute percentage changes of both price and quantity. A change in price *causes* people to change the quantity they demand in a given time period. By putting the quantity changes in the numerator, we can see that if the quantity response is very large in relation to a price change, the elasticity will also be very large. If the quantity response is small in relation to a price change, then demand is price inelastic (elasticity is small).

Be careful! Do not confuse slope and elasticity. The formula for the slope of the demand curve is the *wrong* formula shown above. The formula for the price elasticity of demand is the *right* formula. Remember to take the absolute value of the elasticity too.

4. A flat demand curve has an elasticity of zero. WRONG!

A flat demand curve has an infinite elasticity. RIGHT!

When price remains constant even when quantity changes, the elasticity formula requires us to divide by a zero price change. In fact, as demand curves approach flatness, the elasticity becomes larger and larger. By agreement we say it is infinite.

5. The person for whom a good or service has the greatest utility has the greatest desire for more of it. WRONG!

The good that has the greatest *marginal* utility for a person, with respect to price, is the good that he or she desires more. RIGHT!

Utilities of one good for many people cannot be compared. Utilities of various goods for one person can be compared. Marginal utility with respect to price, not total utility, is the best indicator of how to make a choice.

6. An expected price change has the same effect as a change in the current price. WRONG!

An unexpected price change shifts the demand curve, whereas a current price change is a movement along the demand curve. RIGHT!

If prices are expected to rise in the near future, people will demand more of the commodity today in order to beat the rise in price. Demand increases and the quantity demanded will rise. However, if the price rises today, by the law of demand people reduce the quantity demanded! Furthermore, demand itself does not change. A current price change and an expected price change have very different effects.

7. When a buyer purchases a good, the demand for the good decreases. WRONG!

When a buyer purchases a good, demand is not affected. RIGHT!

Demand refers only to the *willingness* and *ability* of a buyer to buy. The potential for purchase, not the actual purchase, is the focus of demand. Demand is defined over a given period of time. If a buyer buys a good during that period of time, he or she is still counted as demanding the good—even after it is purchased.

8. Both income and cross-price elasticities must be interpreted using absolute values. WRONG!

The absolute value is used only for the price elasticity of demand. RIGHT!

The law of demand guarantees that the price elasticity of demand would always have a negative sign. However, the income and cross-price elasticities may be either positive or negative, and the sign provides important information about the demand for a good. The sign of the income elasticity indicates if a good is a normal good or an inferior good. The sign on the cross-price elasticity indicates whether a good is a substitute or a complement.

•ANSWERS•

Using Key Terms

Across

1. complementary goods
6. diminishing marginal utility
12. law of demand
13. total utility
14. total revenue
15. substitute goods
17. income elasticity of demand
18. cross-price elasticity
19. opportunity cost

Down

2. demand
3. price elasticity of demand
4. optimal consumption
5. marginal utility
7. shift in demand
8. inferior good
9. demand curve
10. normal good
11. *ceteris paribus*
16. utility

True or False

1. T
2. T
3. F Consumers will plan to wait until next month's lower prices to purchase this good. The current demand curve will shift to the left.
4. F The marginal utility will decline. The total utility will increase as long as the marginal utility is positive.
5. T
6. F A rise in the price will result in lower total revenues. A *decrease* in the price will raise total revenues if demand is elastic.
7. F Price elasticity of demand will be more elastic (i.e. consumers more responsive) at higher prices. Elasticity cannot be compared to slope.
8. T
9. T
10. F A *positive* cross-price elasticity indicates substitutes. An *increase* in the price of one good, for example, would result in an *increase* in the demand for the substitute.

Multiple Choice

1.	a	5.	b	9.	b	13.	d	17.	a	21.	c
2.	c	6.	c	10.	b	14.	c	18.	b	22.	c
3.	b	7.	d	11.	b	15.	d	19.	c	23.	d
4.	d	8.	a	12.	a	16.	a	20.	b		

Problems and Applications

Exercise 1

1. d

2. **Figure 5.1 Answer**

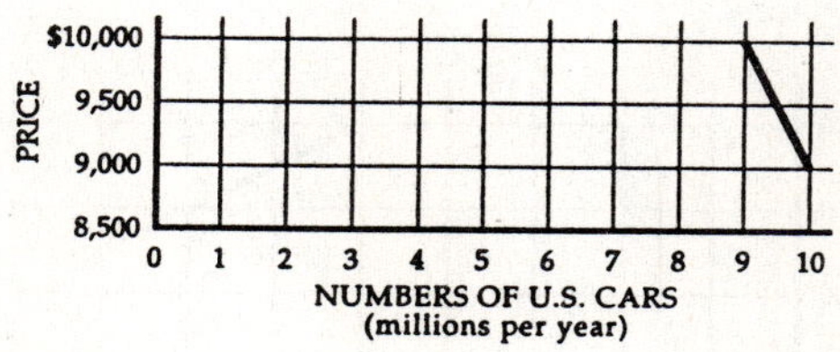

3. **Figure 5.2 Answer**

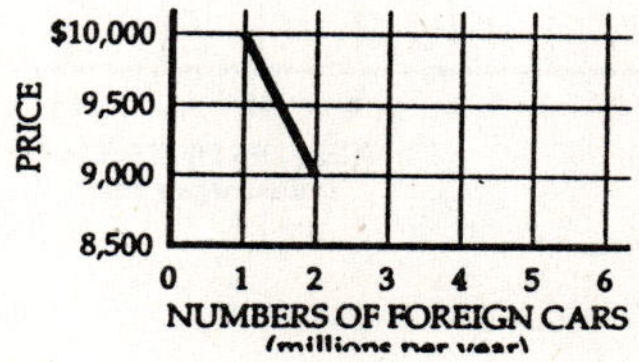

4. **Table 5.3 Answer**

Price	*Number of new cars (millions per year)*
$10,000	10.0
9,000	12.0

5. **Figure 5.3 Answer**

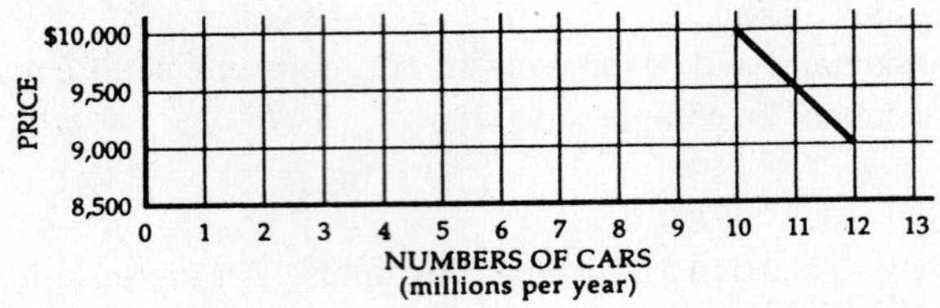

Exercise 2

1. F
2. **Table 5.4 Answer**

Price	*Number of new U.S. cars (millions per year)*	*Elasticity of demand*
$10,000	10.0	---
9,000	12.0	1.64
8,000	14.0	1.25
7,000	16.0	1.00

3. Elastic
4. $112,000
5. Decrease
6. **Figure 5.4 answer**

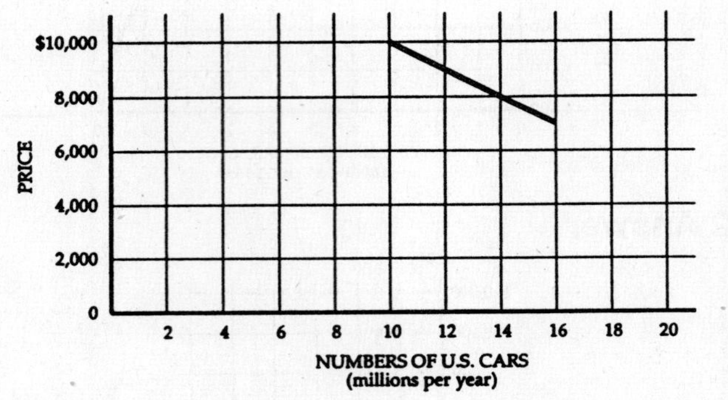

7. T

8. The slope can be estimated by using the coordinates of any two points on the demand curve. The slope is computed by dividing the change in the variable on the y-axis by the change in the variable on the x-axis. For example, using the first two points in Table 5.4, we would have

Regardless of what pair of points is chosen, the slope should be the same (except for differences that result from rounding).

9. b As noted in the previous problem, the slope is the same regardless of which pair of points is tried.

10. T

Exercise 3

1. **Table 5.5 Answer**

	Income (per year)	*Demand for peanut butter (jars per year)*		*Income elasticity of demand*
a	$10,000	12		
b	$20,000	7	a to b	**-0.79**
c	$40,000	3	b to c	**-1.19**
d	$80,000	1	c to d	**-1.49**

2. Inferior, falls, negative

3. **Table 5.6 Answer**

	Price of peanut butter (per jar)	*Demand for jelly (jars per year)*		*Cross-price elasticity of demand*
a	$2.00	12		
b	$3.00	10	a to b	**-0.45**
c	$4.00	7	b to c	**-1.21**
d	$5.00	2	c to d	**-5.05**

4. Complementary, falls, negative

Exercise 4

1. **Table 5.7 Answer**

Days of entertainment per month	Evening at home Marginal utility	Event Marginal utility
0	—	—
1	170	600
2	190	650
3	180	430
4	150	360
5	130	310
6	110	200
7	100	170
8	80	100
9	60	0
10	0	–60
11	–50	–100
12	–100	–200

2. b
3. a

4. **Figure 5.5 Answer**

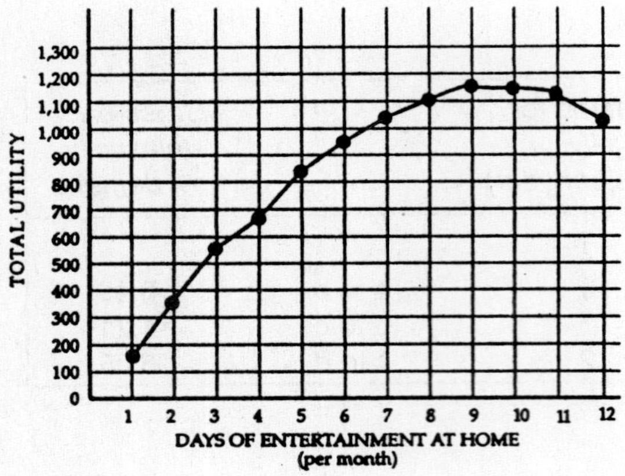

5. **Figure 5.6 Answer**

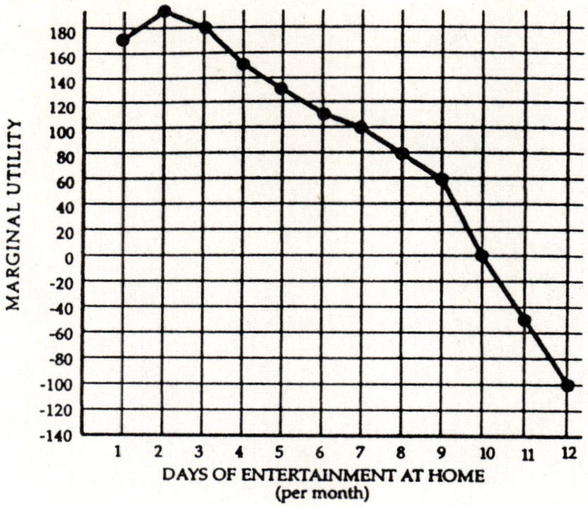

6. b
7. c

Exercise 5

1. c
2. **Table 5.8 Answer**

Days of entertainment per month	*Event entertainment (price = $30)* Marginal utility	MU / price
0	0	0
1	600	20
2	600	20
3	480	16
4	360	12
5	360	12
6	360	12
7	360	12
8	0	0
9	0	0
10	0	0

3. Event entertainment
4. 2
5. $60[=$120-($30x2)]
6. No
7. $30[=$120-$60-(3x$10)]
8. Event entertainment
9. T

Exercise 6

1. 3 cokes, 5 video games
2. 2 cokes, 8 video games
3. c
4. 2 cokes, 5 video games
5. 3 cokes, 4 video games
6. Greater
7. I_2

CHAPTER 6

The Costs of Production

Quick Review

- The production function determines how much output can be obtained from varying amounts of factor inputs. Every point on the production function is efficient, meaning that, given current technology, the maximum output is being produced.

- The output of any factor depends on the amount of other resources available to it. Fixed factors constrain the firm's ability to produce output. As more of a variable input is applied to a fixed input, at some point, the marginal physical product of the variable input begins to get smaller in size. This short-run situation is referred to as the *law of diminishing returns*. In the long run, all factor inputs are variable.

- The dollar costs incurred because of fixed inputs are called fixed costs; those for variable factors are called variable costs. In the short-run, even if output is zero, there are fixed costs. The total cost of producing any level of output is the sum of fixed and variable costs. Because fixed costs do not change as output changes, the rate of increase in total cost is determined by variable costs only.

- Marginal cost (MC) is the increase in total cost associated with a one-unit increase in production. Average total cost (ATC) is the total cost of production divided by the rate of output. The ATC curve starts at a high level and declines as production increases because of fixed costs. At a point, the ATC curve begins to rise because of rising marginal costs that result from the law of diminishing returns. This results in a U-shaped ATC curve.

- Economic costs include both explicit and implicit costs associated with the use of *all* resources in the production process, whether they receive a monetary payment or not. Accounting costs include only those costs for which an explicit payment is made.

- In the short run a producer decides how much output to produce with existing facilities. A producer will supply output only if price at least covers marginal costs. In the long run there are no fixed costs. The producer must decide whether to build, buy, or lease plant and equipment.

- If minimum average costs decrease as the size of the firm increases, then there are economies of scale. If minimum ATC increases as the firm gets larger, then there are diseconomies of scale.

- Advances in technology shift the production function upward and the cost curves downward. Along with improved quality of inputs, technology improvements have historically been the major source of productivity growth in the U.S. economy.

Learning Objectives

After reading Chapter 6 and doing the following exercises, you should:

1. Know the relationship between the production function and the firm's ability to produce goods and services.
2. Understand the nature and determinants of marginal productivity.
3. Be able to draw a graph relating the marginal physical product and total product curves.
4. Be able to define and explain the law of diminishing returns.
5. Understand the relationship between the production function and the short-run cost curves.
6. Understand the difference between variable costs and fixed costs.
7. Know how to define and calculate the total, average, and marginal costs of production and be able to show their relationship to marginal productivity.
8. Understand the relationship between average and marginal cost curves.
9. Understand the distinction between economic costs and accounting costs.
10. Know the distinction between long-run costs and short-run costs.
11. Be able to explain economies of scale, diseconomies of scale, and constant returns to scale.
12. Understand the impact of technological improvements on the production function.

Using Key Terms

Fill in the puzzle on the opposite page with the appropriate term from the list of Key Terms at the end of the chapter in the text.

Across

1. The resources used to produce a good or service.
5. The horizontal curve at $120 in Figure 6.4 in the text.
7. Equals $245 when producing 15 pairs of jeans per day according to Table 6.2 in the text.
9. Equal to the wage rate divided by marginal physical product.
11. The marginal physical product of a variable input declines as more of it is employed with a given quantity of other (fixed) inputs.
13. Maximum output of a good attainable from the resources used.
14. Anytime a dollar payment is made for the use of a resource there is a(an) _______ cost.
15. Average total costs minus average fixed costs.
17. Includes both explicit and implicit costs.
18. Equal to 15 for the first worker hired in Figure 6.1 in the text.
21. Used in Table 6.1 in the text to tell how the output of jeans would change if some sewing machines were leased.
22. Output per unit of input.
23. A period in which some inputs are fixed.

Down

2. Drawn with a U-shape in Figure 6.5 in the text.
3. The most desired forgone alternative.
4. Helps to explain why one large firm dominates the funeral business according to the article in the text titled "Funeral Giant Moves In on Small Rivals."
6. A situation in which an increase in plant size does not reduce minimum average costs.
8. Equal to $6 per pair of jeans at an output rate of 20 pairs per day in Figure 6.5 in the text.
10. The portion of economic cost that does not receive an explicit payment.
12. Determine how fast total costs rise.
16. This curve is typically rising because of the law of diminishing returns.

19. The difference between total revenue and total costs.
20. A period in which all inputs are variable.

Puzzle 6.1

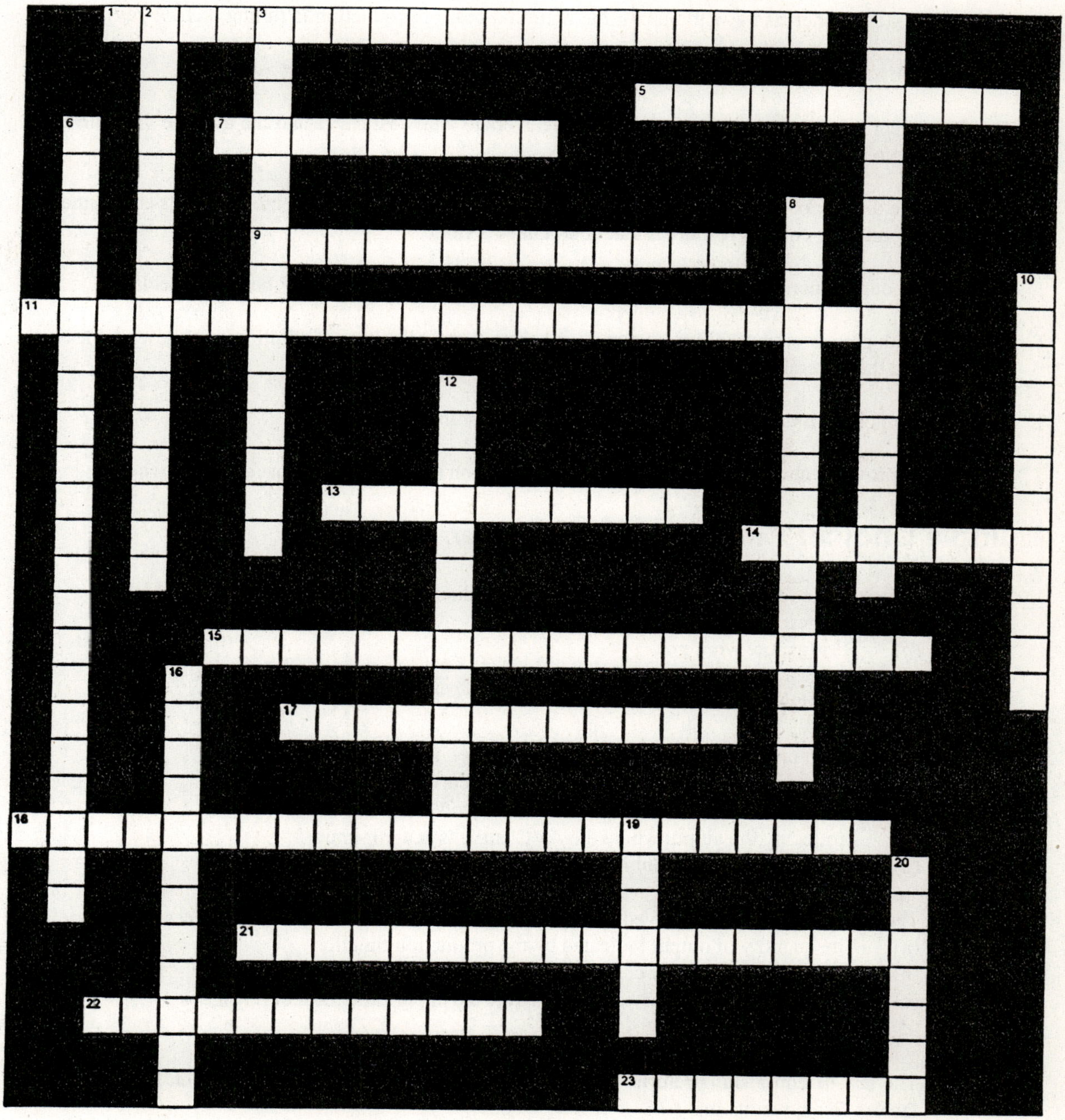

True or False: *Circle your choice and explain why any false statements are incorrect.*

T F 1. The production function can be increased by working the labor input harder.

T F 2. The productivity of labor is affected by changes in the mix of other factors being used in the production process.

T F 3. If MPP is increasing with output, the marginal cost of production is falling, *ceteris paribus*.

T F 4. The total cost at a zero level of output is always the amount of fixed costs.

T F 5. The marginal cost curve can intersect the average total cost curve and the average variable cost curve at any point.

T F 6. The difference between the accountant's and the economist's measurement of costs equals the opportunity costs of resources that do not have a value.

T F 7. As output increases, marginal costs eventually increase because MPP begins to decline.

T F 8. With greater output, falling average fixed costs eventually outweigh falling average variable costs, and then average total cost starts to rise.

T F 9. Economies of scale result from the law of diminishing returns.

T F 10. Improved technology shifts the production function upward and the cost curves downward.

Multiple Choice: *Select the correct answer.*

_____ 1. Which of the following would cause a firm's production function to shift upward?
(a) An increase in production by the firm.
(b) Hiring more workers.
(c) Increased training for the firm's workers.
(d) An increase in factor costs.

_____ 2. When a firm produces at the least-cost output level, it is:
(a) Producing the output at the minimum MC curve.
(b) Using the fewest resources to produce a good or service.
(c) Producing the output where the AVC curve is at a minimum.
(d) Producing the best combination of goods and services.

_____ 3. Technical efficiency is achieved for a given set of resources when a firm produces:
(a) The quantity of output indicated by the production function.
(b) Below the opportunity cost for the resources.
(c) The minimum necessary output to cover the opportunity cost of resources.
(d) All of the above.

_____ 4. The law of diminishing returns indicates that the greater use of a variable input, holding other factors fixed, results in:
(a) A declining rate of increase in total output for each additional unit of input.
(b) A rising MC curve.
(c) A declining MPP curve.
(d) All of the above.

_____ 5. Rising marginal costs are the result of:
(a) The *law of diminishing returns.*
(b) Decreasing MPP.
(c) Adding more variable factors of production to a fixed quantity of other factors of production.
(d) All of the above are correct.

_____ 6. Given the cost of the variable input, marginal cost will increase with greater output if:
(a) Marginal physical product is declining.
(b) Marginal physical product is increasing.
(c) Total variable cost is decreasing.
(d) Total fixed cost is increasing.

_____ 7. For which of the following costs would the cost curve appear as a flat line and the associated average cost curve decline continuously?
(a) Total costs.
(b) Variable costs.
(c) Fixed costs.
(d) Marginal costs.

_____ 8. If an additional unit of labor costs \$20, and has an MPP of 40 units of output, the marginal cost is:
(a) \$0.20.
(b) \$0.50.
(c) \$20.00.
(d) \$800.00.

_____ 9. Which of the following can you compute if you know only the total cost at an output level of zero?
(a) Fixed cost.
(b) Variable cost.
(c) Marginal cost.
(d) Average total cost.

_____ 10. When output increases and the marginal cost curve is:
(a) Below the ATC, the ATC is downward sloping.
(b) Equal to the ATC, the ATC is at its lowest point.
(c) Above the ATC, the ATC is upward sloping.
(d) All of the above.

_____ 11. As output increases, changes in short-run total costs result from changes in:
(a) Variable costs.
(b) Fixed costs.
(c) Profit.
(d) The price elasticity of demand.

_____ 12. Which of the following is equivalent to ATC?
(a) FC + VC.
(b) AFC + AVC.
(c) Change in output divided by change in total cost.
(d) Total cost times the quantity produced.

_____ 13. The ATC at a given output level multiplied by the number of units produced at that output level equals:
(a) Marginal cost.
(b) Total fixed cost.
(c) Total variable cost.
(d) Total cost.

_____ 14. Which one of the following curves is falling when marginal cost is below it?
(a) Average variable cost curve.
(b) Average total cost curve.
(c) Average fixed cost curve.
(d) All of the above.

_____ 15. Which of the following costs will always increase as output increases?
(a) Total costs.
(b) Average total costs.
(c) Marginal costs.
(d) Fixed costs.

_____ 16. Economies of scale are reductions:
(a) In average total cost that result from declining average fixed costs.
(b) In average fixed cost that result from reducing the firm's scale of operations.
(c) In average total cost that result from increasing the firm's scale of operations.
(d) In average fixed cost resulting from improved technology and production efficiency.

_____ 17. Which of the following contributes to the typical U shape of the ATC curve?
(a) The initial dominance of diminishing returns.
(b) The eventual dominance of the rising AVC curve.
(c) The steady impact of a rising AFC curve.
(d) All of the above.

_____ 18. In economics, the long run is the time period in which:
(a) All inputs are fixed.
(b) All inputs are variable.
(c) Some inputs are fixed.
(d) Producers decide how much to produce with existing plant and equipment.

_____ 19. In defining economic costs, economists recognize:
(a) Only explicit costs while accountants recognize only implicit costs.
(b) Only explicit costs while accountants recognize explicit and implicit costs.
(c) Explicit and implicit costs while accountants recognize only implicit costs.
(d) Explicit and implicit costs while accountants recognize only explicit costs.

_____ 20. The long-run average cost curve is constructed from:
(a) The minimum points of the short-run marginal cost curves.
(b) The minimum points of the short-run average cost curves.
(c) The lowest average cost for producing each level of output.
(d) The minimum points of the long-run marginal cost curves.

Problems and Applications

Exercise 1

This exercise shows how to compute and graph the marginal physical product of a factor of production. It also demonstrates the law of diminishing returns.

In Table 6.1 of the text, an example of jeans production was used to show how many sewing machines and workers were needed per day to produce various quantities of jeans per day. A similar table is given here.

Table 6.1
The production of jeans
(pairs per day)

Capital input (sewing machines per day)	*Labor input (workers per day)* 0	1	2	3	4	5	6	7
0	0	0	0	0	0	0	0	0
1	0	15	34	44	48	50	51	46
2	0	20	46	64	72	78	81	80
3	0	21	50	73	82	92	99	102

1. Suppose a firm has two sewing machines and can vary only the amount of labor input. On the basis of Table 6.1, fill in column 2 of Table 6.2 to show how much can be produced at different levels of labor input when there are only two sewing machines.

Table 6.2
The production of jeans with two sewing machines

(1) Labor input (workers per day)	*(2) Production of jeans (pairs per day)*	*(3) Marginal physical product (pairs per worker)*
0	______	—
1	______	______
2	______	______
3	______	______
4	______	______
5	______	______
6	______	______
7	______	______

2. Graph the total output curve in Figure 6.1.

Figure 6.1

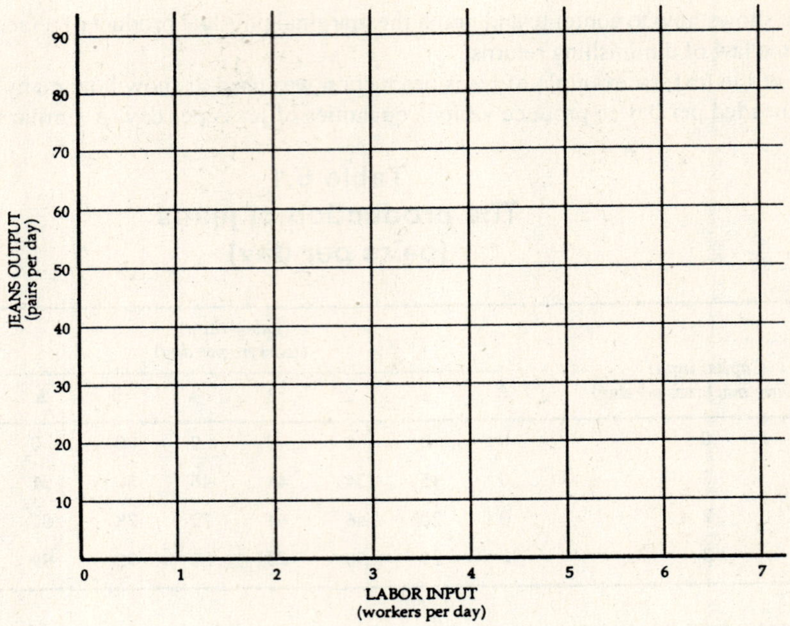

3. Compute the marginal physical product of each extra worker per day. (*Hint:* See Figure 6.2 in the text.) Place the answers in column 3 of Table 6.2.

4. Graph the marginal physical product curve in Figure 6.2.

Figure 6.2

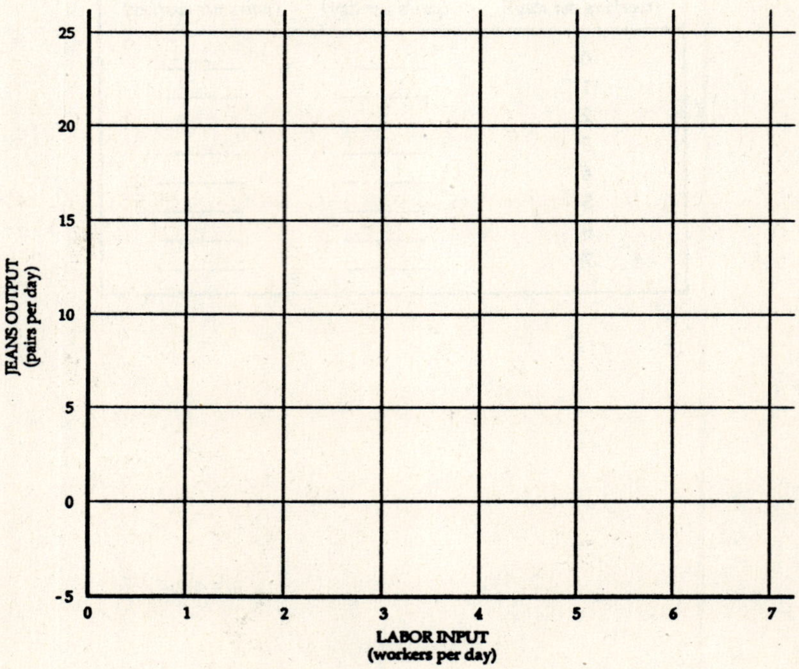

5. The law of diminishing returns states that the marginal physical product of a factor will:
   (a) Become negative as output increases.
   (b) Always decline as output increases.
   (c) Increase and then decline as output increases.
   (d) Begin to decline as more of the factor is used.

6. At what amount of labor input does the law of diminishing returns first become apparent in Figure 6.2?
   (a) 0-1.
   (b) 1-2.
   (c) 2-3.
   (d) 3-4.

7. In Figure 6.1 at 4 units of labor, total output:
   (a) Is rising with increased labor usage.
   (b) Is falling with increased labor usage.
   (c) Remains constant with increased labor.

8. T F When marginal physical product declines, total output declines.

Exercise 2

This exercise shows the relationship between the various costs of production.

1. Complete Table 6.3 using the information given about output and the costs of production. (Hint: Refer to Figure 6.5 in the text if you need help getting started.)

Table 6.3 Costs of Production

Rate of Output	*Fixed Cost*	*Variable Cost*	*Total Cost*	*Average Total Cost*	*Marginal Cost*
0	$ ______	$ ______	$ 10	--------	-------
1	______	6	______	$ ______	$ ______
2	______	10	______	______	______
3	______	16	______	______	______
4	______	______	36	______	______
5	______	40	______	______	______
6	______	______	68	______	______

2. When the average total cost is rising, marginal cost is (above, below, equal to) average total cost.

3. When the average total cost is falling, marginal cost is (above, below, equal to) average total cost.

Exercise 3

This exercise shows the relationship between fixed costs, variable costs, accounting cost, and economic cost.

1. Fixed costs are defined as:
   (a) Costs that do not change with inflation.
   (b) Costs that are set firmly (without escalator clauses) in a contract.
   (c) Costs of production that do not change when the rate of production is altered.
   (d) Average costs that do not change when the rate of production is altered.

2. Variable costs include:
   (a) Costs of production that change when the rate of production is altered.
   (b) All costs in the long run.
   (c) The difference between total and fixed costs.
   (d) All of the above.

Table 6.4 Expense statements for parachute business (dollars per week)

	Parachutes produced per week		
Weekly expense	*0*	*100*	*200*
Lease on building	$1,500	$1,500	$1,500
Sewing machines	600	600	600
Nylon	0	400	700
Utilities (electricity, etc.)	0	150	200
Labor	0	650	750
Testing and certification	800	800	800

Use the information in Table 6.4 to answer the following questions.

3. Which items are considered to be fixed costs? ____________________

4. Calculate variable costs at an output level of 100 parachutes per week. __________

5. Calculate total costs at an output level of 100 parachutes per week. __________

6. Now assume the owner of the parachute business buys the building he is currently leasing so he no longer has a lease expenditure. Calculate the accounting cost at an output level of 200 parachutes per week. __________

7. Assume the owner still owns the building. Calculate the economic cost at an output level of 200 parachutes per week. Explain why there is a difference in the accounting cost at an output level of 200 parachutes and the economic cost. ____________________

Exercise 4

This exercise focuses on average total costs. It will help you solve problems at the end of chapter in the text.

Table 6.5 represents the cost data for producing cement in three different plants, where Plant 1 is the smallest and Plant 3 is the largest.

Table 6.5
Costs associated with three plants

Output (tons per day)	*1*	*2*	*3*	*4*	*5*	*6*	*7*	*8*	*9*	*10*
Average total cost:										
Plant 1	$10	9	8	7	8	9	10	11	12	13
Plant 2	12	10	8	6	5	4	5	6	8	10
Plant 3	13	12	11	9	7	5	3	2	3	4

1. Given the three plant sizes in Table 6.5, the cement industry experiences (economies of scale, diseconomies of scale, constant returns to scale) because as plant size increases the minimum average total cost (increases, decreases, stays the same).

2. Which plant should be used to produce 2 tons of cement per day? ____________

3. Which plant should be used to produce 8 tons of cement per day? ____________

4. For which levels of output is Plant 2 the best choice? ____________________

Exercise 5

Suppose the marginal physical product of worker A is 10 units per hour and her wage is $15 per hour. Suppose the marginal physical product of worker B is 5 units per hour and her wage is $10 per hour. Given this information, answer questions 1-4.

1. Calculate the unit labor cost for worker A. ______________

2. Calculate the unit labor cost for worker B. ______________

3. T F Worker B is less costly per unit because her wage rate is lower.

4. T F Unit labor costs can be used to measure productivity.

Exercise 6

The news media often provide information on events that affect productivity and costs. This exercise will use one of the articles in the text to show the kind of information to look for.

Reread the article in the text titled "Funeral Giant Moves In on Small Rivals," and then answer the following questions.

1. What is the strategy employed by SCI to achieve economies of scale? ____________________
____

2. Which phrase(s) indicates how SCI grew to more than 230,000 units? ____________________
____

3. Which phrase indicates one way that SCI achieves lower costs than its rivals? ______________
____

4. Which phrase demonstrates that economies of scale have allowed SCI to reap greater profits than its smaller rivals? ______________________________

Common Errors

The first statement in each "common error" below is incorrect. Each incorrect statement is followed by a corrected version and an explanation.

1. A rising marginal cost means average cost is rising. WRONG!

   A rising average cost curve means the marginal cost curve is above the average cost curve. RIGHT!

It is important to remember the basic relationships between the average cost curves and the marginal cost curve:

(a) When the average cost curve rises, the marginal cost curve is above the average cost curve.
(b) When the average cost curve falls, the marginal cost curve is below the average cost curve.
(c) When the average cost curve is flat, the marginal cost curve equals the average cost curve.

2. Total output starts falling when diminishing returns occur. WRONG!

Diminishing returns set in when marginal physical product begins to decline. RIGHT!

The law of diminishing returns describes what happens to *marginal physical product,* not total output. Marginal physical product will typically begin to decline long before total output begins to decline. For total output to decline, the marginal physical product must be negative.

3. A firm's productivity increases when labor is willing to accept lower wages. WRONG!

A firm's productivity increases when more output can be produced per unit of labor used. RIGHT!

Productivity is not defined on the basis of the prices of factors of production. Productivity depends simply on the amount of output that is produced by the factors of production.

4. The term "economies of scale" refers to the shape of the short-run average cost curve. WRONG!

The term "economies of scale" refers to the shape of the long-run average cost curve. RIGHT!

The short-run average cost curve and the long-run average cost curve may have similar shapes. But the shape of the short-run curve results from the law of diminishing returns. In the long run, all factors, and therefore all costs, are variable. Thus the shape of the long-run average cost curve is the result of other forces, such as the specialization and division of labor, the use of different sources of power, and so on. Remember, even though the long-run average cost curve is a summary of many short-run average cost curves, and even though the shapes of the two curves may be similar, the reasons for the shapes of the curves are quite different. The term "economies of scale" applies only to the long-run average cost curve.

5. The marginal cost curve rises because factor prices rise when more of a good is produced. WRONG!

The marginal cost curve rises because the marginal productivity of the variable factor declines. RIGHT!

The marginal cost curve moves in the direction opposite to that of marginal product curve. Changes in factor prices would shift the whole marginal cost curve but would not explain its shape and would not affect the marginal product curve.

6. Marginal physical product begins to decline because inferior factors must be hired to increase output. WRONG!

Declining marginal physical product occurs even if all of the factors are of equal quality. RIGHT!

Many people incorrectly attribute diminishing returns to the use of inferior factors of production. Diminishing returns result from an increasing ratio of the variable input to the fixed input. There is always a point where the variable input begins to have too little of the fixed input to work with. Result? Diminishing marginal product! The quality of the factors has nothing to do with it. Generally, factors of production are considered homogeneous in economics.

7. Diminishing returns means there are diseconomies of scale. WRONG!

Diminishing returns refers to the short run shape of a marginal physical product curve and diseconomies of scale refers to the shape of the long run average cost curve. RIGHT!

As suggested in the previous Common Error, diminishing returns is a short run phenomenon; at least one input in the production process is fixed. Diminishing returns is reflected in diminishing marginal productivity and a rising short run marginal cost curve. However, when all factors are variable—as they are in the long run—then it is possible to talk about economies or diseconomies of scale. Diseconomies of scale results in a rising long run average cost curve. It is quite common to have short run diminishing returns and long run economies of scale, particularly in the public utilities.

•ANSWERS•

Using Key Terms

Across

1. factors of production
5. fixed costs
7. total cost
9. unit labor cost
11. law of diminishing returns
13. efficiency
14. explicit
15. average variable cost
17. economic cost
18. marginal physical product
21. production function
22. productivity
23. short run

Down

2. average total cost
3. opportunity cost
4. economies of scale
6. constant returns to scale
8. average fixed cost
10. implicit cost
12. variable costs
16. marginal cost
19. profit
20. long run

True or False

1. F The production function represents the maximum output that can be obtained from a given mix of inputs, i.e., technical efficiency.
2. T

3. T
4. T
5. F The marginal cost curve always intersects the minimum point of the average total cost curve and the minimum point of the average variable cost curve.
6. F The difference is the opportunity costs of resources that are not given an explicit payment.
7. T
8. F Rising AVC (MC) will eventually overcome falling AFC and cause the ATC to increase.
9. F Economies of scale is a long-run phenomenon. The law of diminishing returns does not apply in the long run because there are no fixed inputs in the long run.
10. T

Multiple Choice

1. c
2. b
3. a
4. d
5. d
6. a
7. c
8. b
9. a
10. d
11. a
12. b
13. d
14. d
15. a
16. c
17. b
18. b
19. d
20. c

Problems and Applications

Exercise 1

1. See Table 6.2 Answer, column 2.

Table 6.2 Answer

(1)	(2)	(3)
0	0	---
1	20	20
2	46	26
3	64	18
4	72	8
5	78	6
6	81	3
7	80	- 1

2. **Figure 6.1 Answer**

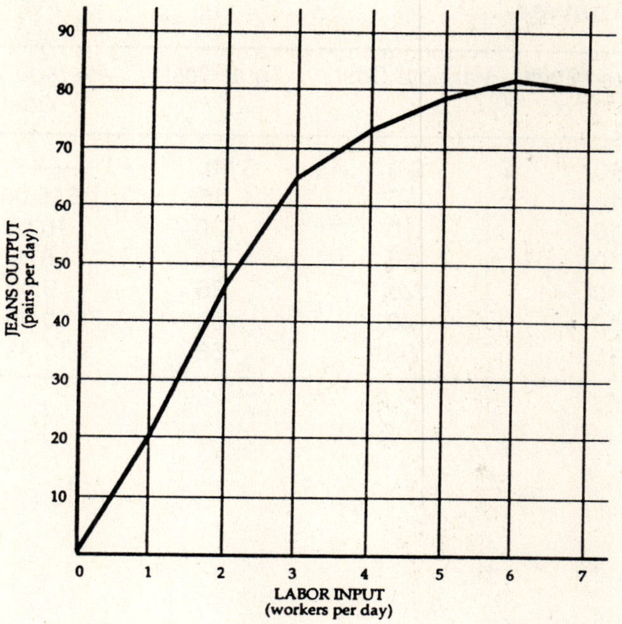

3. See Table 6.2 Answer, column 3.

4. **Figure 6.2 Answer**

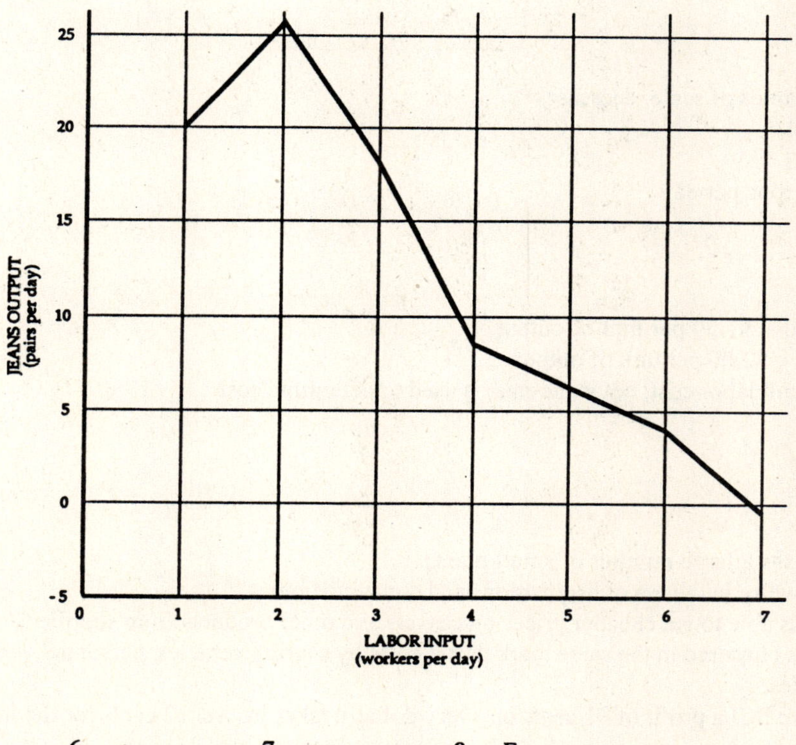

5. d 6. c 7. a 8. F

Exercise 2

1. **Table 6.3 Answer**

Rate of Output	*Fixed Cost*	*Variable Cost*	*Total Cost*	*Average Total Cost*	*Marginal Cost*
0	$ 10	$ 0	$ 10	--------	-------
1	10	6	16	$16.00	$ 6
2	10	10	20	10.00	4
3	10	16	26	8.67	6
4	10	26	36	9.00	10
5	10	40	50	10.00	14
6	10	58	68	11.33	18

2. Above
3. Below

Exercise 3

1. c
2. d
3. Lease on the building, sewing machines, and testing and certification
4. $1,200
5. $4,100
6. $3,050
7. $4,550; The economic cost is greater because it includes the implicit cost of the building; the accounting cost does not.

Exercise 4

1. Economies of scale, decreases
2. Plant 1
3. Plant 3
4. 4 to 6 tons per day

Exercise 5

1. $15/10 = $1.50 per unit of output
2. $10/5 = $2.00 per unit of output
3. F Unit labor cost, not wage rate, is used to determine cost.
4. T

Exercise 6

1. SCI uses a large number of small plants.
2. "But we're in the era of acquisitions and consolidations..."
3. "SCI is able to get cheaper prices on caskets and other products from suppliers," and "if funeral homes clustered in the same markets cut costs by sharing vehicles, personnel, services, and supplies."
4. "...give SCI a profit of 31 cents on every dollar it takes in...vs. 12 cents for the industry as a whole."

PART 3 Market Structure

CHAPTER 7

The Competitive Firm

Quick Review

- Profit is the difference between revenues and costs. Because economists include implicit costs in assessing the costs of production, economic profits are smaller than accounting profits.
- Market power is determined by the number and relative size of firms in an industry. It affects the behavior of producers and influences market outcomes. Market structure ranges from monopoly to perfect competition.
- A perfectly competitive firm cannot influence the price of its output and is referred to as a price taker. It is important to distinguish the firm's demand curve from the market-demand curve. The firm's demand curve is perfectly flat because the firm produces such a small part of total market output, while the market demand curve is downward-sloping, reflecting the law of demand.
- In an effort to maximize profits, in the short run, a competitive firm will choose the rate of output where price equals marginal cost.
- The existence of short-term profits will encourage new firms to enter a competitive market. As they enter, the market supply will increase and push price down along the demand curve. Profit for the competitive firm will decrease.
- In the short run, a firm continues to operate as long as it can cover its variable costs. In the short run a firm *shuts down* if variable costs of production cannot be covered. In the long run a firm must cover all costs, both explicit and implicit, or exit from the market. This is the firm's investment decision.
- A competitive firm's marginal cost curve above the average total cost curve is its short-run supply curve. The competitive market supply curve is the sum of the individual marginal cost curves.
- The determinants of supply include the price of inputs, technology, and expectations. If any of these determinants change, the firm's supply curve will shift. Market supply will shift in response to a change in the supply curve of the individual firms or if the number of firms changes.
- Changes in tax laws can affect both the production decision (short run) and the investment decision (long run).

Learning Objectives

After reading Chapter 7 and doing the following exercises, you should:

1. Know the difference between economic profits and accounting profits, and how profits are maximized.
2. Know the different market structures and the basic characteristics of each.
3. Understand why competitive firms are "price takers" and recognize the differences between the firm's demand and the market demand.
4. Know the relationships among total, average, and marginal costs (or revenue).
5. Recognize the difference between long-run and short-run decisions.
6. Know the profit maximization rule and the importance of marginal revenue and marginal cost.
7. Understand graphically how a firm determines profit, price, and production rate in the short run.
8. Understand how the firm makes the "shutdown" decision and the long-run investment decision.
9. Know how changes in the determinants affect the market supply curve.
10. Understand how various taxes affect the firm's output decision.

Using Key Terms

Fill in the puzzle on the opposite page with the appropriate term from the list of Key Terms at the end of the chapter in the text.

Across

2. The value of all resources used in production.
4. Equal to $10 per day at all rates of output in Figure 7.6 in the text.
6. The competitive _______ _______ _______ is summarized in Table 7.3 in the text.
7. Equal to $13 at every output level in Figure 7.7 in the text.
9. The opportunity cost of capital.
11. The period in which the quantity of some inputs cannot be changed.
12. Equal to $5 at the output rate of one bushel per hour in Figure 7.7 in the text.
13. The ability to alter the market price of a good or service.
14. The long-run decision to enter or exit an industry.
17. Ranges from perfect competition to monopoly in Figure 7.1 in the text.
18. Equal to $52 at an output rate of four bushels per day in Figure 7.7 in the text.
19. The value of resources used, even when no direct payment is made, is the _______ cost.
20. Costs of production that change when the rate of output changes.
21. A period of time long enough for all inputs to be varied.
22. Represented by a direct payment made for the use of a resource.

Down

1. A market in which no buyer or seller has market power.
3. The sole supplier of a good or service.
5. A firm that must take whatever price the market offers for the goods it produces.
6. The choice of a short-run rate of output by Farmer Kitt.
8. Total revenue minus total economic cost.
10. Occurs at a price of $5 in Figure 7.9 in the text.
15. The short-run _______ _______ is equal to the marginal cost curve in Figure 7.10 in the text.
16. Eventually becomes zero in a competitive industry because of market entry.

Puzzle 7.1

True or False: *Circle your choice and explain why any false statements are incorrect.*

T F 1. A firm should increase output as long as the next unit produced will raise marginal revenue above marginal cost.

T F 2. If the price of a good remains the same regardless of the rate of output that a firm produces, the demand curve faced by the firm is perfectly elastic.

T F 3. For a competitive firm, the supply curve is that part of the marginal cost curve that is above the short-run average total cost curve.

T F 4. Since a firm's goal is to maximize profits, it should expand production until total revenue equals total cost.

T F 5. If a firm maximizes revenue, it is maximizing profit.

T F 6. A firm can minimize its losses by continuing to produce in the short run when price is less than ATC but greater than AVC.

T F 7. Normal profit is when a firm's revenues just cover its economic costs.

T F 8. When businesses earn zero economic profit, they have no incentive to stay in business.

T F 9. A change in the tax rate on corporate profits will affect the firm's investment decision.

T F 10. Perfectly competitive firms face horizontal demand curves because they have no market power.

Multiple Choice: *Select the correct answer.*

_____ 1. Whereas consumers try to maximize utility, economists assume that firms try to maximize:
(a) Profits.
(b) Revenues.
(c) Sales.
(d) Production in a given period of time, *ceteris paribus*.

_____ 2. Economic costs and economic profits are typically:
(a) Greater and smaller, respectively, than their accounting counterparts.
(b) Smaller and greater, respectively, than their accounting counterparts.
(c) Both smaller than their accounting counterparts.
(d) Both larger than their accounting counterparts.

_____ 3. When a producer can control the market price for the good it sells:
(a) The producer is an entrepreneur.
(b) The producer is certain to make a profit.
(c) The producer has market power.
(d) The producer is a perfectly competitive firm.

_____ 4. In which of the following types of markets does a single firm have the most market power?
(a) Monopoly.
(b) Monopolistic competition.
(c) Oligopoly.
(d) Perfect competition.

_____ 5. Normal profit implies that:
(a) Economic profit is zero.
(b) All factors employed are earning an amount equal to their opportunity costs.
(c) The factors employed are earning as much as they could in the best alternative employment.
(d) All of the above.

_____ 6. The market equilibrium price occurs where:
(a) Price equals the minimum of average variable cost.
(b) Market supply crosses market demand.
(c) A firm's marginal revenue equals marginal cost.
(d) A firm's marginal cost equals average cost.

_____ 7. A competitive firm:
(a) Has a large advertising budget.
(b) Has output so small relative to the market supply that is has no effect on market price.
(c) Can alter the market price of the good(s) it produces.
(d) Can raise price to increase profit.

_____ 8. If a perfectly competitive firm can sell 100 computers at $500 each, in order to sell one more computer, the firm:
(a) Must lower its price.
(b) Can raise its price.
(c) Can sell the 101st computer at $500.
(d) Cannot sell an additional computer at any price because the market is at equilibrium.

_____ 9. A competitive firm's profits are maximized where:
(a) Market supply crosses the firm's marginal cost.
(b) Price equals the minimum of total cost.
(c) Price equals marginal cost.
(d) Marginal cost equals total revenue.

_____ 10. If price is greater than marginal cost, a perfectly competitive firm should increase output because:
(a) Marginal costs are increasing.
(b) Additional units of output will add to the firm's profits (or reduce losses).
(c) The price they receive for their product is increasing.
(d) Total revenues would increase.

_____ 11. If a perfectly competitive firm wanted to maximize its total *revenues*, it would produce:
(a) The output where MC equals price.
(b) As much output as it is capable of producing.
(c) The output where the ATC curve is at a minimum.
(d) The output where the marginal cost curve is at a minimum.

_____ 12. Total profit is:
(a) $TR - TC$.
(b) $Q \times (P - ATC)$.
(c) $(P \times Q) - TC$.
(d) All of the above.

_____ 13. When price exceeds average variable cost but not average total cost, the firm should, in the short run:
(a) Shut down.
(b) Produce at the rate of output where price = MC.
(c) Minimize per-unit losses by producing at the rate of output where ATC is minimized.
(d) Raise the price it charges.

_____ 14. A firm should shut down (stop producing) whenever:
(a) Minimum average variable cost exceeds price.
(b) Minimum average total cost exceeds price.
(c) It is taking a loss.
(d) Marginal cost exceeds marginal revenue.

_____ 15. A firm that makes an investment decision views all factors of production as:
(a) Variable over the long run.
(b) Variable over the short run.
(c) Fixed over the long run.
(d) Fixed over the short run.

_____ 16. The marginal cost curve:
(a) Will be affected by changes in the cost of inputs.
(b) Will eventually slope upward to the right as output increases.
(c) Above the AVC is the short run supply curve for a competitive firm.
(d) All of the above.

_____ 17. The market supply curve is calculated by:
(a) Summing the quantities supplied of individual supply curves at each price.
(b) Averaging the quantities supplied of individual supply curves at each price.
(c) Summing the prices of individual supply curves at each price.
(d) Averaging the prices of individual supply curves.

_____ 18. The short-run supply curve, for a perfectly competitive firm, is equivalent to the MC curve:
(a) Above ATC.
(b) Above AFC.
(c) Above AVC.
(d) Beyond its minimum point.

_____ 19. Taxes affect average total cost and marginal cost curves as follows:
(a) Profit taxes affect neither, property taxes affect only average total cost, and payroll taxes affect both average and marginal costs.
(b) Payroll taxes affect neither, property taxes affect only average total cost, and profit taxes affect both average and marginal costs.
(c) Payroll taxes affect neither, property taxes affect only marginal cost, and profit taxes affect both average and marginal costs.
(d) Property taxes affect neither, payroll taxes affect only marginal cost, and profit taxes affect both average and marginal costs.

_____ 20. If a perfectly competitive firm finds that economic profits are negative in the short run, it should shut down:
(a) And go out of business.
(b) If price is less than ATC but greater than AVC.
(c) If price is less than MC but greater than AVC.
(d) If price is less than AVC.

Problems and Applications

Exercise 1

This exercise uses total cost and total revenue to determine how much output a competitive firm should produce.

Refer to Figure 7.1 to answer questions 1-5.

Figure 7.1

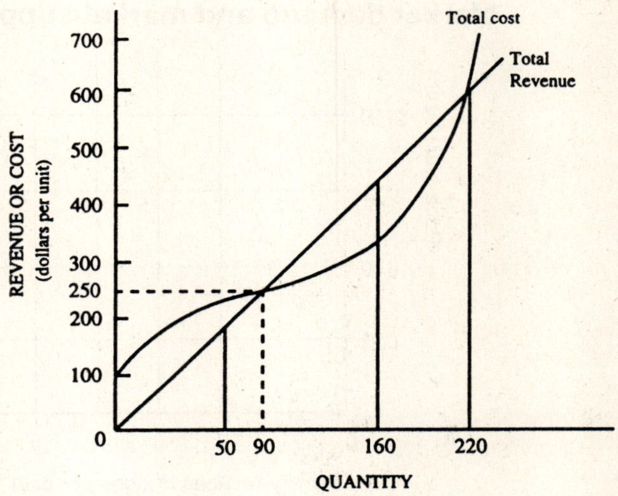

1. Profit is the difference between __________ __________ and __________ __________.
2. This firm earns a profit at all output levels between _______ and _______ units.
3. What is the profit maximizing rate of output for this firm? ________________
4. This firm experiences losses at all rates of output below _______ units.
5. Total costs increase more rapidly after 90 units of output because of the law of ____________________________ __________________.

Exercise 2

This exercise shows how the equilibrium price is determined in a competitive market and how the profit maximizing rate of output is determined in a perfectly competitive market.

1. Using the information in Table 7.1 draw the market demand curve for chicken eggs in Figure 7.2. Label the curve *D*. (Assume the demand curve is linear or a straight line.)

Table 7.1
Market demand for eggs

Quantity (millions of eggs per day)	Price (per dozen)
2	$ 1.00
4	$ 0.50

Figure 7.2
Market demand and market supply curves

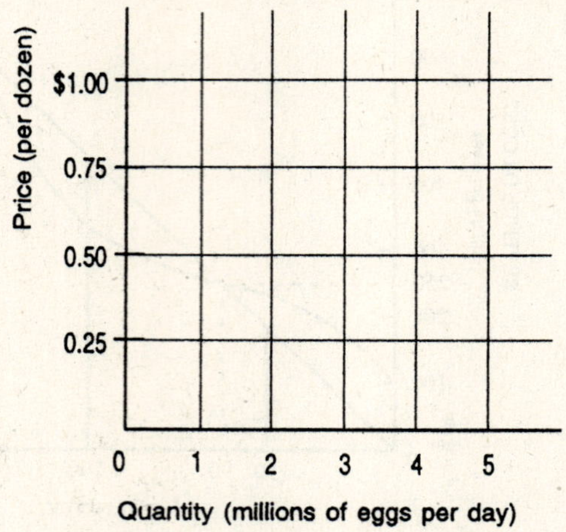

2. Using the information in Table 7.2 draw the market supply curve for chicken eggs in Figure 7.2. Label the curve *S*. (Assume the supply curve is linear or a straight line.)

Table 7.2
Market supply of eggs

Quantity (millions of eggs per day)	Price (per dozen)
4	$ 1.00
2	$ 0.50

3. Use the information in Table 7.3 to determine the marginal cost at each output level for an individual egg farmer.

Table 7.3
Production costs for an individual egg farmer

Quantity (eggs per minute)	*Total cost*	*Marginal cost*
0	$ 4.00	---------
1	$ 4.20	______
2	$ 4.65	______
3	$ 5.40	______
4	$ 6.50	______
5	$ 7.90	______

4. Use the information in Table 7.3 to draw the marginal cost curve for the individual egg farmer in Figure 7.3.

Figure 7.3
Costs of egg production

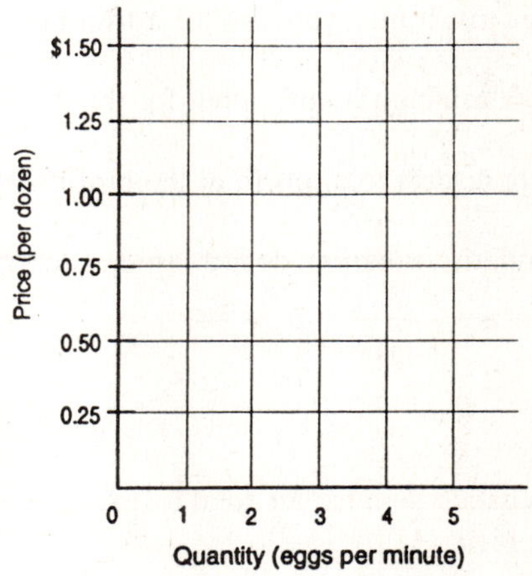

5. Use the market equilibrium price from Figure 7.2 to draw a line at the price that the individual farmer faces in Figure 7.3.

6. For a competitive firm, MR always equals ________.

7. According to the profit-maximization rule, this egg farmer should produce _____ eggs per minute.

8. At an output level of 2 eggs per minute, for the individual farmer, MC is (greater, less) than price and the farmer should (increase, decrease) output in order to maximize profit.

Exercise 3

This exercise provides practice in using graphs in a perfectly competitive market situation.

Figure 7.4
Production costs

1. Label the three curves given in Figure 7.4 for a firm in a perfectly competitive market situation.

2. What is the profit maximizing rate of output for this firm?

3. Shade the area that represents total profit at the profit maximizing rate of output.

4. Given a perfectly competitive market, does this graph depict a short-run or long-run situation? Explain how you know. ______________________________

Exercise 4

This exercise gives you a chance to calculate total revenue, total profit, and marginal cost and to find the output that will yield maximum profit.

1. Complete the following formulas: (a) Price x quantity = ____________
(b) Change in total cost / change in output = ____________
(c) Total revenue - total cost = ____________

2. After checking your answers for question 1, complete Table 7.4.

Table 7.4
Cost and revenue data

Qty.	*Price*	*Total revenue*	*Total cost*	*Profit*	*Marginal cost*
0	$7	$_____	$ 5.00	$_____	--------
1	7	_____	7.00	_____	_____
2	7	_____	11.00	_____	_____
3	7	_____	18.00	_____	_____
4	7	_____	27.00	_____	_____
5	7	_____	39.00	_____	_____

3. In Figure 7.5, graph price and marginal cost.

Figure 7.5

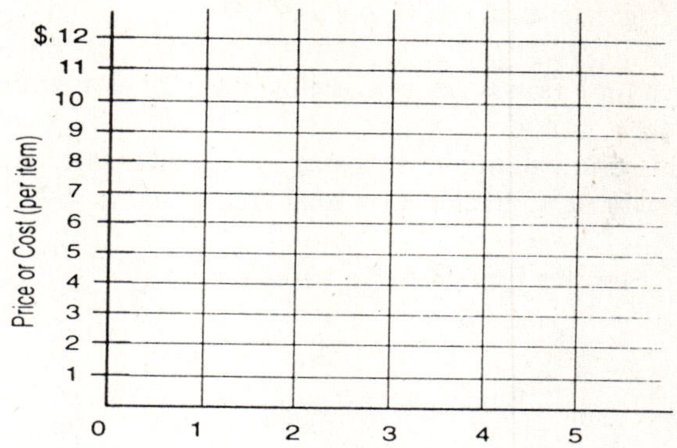

4. What is the profit maximizing level of output for this firm? ________________

5. At an output level of 4 items this firm would (increase, decrease) profit by producing more.

Exercise 5

This exercise focuses on the shutdown decision.

Refer to Figure 7.6 to answer questions 1-6.

Figure 7.6

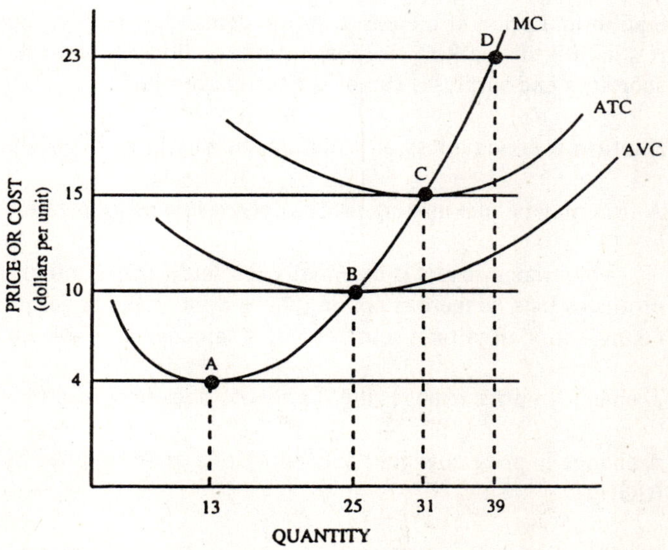

1. What is the profit-maximizing production rate for the firm if the price is $23? ________

2. What is the profit-maximizing production rate for the firm if the price is $15? ________

3. At a price of $12 this firm is earning a (profit, loss) and should (continue to produce, shut-down) because the price is greater than (ATC, AVC).

4. The shutdown price for a firm is any price below the minimum of the ________ curve.

5. At a price of $8 this firm will minimize losses by (continuing to produce, shutting down). In this case total revenues are (less, greater) than total variable costs.

6. The shutdown point for this firm occurs at a price of ________.

Common Errors

The first statement in each "common error" below is incorrect. Each incorrect statement is followed by a corrected version and an explanation.

1. Higher prices yield greater profits. WRONG!

   The effect of price increases on total revenue depends on the elasticity of demand. RIGHT!

   The law of demand tells us that when prices rise, quantity falls; total revenues may actually decrease (remember the $4 ice cream cones). Costs also change; if they don't fall as quickly as total revenues, then *profits* fall.

2. Surpluses and shortages are determinants of demand and supply that shift demand and supply curves. WRONG!

   Surpluses and shortages often result from shifts of demand or supply curves, but they do not cause such shifts themselves. RIGHT!

   Surpluses or shortages may appear in a market if the market price does not adjust to the equilibrium price. If there is a shift in demand or supply, shortages or surpluses may temporarily result until the market price reaches its equilibrium. Nevertheless, expectations of future shortages and surpluses can affect current demand.

3. If a firm is taking a loss, it is not maximizing profits. WRONG!

   A firm may be maximizing profits even if it is making zero profits or taking a loss. RIGHT!

   Minimizing losses is essentially the same as maximizing profits. A firm is maximizing profits as long as there is nothing it can do to make larger profits. Remember, even if the firm is taking a loss, it will not shut down if it can cover variable costs.

4. A change in price changes the supply of goods produced by a firm. WRONG!

   A change in price changes the quantity of a good supplied by a firm in a given time period. RIGHT!

   Be careful! Economists differentiate between the terms "quantity supplied" and "supply." A change in the quantity supplied usually refers to a movement along a supply curve as a result of a change in price or production rate. A change in supply refers to a shift of the supply curve as a result of a change in technology, the price of a resource, or the number of sellers.

5. A firm should always increase the rate of production as long as it is making a profit. WRONG!

A profitable firm should increase production rates only as long as additional revenues from the increase in production exceed the additional associated costs. RIGHT!

If the increase in production rates generates more costs than revenue, the firm will be less profitable. In this case, continued expansion will ultimately result in zero profits.

•ANSWERS•

Using Key Terms

Across

2. economic cost
4. fixed costs
6. profit maximization rule
7. marginal revenue
9. normal profit
11. short run
12. marginal cost
13. market power
14. investment decision
17. market structure
18. total revenue
19. implicit
20. variable costs
21. long run
22. explicit cost

Down

1. perfect competition
3. monopoly
5. competitive firm
6. production decision
8. economic profit
10. shutdown point
15. supply curve
16. profit

True or False

1. T
2. T
3. F The supply curve is that part of the marginal cost curve above the AVC curve.
4. F A firm should expand production until MR equals MC. To produce where total revenue equals total cost yields a profit of zero.

5. F To maximize revenue, a firm would produce as much output as it possibly can. To maximize profit, the firm should produce the output where the difference between TR and TC is the greatest.

6. T
7. T
8. F A firm that earns zero economic profits is covering all its economic costs, including a normal profit to the entrepreneur. There is no better use for the firm's resources (i.e., it is earning exactly what it could earn in the next best option).

9. T
10. T

Multiple Choice

1. a	5. d	9. c	13. b	17. a
2. a	6. b	10. b	14. a	18. c
3. c	7. b	11. b	15. a	19. a
4. a	8. c	12. d	16. d	20. d

Problems and Applications

Exercise 1

1. Total revenue, total cost
2. 90, 220
3. 160 units
4. 90
5. Diminishing returns

Exercise 2

Figure 7.2 Answer

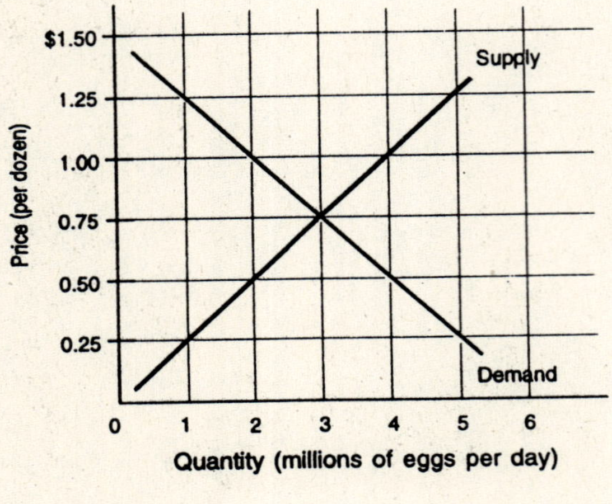

1. See Figure 7.2 answer.
2. See Figure 7.2 answer.

3. **Table 7.3 Answer**

Quantity	*Marginal cost*
0	$ ------
1	0.20
2	0.45
3	0.75
4	1.10
5	1.40

Figure 7.3 Answer

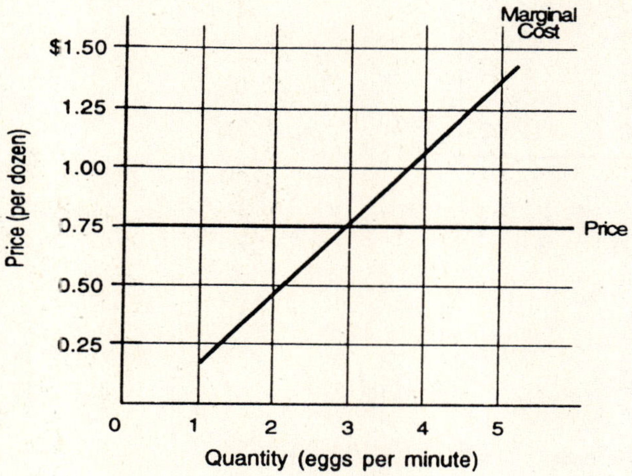

4. See Figure 7.3 answer.
5. See Figure 7.3 answer.
6. Price
7. 3
8. Less, increase

Exercise 3

1. **Figure 7.4 Answer**

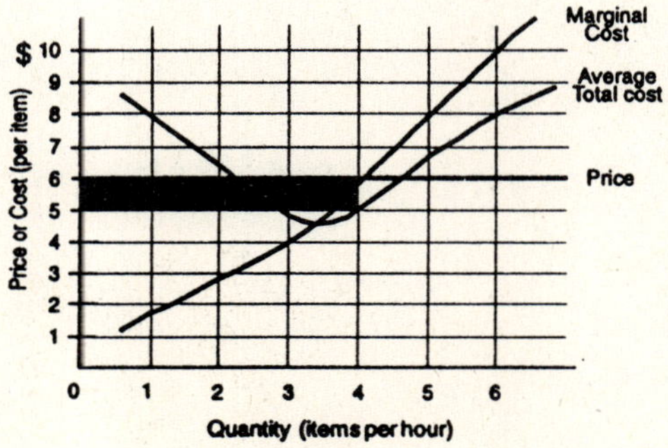

2. 4 items per hour
3. See Figure 7.4 answer.
4. Short run, there is an economic profit (price is greater than minimum ATC)

Exercise 4

1. a. Total revenue
   b. Marginal cost
   c. Profit

2. **Table 7.4 Answer**

Quantity	*Total revenue*	*Profit*	*Marginal cost*
0	$ 0.00	$ -5.00	-------
1	7.00	+ 0.00	$ 2.00
2	14.00	+ 3.00	4.00
3	21.00	+ 3.00	7.00
4	28.00	+ 1.00	9.00
5	35.00	- 4.00	12.00

3. **Figure 7.5 Answer**

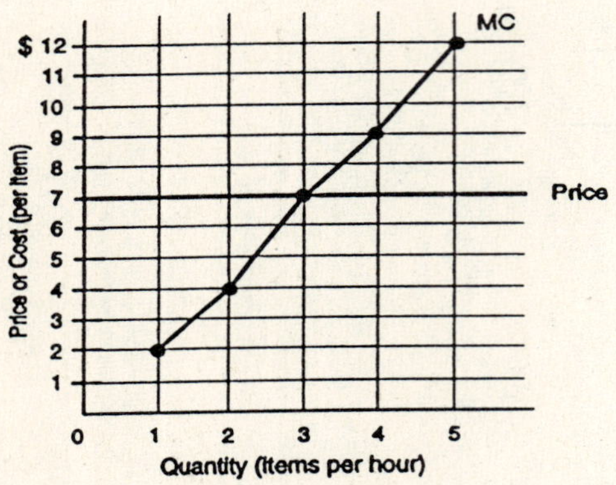

4. 3 items per day
5. Decrease

Exercise 5

1. 39 units
2. 31 units
3. Loss, continue to produce, AVC
4. AVC
5. Shutting down, less
6. $10

CHAPTER 8

Competitive Markets

Quick Review

- Economic profits encourage new firms to enter a competitive market. As entry occurs, the market supply curve shifts to the right and the equilibrium price decreases.

- A perfectly competitive market is characterized by many firms, perfect information, low barriers to entry, identical products, and zero economic profit in the long run.

- The short-run production decision leads perfectly competitive firms to produce where price equals MC.

- The limit to the competitive price and profit squeeze is reached when price is driven down to the level of minimum average total cost (ATC). If the market price falls below the minimum ATC, firms will exit from the industry. Price stabilizes when entry and exit cease. This long-run equilibrium occurs when economic profits reach zero.

- In an effort to earn economic profits, competitive firms are always searching for better and more efficient production methods. Technological advances cause MC and ATC to decrease.

- As long as a firm can cover its AVC it will minimize losses by continuing to operate in the short run. The point where price equals minimum AVC is the shutdown point.

- The process of competition benefits consumers because it results in the optimal mix of output and the most efficient use of resources.

- In competitive markets there is a persistent pressure on prices and profits. Firms must keep costs as low as possible by adopting the most efficient technologies. Competitive firms must also respond quickly to changes in demand by producing the goods and services demanded by buyers in order to earn a profit. The penalties for not responding are losses and the potential failure of the firm.

Learning Objectives

After reading Chapter 8 and doing the following exercises, you should:

1. Know how the absence of market power relates to the shape of demand and supply curves from the point of view of buyers and sellers.
2. Be able to tell why the demand curve facing a competitive firm is flat.
3. Be able to list the characteristics of the competitive market structure and describe the role of competition in the U.S. economy.
4. Know how barriers to entry influence the competitive process.
5. Know the difference between the firm's demand curve and the market demand curve.
6. Know why above-normal profits disappear in competitive industries.
7. Understand how a competitive market structure affects prices, cost, output, and profits in the short and long run.
8. Be able to identify the signals for the entry and exit of firms.
9. Be able to show the effects of shifts of market demand or supply on individual demand or supply.
10. Describe how marginal cost pricing leads to efficiency in the allocation of resources.

Using Key Terms

Fill in the puzzle on the opposite page with the appropriate term from the list of Key Terms at the end of the chapter in the text.

Across

3. The choice of a short-run rate of output by catfish farmers.
4. The offer of goods at a price equal to their marginal cost.
6. Competitive markets promote _____________ because price is driven down to the level of minimum average costs.
7. According to Table 8.2 in the text, firms will enter an industry if ______ ______ exists.
8. A market in which no buyer or seller has market power.
10. Equal to $300 at an output rate of 600 computers per month in Table 8.1 in the text.
11. This curve shifts to the right in Figure 8.2 in the text as more firms enter the industry.
12. The rate of output at which price equals minimum AVC.
13. The price signal the consumer receives in a competitive market is an accurate reflection of ______ ______.
14. Equal to marginal revenue at an output rate of 600 computers per month in Table 8.1 in the text.
15. Total cost divided by the quantity produced.
16. Determined by the intersection of market demand and market supply.
17. Allows for indirect communication between producers and consumers by way of market sales and purchases.

Down

1. Occurs where price equals minimum ATC in Figure 8.6 in the text.
2. Occurs where price equals marginal cost in Figure 8.6 in the text.
5. Obstacles that make it difficult or impossible for new firms to enter an industry.
9. The decision to build, buy, or lease plant and equipment.

Puzzle 8.1

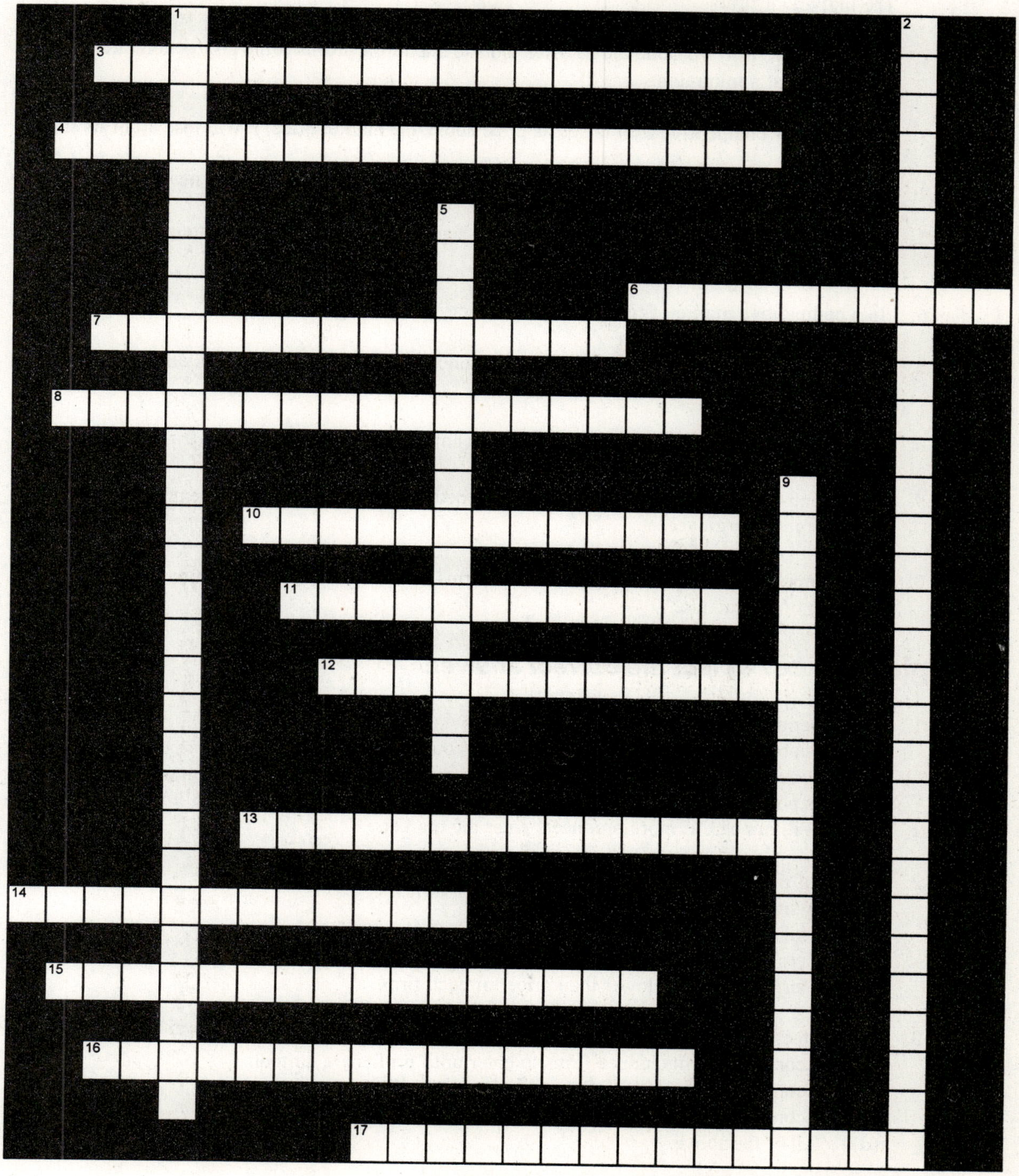

True or False: *Circle your choice and explain why any false statements are incorrect.*

T F 1. The market supply curve is a horizontal summation of the *MC* curves above minimum *AVC* of the individual firms.

T F 2. A competitive firm's production decision aims to maximize profits at the production rate where the ATC is at a minimum.

T F 3. If a perfectly competitive firm raises its price above the market price, it will lose all of its sales.

T F 4. As long as an economic profit is available, a market will continue to attract new entrants.

T F 5. In competitive markets, economic losses are a signal to firms that better options are available for its resources.

T F 6. In a competitive market, firms sell their products at a price greater than MC.

T F 7. Since perfectly competitive firms earn zero economic profits in the long run, all firms will leave the industry.

T F 8. Perfectly competitive firms are forced to be technically efficient by government regulations.

T F 9. In the long-run equilibrium for a perfectly competitive market, the price of the product will equal the minimum marginal cost.

T F 10. In a competitive market, competition forces firms to continually search for more efficient methods of production.

Multiple Choice: *Select the correct answer.*

_____ 1. A competitive firm:
- (a) Is able to keep other potential producers out of the market.
- (b) Would like to keep other potential producers out of the market but cannot do so.
- (c) Is powerless to alter its own rate of production.
- (d) Will not care if more producers enter the market.

_____ 2. Which of the following is consistent with a competitive market?
- (a) A small number of firms.
- (b) Exit of small firms when profits are high for large firms.
- (c) Zero economic profit in the long run.
- (d) Marginal revenue lower than price for each firm.

_____ 3. In a perfectly competitive market in the long run:
- (a) Economic profits induce firms to enter until profits are normal.
- (b) Economic losses induce firms to exit until profits are normal.
- (c) Economic profit is zero at equilibrium.
- (d) All of the above.

_____ 4. The exit of firms from a market:
(a) Shifts the market supply curve to the right.
(b) Reduces profits of existing firms in a market.
(c) Reduces the equilibrium output in the market.
(d) All of the above.

_____ 5. Which of the following conditions is *not* characteristic of a perfectly competitive market?
(a) The market price is determined by an organization of sellers.
(b) Products are homogeneous.
(c) Barriers to enter the industry are low.
(d) There are many firms.

_____ 6. In a competitive market, if the market demand curve is tangent to the minimum point of the ATC curve, a firm may seek to earn economic profits by:
(a) Producing at the rate of output where price equals demand.
(b) Decreasing production costs through technological improvements.
(c) Decreasing price.
(d) Increasing price.

_____ 7. The entry of firms into a market:
(a) Pushes the equilibrium price downward.
(b) Reduces profits of existing firms in the market.
(c) Shifts the market supply curve rightward.
(d) All of the above.

_____ 8. The exit of firms from a market:
(a) Shifts the market supply curve to the right.
(b) Reduces the profits of existing firms in the market.
(c) Reduces the equilibrium output in the market.
(d) All of the above.

_____ 9. A competitive market promotes technical efficiency in the long run by pushing prices to the minimum of:
(a) Short-run AVC.
(b) Short-run MC.
(c) Long-run ATC.
(d) Long-run TC.

_____ 10. Which of the following conditions always characterizes a firm that is in short-run competitive equilibrium where profits are maximized?
(a) Price equals minimum average total cost.
(b) Price equals marginal cost.
(c) There are no economic profits.
(d) All of the above characterize such a firm.

_____ 11. The market supply curve will shift as a result of all of the following *except:*
(a) Changes in technology.
(b) Changes in the number of supplying firms.
(c) Changes in expectations about making profits in an industry.
(d) Changes in the current income of buyers.

_____ 12. In a competitive market where firms are incurring losses, which of the following should be expected as the industry moves to long-run equilibrium, *ceteris paribus?*
(a) A higher price and fewer firms.
(b) A lower price and fewer firms.
(c) A higher price and more firms.
(d) A lower price and more firms.

_____ 13. In long-run competitive equilibrium, price equals:
(a) The minimum of the long-run average total cost curve.
(b) The minimum of the long-run average variable cost curve.
(c) Long-run marginal cost.
(d) All of the above.

_____ 14. In which of the following cases would a firm enter a market?
(a) P = short-run ATC.
(b) P > long-run ATC.
(c) P < short-run ATC.
(d) P < long-run ATC.

_____ 15. The constant quest for profits in competitive markets results in:
(a) Zero economic profits in the long run.
(b) The production of goods and services that consumers demand.
(c) Product and technological innovation.
(d) All of the above are correct.

_____ 16. When economic profits exist in the market for a particular product, this is a signal to producers that:
(a) Consumers would like more scarce resources devoted to the production of this product.
(b) The market is oversupplied with this product.
(c) The best mix of goods and services are being produced with society's scarce resources.
(d) Price is at the minimum of the ATC curve.

_____ 17. In a competitive market where firms are experiencing economic losses, which of the following would not be expected?
(a) A decrease in MR for the remaining firms.
(b) A decrease in market supply.
(c) An increase in total revenue for the remaining firms.
(d) An increase in output for the remaining firms.

_____ 18. In a perfectly competitive market, efficiency in production occurs because of:
(a) The profit motive.
(b) The competition from many other firms selling an identical product.
(c) Low barriers to entry.
(d) All of the above.

_____ 19. When a computer firm is producing an output where the price is greater than the MC, then from society's standpoint:
(a) The firm is producing too much because society is giving up more to produce additional computers than the computers are worth.
(b) The firm is producing too much because society would be willing to give up more alternative goods in order to get additional computers.
(c) The firm is producing too little because society is giving up more to produce additional computers than the computers are worth.
(d) The firm is producing too little because society would be willing to give up more alternative goods in order to get additional computers.

_____ 20. Marginal cost pricing results in the most desirable mix of output from the consumer's standpoint because:
(a) Firms are forced by law to produce at the most technically efficient output level.
(b) The price consumers are willing to pay reflects the value of the output which is given up.
(c) Prices are forced down to the lowest possible level.
(d) Economic profits are zero.

Problems and Applications

Exercise 1

This exercise focuses on the market supply curve and how a competitive industry adjusts to long-run equilibrium.

Assume the HDTV industry is a competitive market and initially there are economic profits in the industry.

1. The lure of economic profits will cause (more, less) firms to enter the industry over time which will cause the market supply curve to ______________________________.
2. Market price is determined by the intersection of ______________________________ ______________________________.
3. If the market supply shifts to the right, *ceteris paribus*, market price will (increase, decrease).
4. As long as new producers enter the market, market output will (expand, contract) and economic profits will (increase, decrease).
5. Economic profits will approach _________ for this industry in the long run.
6. In long-run competitive equilibrium, price will be equal to minimum _____________.

Exercise 2

This exercise uses information from a table to determine revenues, costs, and profits.

Use Table 8.1 to answer questions 1-9.

Table 8.1

Output	Price	Total revenue	Total cost	Total profit	Marginal revenue	Marginal cost	Average total cost
0	----	----	$10	_____	----	----	----
1	$13	_____	15	_____	_____	_____	_____
2	13	_____	22	_____	_____	_____	_____
3	13	_____	31	_____	_____	_____	_____
4	13	_____	44	_____	_____	_____	_____
5	13	_____	61	_____	_____	_____	_____

1. It is obvious that Table 8.1 refers to a perfectly competitive firm because ___________ is constant regardless of the level of output.

2. The fixed cost for this firm is equal to __________.

3. Calculate total revenue, total profit, marginal revenue, marginal cost, and average total cost for this firm.

4. What is the profit maximizing rate of output for this firm? ______________

5. The short-run competitive equilibrium occurs where ____________________________.

6. The long-run competitive equilibrium occurs where ____________________________.

7. The minimum for average total cost for this firm is __________. This amount is (greater, less) than the current price so this firm is operating in the (short, long) run.

8. In this case, firms will ______________ the industry because economic ______________ exist.

9. What happens to price as new firms enter the market? ______________________________

Exercise 3

When the hand-held calculator was invented in the 1970s, the market responded in competitive fashion. This exercise focuses on the adjustments made in a competitive market in both the short run and the long run.

Figure 8.1 presents the cost curves that are relevant to a firm's production decision, and Figure 8.2 shows the market demand and supply curves for the calculator market. Use Figures 8.1 and 8.2 and the knowledge of cost curves that you have gained from the text to answer questions 1-10.

Figure 8.1
Firm

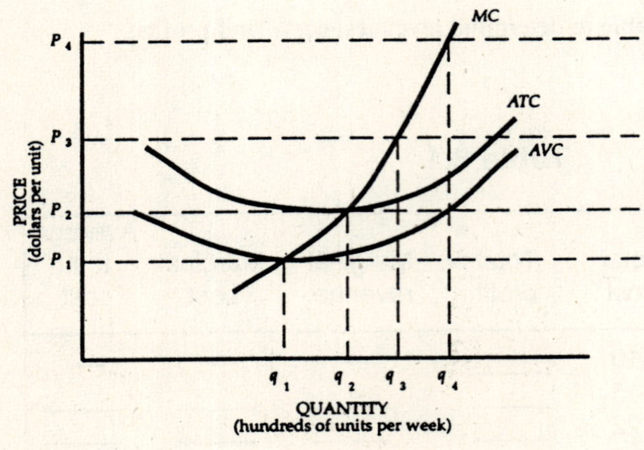

Figure 8.2
Market (all firms)

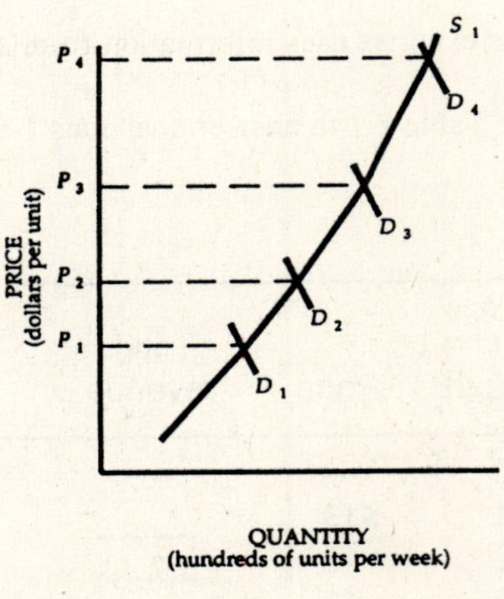

1. If the market demand and supply curves are S_1 and D_1, the market equilibrium price will be:
   (a) P_1.
   (b) P_2.
   (c) P_3.
   (d) P_4.

2. Suppose the demand for calculators shifts to D_4. This shift might be caused by:
   (a) An increase in the number of consumers.
   (b) An increase in consumers' incomes.
   (c) A rise in the price of a substitute good.
   (d) All of the above.

3. If the demand curve is at D_4, the quantity supplied by the *firm* will be:
   (a) q_1.
   (b) q_2.
   (c) q_3.
   (d) q_4.

4. Suppose a recession results in a shift in the demand curve for calculators to D_1. Then the *firm* will produce:
   (a) q_1.
   (b) q_2.
   (c) q_3.
   (d) q_4.

5. In the short run, the firm will continue to produce some output until demand changes enough to drive price below:
   (a) P_1.
   (b) P_2.
   (c) P_3.
   (d) P_4.

6. At prices below P_1, the firm will shut down (produce no output) because:
   (a) Its loss will be less than if it produces at any level of output.
   (b) Its loss will be limited to its fixed costs.
   (c) Total revenue is less than total variable cost.
   (d) All of the above are the case.

7. The fact that the quantity supplied by the firm changes whenever the market price changes indicates that:
   (a) The firm is a price setter.
   (b) The firm is a price taker.
   (c) The firm has monopoly power.
   (d) The firm has no control over the quantity it produces.

8. Since the firm will not produce any output if the market price falls below P_1:
   (a) The firm's supply curve is that part of the *MC* curve above the minimum point on the *ATC* curve.
   (b) The average variable cost curve is the firm's supply curve.
   (c) The average total cost curve is the firm's supply curve.
   (d) The firm's supply curve is that part of its marginal cost curve that lies above its average variable cost curve.

9. If the price is P_3, and the demand curve is D_3 in the long run:
   (a) Returns to the firm are below average, and firms will leave the industry.
   (b) Returns are above average, and new firms will have an incentive to enter the market.
   (c) Returns are about average, and there is no incentive for firms to move into or out of the industry.
   (d) We really can't say without more information.

10. Long-run competitive equilibrium occurs at a price of:
   (a) P_1.
   (b) P_2.
   (c) P_3.
   (d) P_4.

Exercise 4

Many newspapers provide information from competitive markets, such as the want ads, market prices, and advertising.

Reread the article in the text entitled "Whiskered Catfish Stir a New Trade Controversy." Then answer the following questions.

1. Which phrase indicates the change in the U.S. catfish market? ______________________________________.

2. Which passage indicates entry into the catfish market? ______________________________________

3. What causes entry into a competitive market? ______________________

4. As more producers enter the catfish industry, what will happen to profits? ______________

5. On the basis of information in the article, the catfish market appears to be:
   (a) A local market.
   (b) A regional market.
   (c) A national market.
   (d) An international market.

Common Errors

The first statement in each "common error" below is incorrect. Each incorrect statement is followed by a corrected version and an explanation.

1. The demand curve for a competitive market is flat. WRONG!

   The demand curve for a competitive firm is flat. RIGHT!

   The error above results from failure to distinguish between the market and the firm. Review Exercise 3 if this distinction is not clear.

2. Competitive firms do not make profits. WRONG!

Competitive firms can make economic profits in the short run. RIGHT!

In the long run, firms enter an industry and compete away economic profits. In the short run, a change in demand or supply may cause price to change and may bestow temporary economic profits on a firm. In the personal computer example in the text, technological changes shifted the supply curve and provided temporary profits.

Be careful! Always distinguish between short-run profit-maximizing production rates and price levels and long-run equilibrium production rates and price levels. While industries have a tendency to move toward long-run equilibrium, they may never reach it because of shocks that buffet a market.

3. Since competitive firms make zero profits in the long run, they cannot pay their stockholders and so they should shut down. WRONG!

Since competitive firms make zero economic profits in the long run, they are able to pay all factors of production, including the entrepreneurs, to keep the firms in existence. RIGHT!

Be careful! Keep the accounting and economic definitions of such words as "profit" separate and distinct. Keep movements along the supply curve (firms increase production rates) separate from shifts of the supply curve (firms enter or exit). Avoid confusing short-run responses (increasing production rates in existing plants) with long-run responses (entry or exit).

•ANSWERS•

Using Key Terms

Across

3. production decision
4. marginal cost pricing
6. efficiency
7. economic profit
8. competitive market
10. profit per unit
11. market supply
12. shutdown point
13. opportunity cost
14. marginal cost
15. average total cost
16. equilibrium price
17. market mechanism

Down

1. long-run competitive equilibrium
2. short-run competitive equilibrium
5. barriers to entry
9. investment decision

True or False

1. T
2. F The firm maximizes profits at the output rate where price (MR) = MC.
3. T
4. T
5. T
6. F In a competitive market, firms sell their products at a price equal to MC.
7. F Zero economic profits are an indication that there is no better use for a firm's resources. As a result, once economic profits reach zero, there is no further exit (or entry).
8. F Competition forces perfectly competitive firms to be technically efficient.
9. F The price of the product will equal the minimum ATC.
10. T

Multiple Choice

1. b
2. c
3. d
4. c
5. a
6. b
7. d
8. c
9. c
10. b
11. d
12. a
13. a
14. b
15. d
16. a
17. a
18. d
19. d
20. b

Problems and Applications

Exercise 1

1. More, shift to the right
2. Market supply and market demand
3. Decrease
4. Expand, decrease
5. Zero
6. ATC

Exercise 2

1. Price
2. $10
3. **Table 8.1 Answer**

Output	Price	Total revenue	Total cost	Total profit	Marginal revenue	Marginal cost	Average total cost
0	----	----	$10	$-10	----	----	----
1	$13	$13	15	-2	$13	$5	$15.00
2	13	26	22	4	13	7	11.00
3	13	39	31	8	13	9	10.33
4	13	52	44	8	13	13	11.00
5	13	65	61	4	13	17	12.20

4. 4 units of output
5. p=MC
6. p=MC=minimum ATC
7. $10.33, less, short
8. Enter, profits
9. Decreases

Exercise 3

1. a	3. d	5. a	7. b	9. b
2. d	4. a	6. d	8. d	10. b

Exercise 4

1. ". . . the U.S. catfish production has plunged in the past year."
2. ". . . imports from Vietnam have soared from 575,000 pounds in 1998 to as much as 20 million pounds this year."
3. Economic profit
4. Decrease
5. d

CHAPTER 9

Monopoly

Quick Review

- Market power is the ability to alter the price of a good or service. A monopolist is the sole supplier in a given market and has market power, which it can use to influence price and output.

- The demand curve faced by a monopolist is the downward-sloping market demand curve. As a result, in order to sell more output a monopolist must lower its price for all output, so the marginal revenue curve is always less than price.

- In making the production decision, monopolists attempt to maximize profits. They produce the level of output at which marginal cost equals marginal revenue. When compared to the competitive producer, the monopolist will charge a higher price and will produce a smaller output.

- If market demand is sufficient, monopolists will reap economic profits that are a signal for other firms to enter the market. In order to maintain its monopoly status, barriers to entry such as patents, legal harassment, exclusive licensing, bundled products, and government franchises are necessary.

- The existence of market power in the economy influences the answers we get to the WHAT, HOW, and FOR WHOM questions. By restricting output, the monopolist forces some resources to move where they will earn less and keeps economic profits for itself. Monopolists tend to be less efficient than competitive firms are since they are not compelled by competitive forces to adopt the newest and most efficient technologies.

- Arguments in favor of a monopoly include: 1) economic profits give the firm the financial resources to pursue research and development, 2) monopoly profits may encourage entrepreneurial activity, 3) if economies of scale exist over the entire market, society will be best served by having a single firm (a natural monopolist) produce all the output, 4) potential competition, perhaps from foreign producers attracted by economic profits, is sufficient to constrain the monopolist from exploiting its market power. If a market is contestable, the economic outcomes may be more like that of the perfectly competitive market.

- The government is empowered to prevent or regulate the abuse of market power. The Sherman Act, the Clayton Act, and the Federal Trade Commission Act form the legal foundation for antitrust activities.

Learning Objectives

After reading Chapter 9 and doing the following exercises, you should:

1. Know the meaning of market power.
2. Know why a monopolist has market power and a downward-sloping demand curve, and why price and marginal revenue diverge.
3. Be able to show the relationship between the market demand and individual demand curve for a monopolist.
4. Know the difference between marginal cost pricing for a competitive firm and profit maximization for a monopoly.
5. Be able to determine a monopolist's most profitable rate of production.
6. Be able to show why a monopoly typically results in higher profits, less output, and higher prices than would occur in a competitive market.
7. Be able to contrast the long-run results in a competitive market with that of a monopoly.
8. Be able to describe the advantages and disadvantages of monopoly versus competition.
9. Be able to distinguish price discrimination from other types of pricing.
10. Be able to distinguish economies of scale from constant returns to scale and diseconomies of scale.
11. Understand why a natural monopoly occurs.
12. Know how and why antitrust policy is used to control monopoly.
13. Understand the idea of "contestable" markets.

Using Key Terms

Fill in the puzzle on the opposite page with the appropriate term from the list of Key Terms at the end of the chapter in the text.

Across

2. This curve lies below the demand curve at every point except the first in Figure 9.2 in the text.
7. Used to determine that the most profitable rate of production is four bushels per hour in Figure 9.3 in the text.
9. The ability to alter the market price of a good or service.
10. An industry in which one firm can achieve economies of scale over the entire range of market supply.
11. Total cost divided by the quantity produced in a given time period.
12. Government intervention to alter market structure or prevent abuse of market power.
13. For a monopolist, this short-run choice is made by locating the intersection of marginal cost and marginal revenue.

Down

1. The sale of an identical good at different prices to different consumers by a single seller.
2. The market structure that Pepsi accuses Coke of trying to duplicate in the article titled "Pepsi Takes Coke to Court" in the text.
3. The percentage change in quantity demanded divided by the percentage change in price.
4. According to the article "Foxy Soviets Pelt the West" in the text, the Soviet Union erected __________ by not letting live sables leave the country.
5. Gives one producer an advantage over several smaller producers and acts as a barrier to entry.
6. An imperfectly competitive industry which is restrained by potential competition.
8. The pricing method characteristic of competitive markets but not a monopoly.

Puzzle 9.1

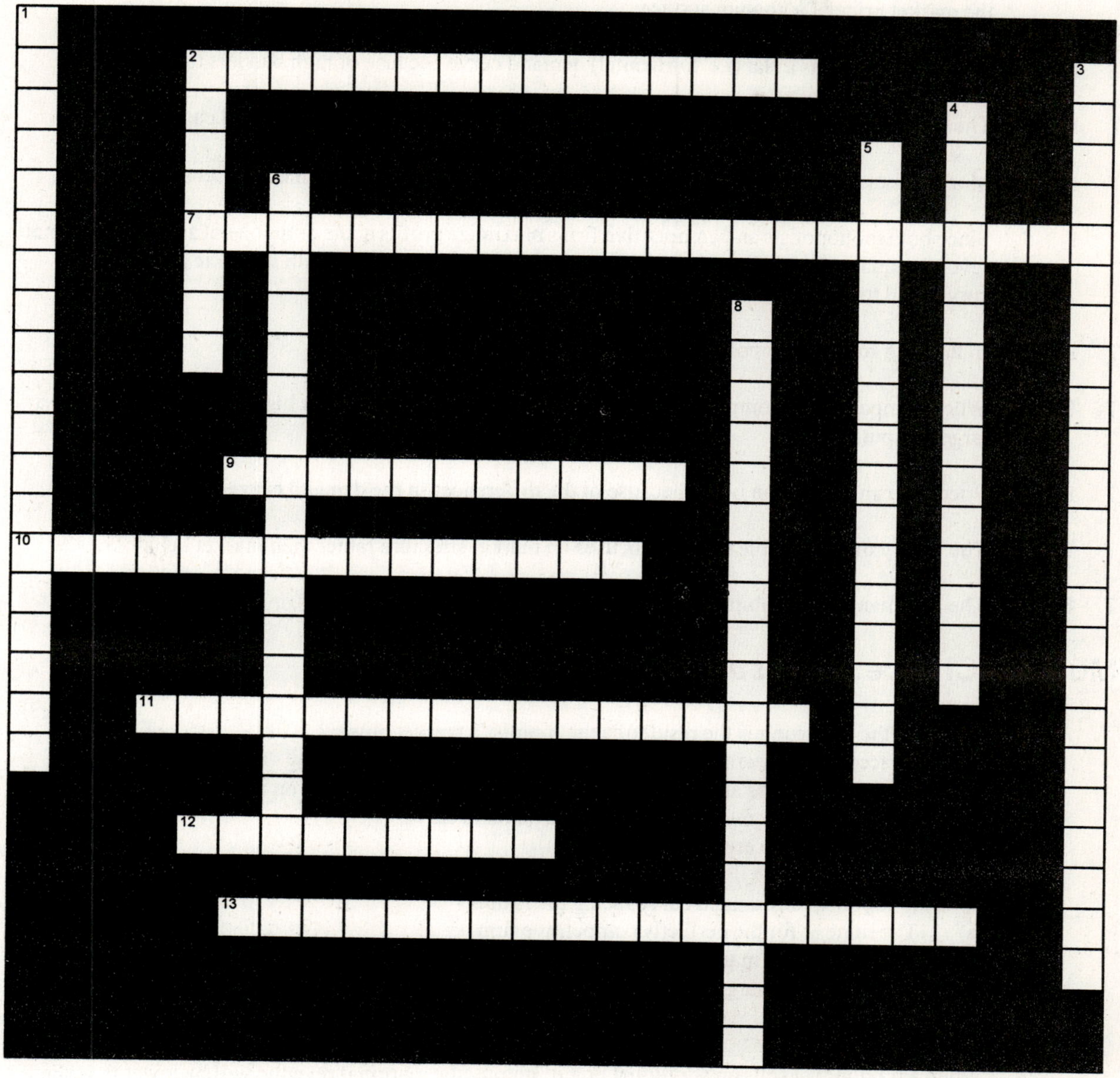

True or False: *Circle your choice and explain why any false statements are incorrect.*

T F 1. Since a competitive firm can sell unlimited quantities of output at the prevailing price, it can affect the market price of a good or service.

T F 2. The monopolist has a flat (i.e. horizontal) demand curve because of high barriers to entry.

T F 3. The demand curve for the monopolist is exactly the same as the market demand curve.

T F 4. Monopolists maximize profits at the output level at which price equals marginal cost.

T F 5. Since both monopolists and competitive firms maximize profits at the output level at which marginal revenue equals marginal cost, monopolists and competitive markets with the same marginal cost curves and market demand curves will produce the same output.

T F 6. In the long run, a monopolist can continue to earn economic profits.

T F 7. When compared to a competitive market, monopolists tend to charge a higher price and produce a larger output.

T F 8. Price discrimination can occur because of the differences in the demand curves among buyers.

T F 9. The theory of contestable markets focuses on market structure rather than market behavior.

T F 10. The Sherman Act prohibits price discrimination.

Multiple Choice: *Select the correct answer.*

_____ 1. Which of the following is the result of a monopolist's market power?
(a) It faces a downward-sloping demand curve.
(b) When it produces an extra unit of output, it must lower its price on all of its units.
(c) Its marginal revenue curve is below its demand curve.
(d) All of the above are results.

_____ 2. For a monopolist, the demand curve facing the firm is:
(a) The same as for the perfectly competitive firm.
(b) The same as the market-demand curve.
(c) Always below marginal revenue.
(d) Perfectly elastic.

_____ 3. When a monopolist sells an additional unit of output, the marginal revenue will be lower than the price because:
(a) The price of all the units sold will have to be lowered in order to sell the additional unit.
(b) The monopolist faces a flat (horizontal) demand curve for its product.
(c) Costs increase as more output is produced.
(d) Economies of scale exist for monopolists.

_____ 4. Which of the following is most likely *not* a monopolist?
(a) The only doctor in a small community.
(b) A large soft-drink firm such as Coca-Cola.
(c) The electric power company in your area.
(d) The water company in your area.

_____ 5. Which of the following rules will always be satisfied when a firm has maximized profit?
(a) P = lowest level of long-run average costs.
(b) P = MC.
(c) MR = MC.
(d) P = ATC.

_____ 6. In a monopoly and perfect competition, a firm should expand production when:
(a) Price is below marginal cost.
(b) Price is above marginal cost.
(c) Marginal revenue is below marginal cost.
(d) Marginal revenue is above marginal cost.

_____ 7. Suppose a monopoly produces a drug and sells 100 prescriptions at $100 each. In order to sell 101 prescriptions, the firm must lower the price to $99. What is the marginal revenue of the 101st unit sold?
(a) $-1.
(b) $1.
(c) $99.
(d) $9999.

_____ 8. Monopoly might be considered to be more desirable than perfect competition because:
(a) The monopolist has more incentive to keep costs down.
(b) Economies of scale can only be fully realized by a single firm in a natural monopoly.
(c) Marginal revenue is less than price for a monopoly.
(d) It is the best way to increase output above the competitive level of production.

_____ 9. Which of the following can help a firm maintain a monopoly situation?
(a) A license.
(b) Exclusive control over important resources.
(c) A patent.
(d) All of the above.

_____ 10. A monopolist with many plants produces less than would be produced if all of the plants were competing with one another in a competitive market:
(a) Because the market demand curve is perfectly inelastic for the monopolistic firm but not for the competitive firms.
(b) Because the market demand curve slopes downward for the monopolistic market and for the competitive market.
(c) Because the marginal revenue curve is below the demand curve for the monopolistic firm but not for the competitive firms.
(d) Because profit is maximized where MR = MC for the monopolistic firm but not for the competitive firms.

_____ 11. The price charged by a profit-maximizing monopolist in the long run occurs:
(a) At the minimum of the long-run average cost curve.
(b) Where P = MR = MC.
(c) At a price on the demand curve above the intersection where MR = MC.
(d) At a price on the long-run average cost curve below the point where MR = MC.

_____ 12. When a monopoly continues to make above-normal profits in the long run, you can be sure that:
(a) It produces more efficiently than a competitive market can.
(b) Barriers to entry prevent other firms from competing away the above-normal profits.
(c) There is a conspiracy between the government and the monopolist to maintain high prices.
(d) It has an inelastic demand curve, which gives it greater revenues at every price.

_____ 13. If a monopoly used marginal cost pricing to determine its output and price, which of the following statements would be true?
(a) The monopolist would not be maximizing its profits.
(b) The monopolist would produce a higher level of output than it would if it was maximizing its profits.
(c) The monopolist would produce the optimal level of output from the consumer's standpoint.
(d) All of the above would be true.

_____ 14. Monopolists are:
(a) Price setters, but competitive firms are price takers.
(b) Price takers, as are competitive firms.
(c) Price takers, but competitive firms are price setters.
(d) Price setters, as are competitive firms.

_____ 15. Price discrimination allows a producer to:
(a) Reap the highest possible average price for the quantity sold.
(b) Increase the elasticity of consumer demand.
(c) Minimize marginal costs.
(d) Decrease total costs.

_____ 16. Which of the following is an example of price discrimination by a "10-Minute Oil Change" firm?
(a) Charging a lower price if the customer does not want their car vacuumed.
(b) Charging a lower price for cars that use 4 quarts of oil instead of the typical 5 quarts.
(c) Charging women a lower price because it is Tuesday.
(d) All of the above.

_____ 17. The argument that concentration of market power enhances research and development efforts may be weak because:
(a) Monopolies cannot afford basic research.
(b) A monopoly may have no clear incentive to pursue new research and development.
(c) No one has attempted to gather any empirical evidence.
(d) No existing monopoly has a research and development program.

_____ 18. According to the theory of contestable markets, monopoly may *not* be a problem if:
(a) The structure of a market is competitive.
(b) Firms can exit from the market.
(c) Antitrust regulations are enforced.
(d) Potential competition exists.

_____ 19. The primary purpose of anti-trust policy in the United States is to:
(a) Issue patents.
(b) Encourage competition.
(c) Limit foreign competition.
(d) Regulate monopolies.

_____ 20. Which of the following was the first to prohibit conspiracies in restraint of trade?
(a) The Sherman Act.
(b) The Clayton Act.
(c) The Federal Trade Commission Act.
(d) The Gramm-Rudman Act.

Problems and Applications

Exercise 1

This exercise provides practice in calculating total revenue and marginal revenue, and shows the relationship between marginal revenue and demand.

1. Use the information given in Table 9.1 to calculate total revenue and marginal revenue.

Table 9.1 Revenue data

	Quantity	Price	Total Revenue	Marginal Revenue
A	0	$12.00	$_____	-------
B	1	11.00	_____	$_____
C	2	10.00	_____	_____
D	3	9.00	_____	_____
E	4	8.00	_____	_____
F	5	7.00	_____	_____
G	6	6.00	_____	_____

2. Use the information from Table 9.1 to graph the demand curve and the marginal revenue curve in Figure 9.1. Label each curve and label the points (B through G) on the demand curve.

Figure 9.1 Demand and marginal revenue curves

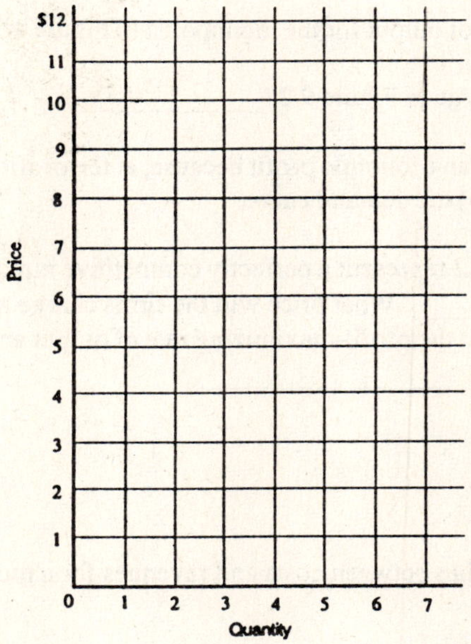

3. For a monopoly, price is determined from the ________________ curve, directly above the point where ________________ .

4. For a monopoly, marginal revenue is always (greater, less) than price, after the first unit, because the firm must (raise, lower) its price to sell additional output.

Exercise 2

This exercise reviews costs and revenues and provides further experience with profit maximization.

Figure 9.2 represents cost curves for a monopolist. Use Figure 9.2 to answer questions 1-4.

Figure 9.2 Cost curves and profit maximization

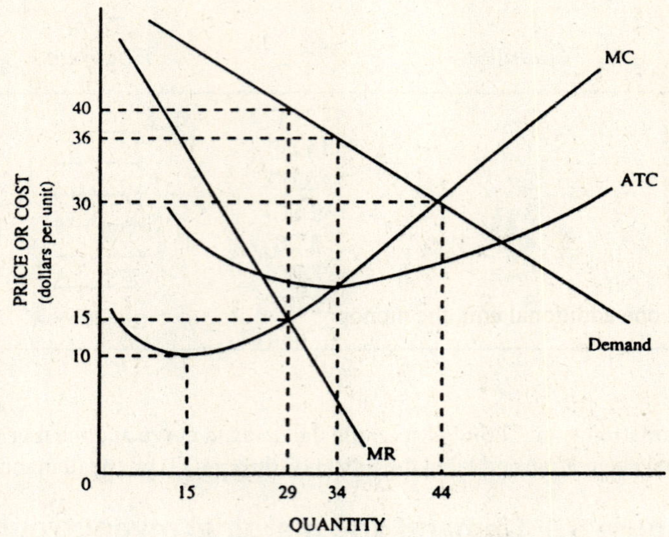

1. What is the profit-maximizing rate of output for the monopolist in Figure 9.2? ___________

2. What price will the monopolist charge in Figure 9.2? ___________

3. This monopolist (is, is not) earning an economic profit because, at the profit-maximizing rate of output in Figure 9.2, ATC is (above, below) the demand curve.

4. Now assume the curves in Figure 9.2 represent a perfectly competitive market. What is the profit-maximizing rate of output? __________ What price will the firms charge at this output? ________ How do price and output compare to the profit-maximizing rate of output and price for a monopolist?
____

Exercise 3

This exercise emphasizes the relationship between costs and revenues for a monopolist and determination of profit maximization.

1. Use the data in Table 9.2 to calculate total revenue, marginal revenue, and marginal cost for a monopolist.

Table 9.2 Revenue and cost data

Quantity	Price	Total revenue	Marginal revenue	Total cost	Marginal cost
0	$14	$____	----	$13	—
1	13	____	$____	15	$____
2	12	____	____	18	____
3	11	____	____	23	____
4	10	____	____	30	____
5	9	____	____	39	____
6	8	____	____	51	____

2. For a monopolist, the profit-maximizing rate of output occurs where marginal revenue equals________.

3. In this case, the profit-maximizing rate of output is ________ units.

4. At the profit-maximizing rate of output, the monopolist will charge _________ for the product.

5. At the profit-maximizing rate of output, this monopolist earns a profit of__________.

6. In order to sell one additional unit, the monopolist would have to (decrease, increase, make no change in) price.

7. Since this monopolist is earning a profit, the ATC curve must be (above, below, equal to) the demand curve at the profit-maximizing rate of output.

8. Now suppose the data in Table 24.2 represent a perfectly competitive market. The profit-maximizing rate of output occurs where marginal cost equals ________________________.

9. In this case, the profit-maximizing rate of output would be ______ units at a price of______.

10. At the competitive profit-maximizing rate of output, profits equal______.

11. Compared to a perfectly competitive market, a monopoly charges a (higher, lower) price, produces a (higher, lower) output, and earns a (greater, smaller) profit.

Exercise 4

Reread the article titled "New Competition May Mean Bad News for CNN" and then answer the following questions.

1. What phrase indicates that CNN has monopoly power in the 24-hour news market? _______________
____

2. What barriers to entry have kept other networks from competing with CNN? __________________
____

3. Why are competitors trying to overcome the barriers to entry? ___________________________
____

Common Errors

The first statement in each "common error" below is incorrect. Each incorrect statement is followed by a corrected version and an explanation.

1. Monopolists have supply curves. WRONG!

   Monopolists have marginal cost curves, but not supply curves. RIGHT!

   The marginal cost indicates the quantity that a competitive firm will supply at a given price. (*Remember*: Price equals marginal cost for the profit maximizing competitive firm.) But we cannot tell what a monopolist will supply at a given price by looking at the marginal cost curve. We need to know marginal revenue, and therefore the demand curve, before we can tell what quantity the firm will supply. (*Remember*: Marginal cost equals marginal revenue when profits are maximized.)

   Be careful! Do not label the marginal cost curve of a monopolist (or any noncompetitive firm) as a "supply" curve in your diagrams.

2. When there are economies of scale, a firm can simply increase production rates in the short run and unit costs will decline. WRONG!

   When there are economies of scale, a firm can choose a plant size designed for increased production rates at lower unit costs. RIGHT!

   Economies of scale are not realized through production decisions in the short run. They are realized through investment decisions, by the choice of an optimal-sized plant for higher production rates. Scale refers to plant size or capacity, not to production rates within a plant of a given size. Think of economies of scale in terms of investment decisions concerning choices of optimal capacity for the long run, not production decisions concerning the lowest cost production in the short run.

3. The profit maximizing and shutdown rules are different for a monopoly than for a competitive firm. WRONG!

   The profit maximizing and shutdown rules are the same for a monopoly as they are for all other profit maximizing firms. RIGHT!

   All firms that want to maximize profits should produce at the output level where MC=MR, regardless of the market structure. In addition, all firms should continue to produce in the short run only if they can cover variable costs. The shutdown point occurs where price equals AVC.

•ANSWERS•

Using Key Terms

Across

2. marginal revenue
7. profit maximization rule
9. market power
10. natural monopoly
11. average total cost
12. antitrust
13. production decision

Down

1. price discrimination
2. monopoly
3. price elasticity of demand
4. barriers to entry
5. economies of scale
6. contestable market
8. marginal cost pricing

True or False

1. F A competitive firm has no control over the market price because it is such a tiny part of the relatively huge market. Because it is relatively insignificant, it can sell as much as it wants at the market price.
2. F The monopolist typically has a relatively inelastic demand curve because of barriers to entry, i.e., few substitutes.
3. T
4. F Monopolists maximize profits where MR = MC.
5. F Monopolists will tend to produce less than the output that would be produced in a competitive market because the MR curve is below the demand curve for the monopolist.
6. T
7. F When compared to a competitive market, monopolists tend to charge a higher price and produce a lower output.
8. T
9. F The theory focuses on behavior rather than structure, i.e. not how many producers exist in a market but how many could potentially exist.
10. F The Clayton Act prohibits price discrimination.

Multiple Choice

1.	d	5.	c	9.	d	13.	d	17.	b
2.	b	6.	d	10.	c	14.	a	18.	d
3.	a	7.	a	11.	c	15.	a	19.	b
4.	b	8.	b	12.	b	16.	c	20.	a

Exercise 1

1. **Table 9.1 Answer**

Quantity	*Total revenue*	*Marginal revenue*
0	$ 0.00	-----
1	11.00	$ 11.00
2	20.00	9.00
3	27.00	7.00
4	32.00	5.00
5	35.00	3.00
6	36.00	1.00

2. **Figure 9.1 Answer**

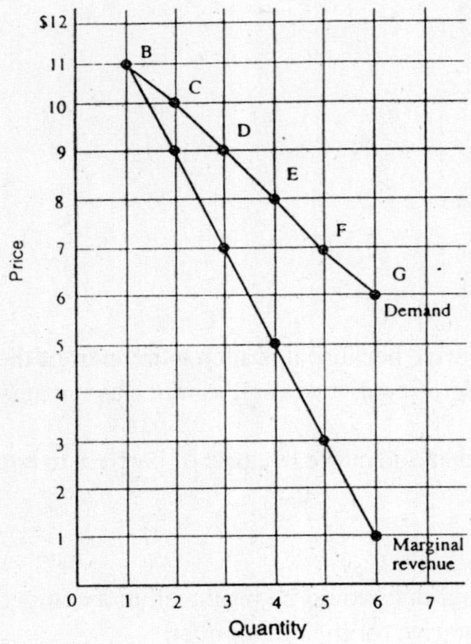

3. Demand, MC = MR
4. Less, lower

Exercise 2

1. 29 units
2. $40
3. Is, below
4. 44 units, $30, price is less and output is greater for the perfectly competitive firm

Exercise 3

1. **Table 9.2 Answer**

Quantity	Price	Total revenue	Marginal revenue	Total cost	Marginal cost
0	$14	$ 0	----	$13	—
1	13	13	$ 13	15	$ 2
2	12	24	11	18	3
3	11	33	9	23	5
4	10	40	7	30	7
5	9	45	5	39	9
6	8	48	3	51	12

2. Marginal cost
3. 4
4. $10

5. $10
6. Decrease
7. Below
8. Price
9. 5, $9
10. $6
11. Higher, lower, greater

Exercise 4

1. ". . . with the market to itself . . . "
2. ". . . huge distribution hurdles caused by lack of space on crowded cable systems . . . "
3. "Last year . . . CNN . . . generated about $227 million in operating profit for Turner Broadcasting System Inc."

CHAPTER 10

Oligopoly

Quick Review

- Market structure is based on the number and relative size of firms in an industry. Three structures are referred to as imperfectly competitive—duopoly, oligopoly, and monopolistic competition.

- The determinants of market power, that is, the extent to which the firm can influence market outcomes, are determined by the number of producers, the size of each firm, barriers to entry, and the availability of substitute products.

- Market power is commonly measured by calculating the concentration ratio: the proportion of total market output produced by the largest producers, typically the top four.

- An oligopoly is a market structure consisting of a few interdependent firms. Because of the small number of firms involved in an oligopoly, it can potentially behave as a shared monopoly.

- An oligopoly is often depicted with a kinked demand curve. This reflects the idea that rival firms will follow price decreases but will not follow price increases. This leads to a demand curve that is flatter above the equilibrium price and steeper below.

- If oligopolists are successful in coordinating their efforts, they can restrict industry output and reap monopoly-like profits. Strategies such as collusion, price leadership, and price-fixing can be used to accomplish this goal.

- Barriers to entry are the key to maintaining economic profits in the long run. Patents, control of a distribution system, government regulation, and nonprice competition are used to eliminate competition. Mergers and acquisitions can also be used to limit entry.

- Market power contributes to market failure when it results in significant misallocation of resources. Antitrust laws explicitly forbid many of the practices described in this chapter.

- The Herfindahl-Hirshman Index (HHI) is used to measure industry concentration. The Justice Department also examines market structure, barriers to entry, and consumer welfare to determine if government intervention is necessary.

Learning Objectives

After reading Chapter 10 and doing the following exercises, you should:

1. Be able to describe the different market structures.
2. Know the determinants of market power.
3. Be able to calculate and interpret concentration ratios and the Herfindahl-Hirshman Index.
4. Be aware of some of the economy's most concentrated industries.
5. Know how market structure affects market behavior and market outcomes.
6. Understand and be able to describe the kinked demand curve model of oligopoly.
7. Know the difference between the long-run market outcomes resulting from perfectly competitive markets and oligopoly.
8. Understand the setting in which game theory is useful in studying business decision making.
9. Be able to describe the coordination problem inherent in the shared-monopoly idea of oligopoly.
10. Know some techniques which oligopolists have used to implement coordination and enforcement of market shares.
11. Be able to list and describe several barriers to entry.
12. Know three prominent antitrust laws and their major provisions.
13. Understand the significance of the Herfindahl-Hirshman Index.
14. Know the criteria used by the Justice Department to determine if an antitrust case should be prosecuted.

Using Key Terms

Fill in the puzzle on the opposite page with the appropriate term from the list of Key Terms at the end of the chapter in the text.

Across

1. The number and relative size of firms in an industry.
4. Trans World Airlines, Delta Air Lines, and Northwest Airlines were accused of using this tactic in an *In the News* article in the text.
7. Government intervention to prevent the abuse of market power.
8. One way a firm can establish the market price for all firms in the industry.
9. A measure of industry concentration that accounts for the number of firms and the size of each.
11. One of the dominant firms in an oligopoly.
15. Used by a firm to make its product appear different and superior to other products.
16. The curve drawn with a gap in Figure 10.6 in the text.
17. Obstacles that help to keep potential competitors out of an industry.
18. A market structure with high barriers to entry, substantial market power, and a few firms.

Down

2. A group of firms with an explicit agreement to fix prices and output shares.
3. Firms produce at the rate of output where MR=MC.
5. An imperfectly competitive industry subject to potential entry if prices or profits increase.
6. The study of how decisions are made when strategic interaction exists.
10. The proportion of total industry output produced by the largest firms.
12. Occurs when market power leads to resource misallocation or greater inequity.
13. The percentage of total market output produced by a firm.
14. An explicit agreement among producers regarding the price at which a good is to be sold.

Puzzle 10.1

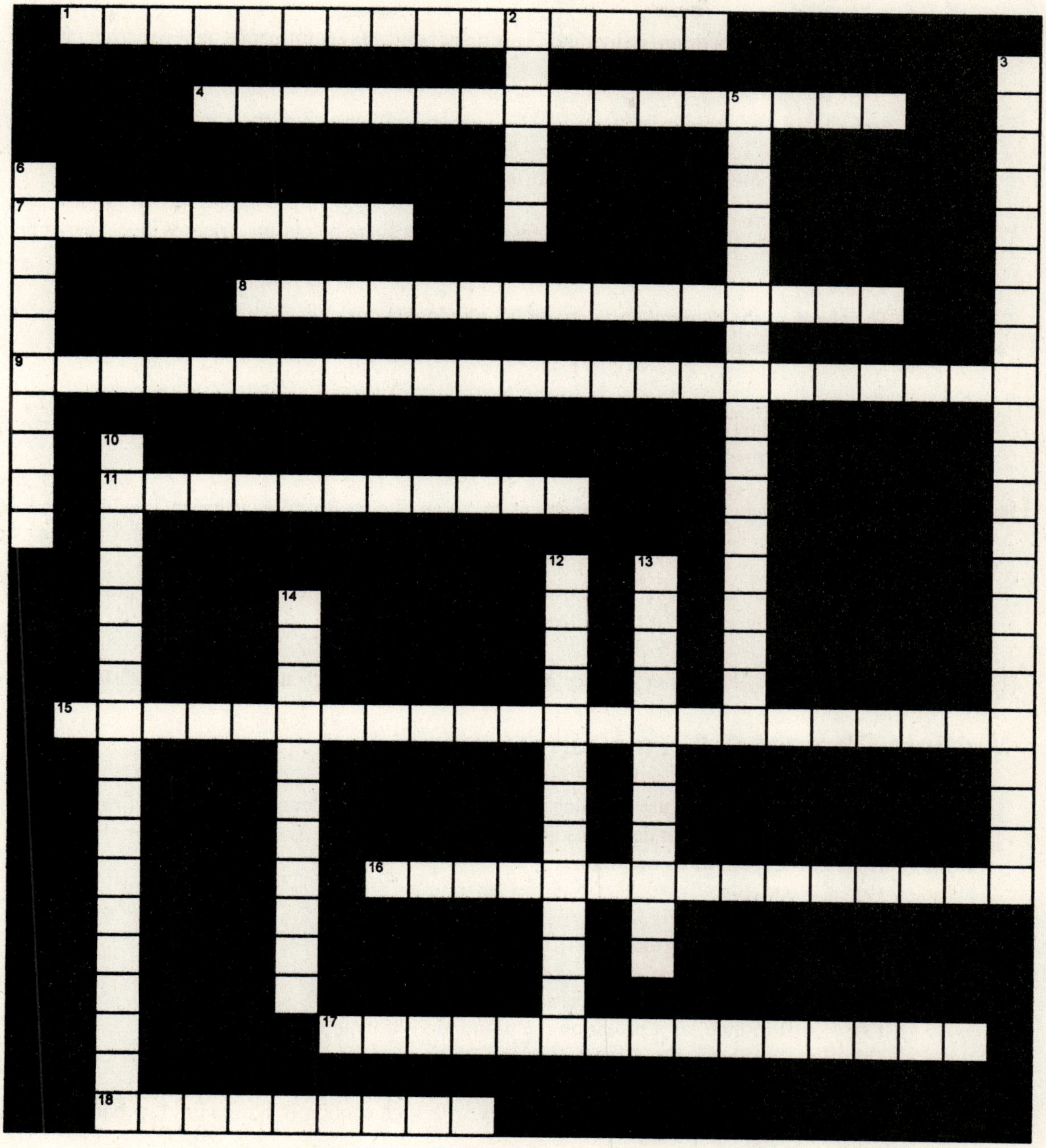

True or False: *Circle your choice and explain why any false statements are incorrect.*

T F 1. Firms are divided into specific market structures based on their ability to earn a profit.

T F 2. In imperfect competition, individual firms do not have direct influence on the market price of a particular product.

T F 3. Firms in an oligopoly market are highly independent because of their relatively small number.

T F 4. When OPEC members set the price of oil they are participating in price-fixing.

T F 5. An attempt by one oligopolist to increase its market share by cutting prices will leave competitors unaffected.

T F 6. The shape of the demand curve facing an oligopolist does not depend on the responses of its rivals to a change in the price of its own output.

T F 7. The reason that changes in marginal cost may have no effect on the output of an oligopoly characterized by a kinked demand curve is that the accompanying marginal revenue curve contains a vertical segment or gap.

T F 8. The kinked demand curve demonstrates that if an oligopolist raises its price, it is likely to lose market share.

T F 9. An increase in the market share of one oligopolist will not necessarily reduce the shares of the remaining oligopolists if the industry is growing.

T F 10. One example of a barrier to entry into an oligopoly market is the control of a distribution process.

Multiple Choice: *Select the correct answer.*

_____ 1. The only market structure in which there is significant interdependence among firms with regard to their pricing and output decisions is:
(a) Monopolistic competition.
(b) Monopoly.
(c) Oligopoly.
(d) Perfect competition.

_____ 2. Which of the following firms has significant market power?
(a) A firm that has a patent on the production of its unique product.
(b) A firm that is the same size as the 1,000 other firms in the industry.
(c) A firm that produces a product with many close substitutes.
(d) A firm that produces in an industry with high economic profits but low barriers to entry.

_____ 3. Which of the following is evidence of the interdependence that characterizes the relationship among oligopolists?
(a) Retaliation.
(b) Price wars.
(c) Gamesmanship.
(d) All of the above.

_____ 4. Characteristics of an oligopolistic market include:
   (a) Tacit collusion.
   (b) High barriers to entry.
   (c) High concentration ratios.
   (d) All of the above.

_____ 5. A kinked demand curve indicates that rival oligopolists match:
   (a) All price changes.
   (b) No price changes.
   (c) Price reductions but not price increases.
   (d) Price increases but not price reductions.

_____ 6. The gap in the marginal revenue curve of an oligopolist is caused by:
   (a) The existence of two alternative demand curves that apply to the oligopolist, depending on whether it raises prices or lowers prices.
   (b) The failure of the marginal cost curve to intersect the demand curve at the profit-maximizing level.
   (c) The ability of oligopolists to make above-normal profits if they cooperate with each other.
   (d) All of the above.

_____ 7. Because of the gap in the marginal revenue curve, when the marginal cost curve rises, the kinked demand curve oligopolist may have an incentive to:
   (a) Speed up production and lower prices—behavior that leads to greater profits.
   (b) Maintain both production rates and prices—behavior that leads to lower profits but not necessarily to losses.
   (c) Lower production rates and maintain prices—actions that raise profits by counteracting cost increases.
   (d) Speed up production rates and maintain prices—actions that result in losses.

_____ 8. If an oligopolist is going to change its price or output, its concern is:
   (a) The response of consumers.
   (b) The possibility of losing market share.
   (c) Gamesmanship practiced by its competitors.
   (d) All of the above are concerns.

_____ 9. If a firm is producing at the kink in its demand curve and increases its price, according to the kinked-demand model:
   (a) It will lose market share to the firms that do not follow the price increase.
   (b) It will gain market share.
   (c) Its market share will not be affected.
   (d) It will not gain market share but it will definitely increase profits.

_____ 10. Which of the following is an explanation of why oligopolists have an incentive to collude?
   (a) The demand for each firm's product would be kinked.
   (b) Each firm would face a perfectly inelastic demand for its product.
   (c) Each firm would face a relatively inelastic demand for its product rather than a relatively elastic demand when firms raise prices independently.
   (d) The market demand curve would become perfectly inelastic.

_____ 11. Game theory is:
   (a) The study of price fixing and collusion.
   (b) The study of how decisions are made when interdependence between firms exists.
   (c) An explanation of how oligopolists become monopolists.
   (d) Only useful in perfectly competitive markets.

_____ 12. Oligopolists will maximize total market profits at the rate of output where:
- (a) MR = MC for the largest firms.
- (b) MR = MC for the average firm.
- (c) The market's MC equals the market's MR.
- (d) MR = MC for the marginal firm.

_____ 13. Open and explicit agreements concerning pricing and output shares transform an oligopoly into a:
- (a) Monopoly.
- (b) Cartel.
- (c) Differentiated oligopoly.
- (d) Perfectly competitive firm.

_____ 14. Price leadership:
- (a) Typically results in greater price stability in oligopolistic markets.
- (b) Is observed in oligopolistic markets.
- (c) Permits oligopolistic firms in a given market to coordinate market-wide price changes without formal collusion.
- (d) All of the above.

_____ 15. For an oligopoly, above-normal profit cannot be maintained in the long run unless:
- (a) A cartel is formed.
- (b) Barriers to entry exist.
- (c) A firm has a high concentration ratio.
- (d) The market is contestable.

_____ 16. An example of nonprice competition in the computer market is:
- (a) Advertising.
- (b) Availability of service on weekends.
- (c) Providing financing for the purchase of a computer.
- (d) All of the above.

_____ 17. Barriers to entry into an imperfectly competitive market include:
- (a) Patents.
- (b) Control of the distribution process.
- (c) Government regulation.
- (d) All of the above.

_____ 18. Market power leads to market failure when it results in:
- (a) Decreased market output.
- (b) Increased market prices.
- (c) Long lasting, above normal economic profits.
- (d) All of the above.

_____ 19. Which of the following are problems associated with pursuing anti-trust policy based on the behavior of firms rather than the structure of a market?
- (a) It is more expensive to investigate behavior rather than structure.
- (b) It is more difficult to prove anti-competitive behavior.
- (c) The general absence of public awareness and interest in the problem of collusion.
- (d) All of the above are problems.

_____ 20. Since 1996, anti-trust guidelines adopted by the Justice Department and the Federal Trade Commission have focused on:
(a) The concept of "unfair competition."
(b) The HHI.
(c) Increased government regulation.
(d) All of the above.

Problems and Applications

Exercise 1

This exercise shows how to compute concentration ratios and market shares for an industry.

1. Market share is:
   (a) The percentage of total market output produced by the largest firms (usually the four largest).
   (b) The percentage of total market output produced by the largest firm.
   (c) The percentage of total market output produced by a given firm.
   (d) A type of stock issued by the firms in a market.

2. Concentration usually refers to:
   (a) The percentage of total market output produced by the four largest domestic firms.
   (b) The percentage of total market output produced by any four large domestic firms.
   (c) The percentage of total market output produced by a given domestic firm.
   (d) The percentage of total market output produced by the four largest domestic or foreign firms.

3. Table 10.1 gives the sales of the top four firms (A, B, C, D) in a market. Insert the total sales for the top four firms and total sales for the market. Then, using this information, compute the market share for each firm separately, the market share for the "Top four firms," and the market share for "All other firms."

Table 10.1
Sales and market shares of top four firms, by company

Firm	*Sales (millions of dollars per year)*	*Market share*
A	$ 60	____%
B	40	____
C	30	____
D	20	____
Top four firms	$____	____%
All other firms	50	____%
All firms	$____	100 %

4. T F The sum of the market shares of the top four firms is the same as the four-firm concentration ratio.

Exercise 2

This exercise illustrates the differences between using the concentration ratio and the Herfindahl-Hirshman Index to measure market power. It also will help you complete a problem in the text.

Table 10.2 presents the market shares for two separate markets. Each market has only four firms.

Table 10.2
Market shares for calculating concentration ratios and the Herfindahl-Hirshman Index

First market		*Second market*	
Firm	*Market share*	*Firm*	*Market share*
A	25%	E	97%
B	25%	F	1%
C	25%	G	1%
D	25%	H	1%

1. The four-firm concentration ratio for the first market is __________ and for the second market is __________.

2. The Herfindahl-Hirshman Index for the first market is __________ and for the second market is __________.

3. Would you expect the market power exerted in the two markets to be the same? __________
Why or why not? ____
____

4. According to the Justice Department guidelines:
(a) Mergers would be permitted in both markets.
(b) A merger would be permitted only in the first market.
(c) A merger would be permitted only in the second market.
(d) Mergers would not be permitted in either market.

Exercise 3

This exercise reviews costs and revenues and provides further experience with profit maximization.

Figure 10.1 represents cost curves for an oligopolist. Use Figure 10.1 to answer questions 1-4.

Figure 10.1

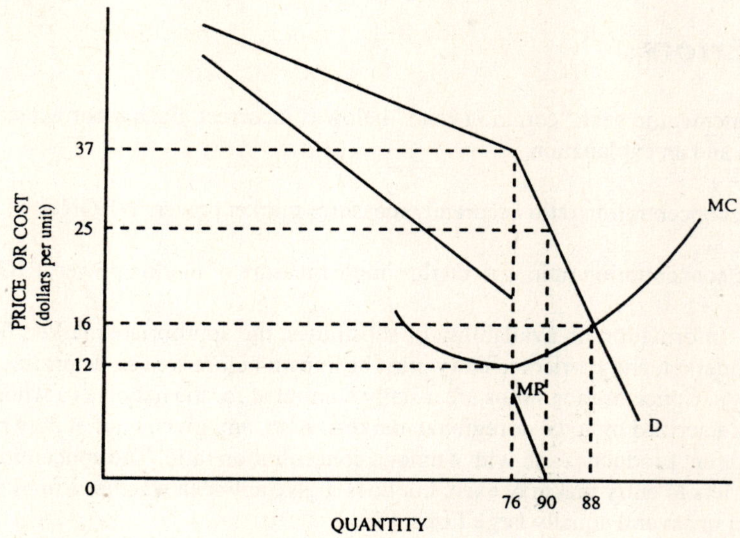

1. What is the profit-maximizing rate of output for the oligopolist in Figure 10.1? ____________

2. What price will the oligopolist charge in Figure 10.1? ____________

3. If the MC curve shifts up by a small amount, $4 or less, the profit maximizing oligopolist will (increase, decrease, not change) price because of the gap in the (MR, demand) curve.

4. The demand curve for the oligopolist is kinked because rival oligopolists will match price (increases, reductions) but not price (increases, reductions).

Exercise 4

The media often provide information about the strategies, both successful and unsuccessful, employed by oligopolists as they attempt to compete in the marketplace. By using one of the articles in the text, this exercise will show you what to look for.

Reread the article in the text entitled "Pop Culture: RC Goes for the Youth Market" and then answer the following questions.

1. What is the concentration ratio in the U.S. soft drink market? ____________

2. What was the Royal Crown strategy in the 1980s? Which phrase indicates the result? ____________
____

3. What is the new Royal Crown strategy? What is their target? ____________
____

4. What barriers to entry exist in the soft drink market? ______________________________
____

5. Calculate an HHI on the basis of the information in the pie chart in the article.______________

6. Would game theory be useful in analyzing behavior in this market? Why? __________________
____

Common Errors

The first statement in each "common error" below is incorrect. Each incorrect statement is followed by a corrected version and an explanation.

1. The concentration ratio accurately measures market power. WRONG!

   The concentration ratio is a rough, simple measure of market power. RIGHT!

   Information on availability of substitutes, the appropriate market, the relative size of firms in the market, and barriers to entry must be known before we can determine whether market power exists. Concentration ratios are usually computed for the nation as a whole, but many industries are characterized by local or regional markets. Also, any given market may produce a variety of different products, each with a unique concentration ratio. The concentration ratio gives no idea of barriers to entry that may exist, nor does it give any idea whether a market contains one dominant firm or several equally large firms.

2. American industry consists mostly of monopolies. WRONG!

   There are only a few monopolies in the U.S. economy. RIGHT!

   The text has shown that many U.S. markets are imperfectly competitive, but concentration ratios of 100 percent are rare. Monopolies are most likely to occur in the utility industries, which are then heavily regulated by government.

3. All large firms have market power. WRONG!

   The largest firms in concentrated markets are *likely* to have market power. RIGHT!

   Control of a market is more important than actual firm size in determining market power. Relative size as measured by concentration is more important than absolute size as measured by sales. For example, while conglomerates may be very large, they may play only small roles in many different markets and have no ability to influence prices in any of them.

4. Oligopolists have unlimited power to raise prices and curtail production to make large profits. WRONG!

   Oligopolists' ability to raise prices is limited by demand and their competitive rivalry. RIGHT!

   The demand for oligopolists' products is limited by foreign competition, availability of substitutes, and potential entry by other firms. Such markets as the railroad-car market, the market for rifles, and the auto market contain only a few large firms, but they are limited by potential competition from other countries or at home.

Furthermore, there is no guarantee that oligopolists will cooperate with each other. Oligopolists may use their market power cooperatively through collusion, price leadership, or indirect means of supporting prices above competitive levels. Such cooperative activity *may* lead to profits in the long run as well as in the short run. Changes in demand and costs, however, can force oligopolists to take losses or even to fail. Most importantly, oligopolists may not cooperate with each other. They may conduct price wars and engage in nonprice competition in order to erode each other's market share. Such conduct often leads to instability and substantial losses.

5. Oligopolistic firms compete with each other. MISLEADING!

   Oligopolies are often characterized by competitive rivalry. RIGHT!

   When firms have market power, they become aware of their interdependence. The often warlike or conspiratorial conduct—rivalry—that occurs is quite different from the conduct of competitive firms. Since no competitive firm can affect market prices, no one firm sees any other as a threat, nor is there any possibility of colluding to fix prices. True competition is often marked on the one hand by independent behavior of the competing firms and on the other by cooperation to hold down costs. For example, while farmers rarely succeed in increasing the prices of farm products by cooperative efforts, they may share the use of farm equipment with neighboring farmers to lower costs. There is certainly no reason for one farmer to engage in a price war with another farmer, since both represent such a small part of the market.

•ANSWERS•

Using Key Terms

Across

1. market structure
4. predatory pricing
7. antitrust
8. price leadership
9. Herfindahl-Hirshman Index
11. oligopolist
15. product differentiation
16. marginal revenue
17. barriers to entry
18. oligopoly

Down

2. cartel
3. profit maximization rule
5. contestable market
6. game theory
10. concentration ratio
12. market failure
13. market share
14. price fixing

True or False

1. F The division is based on market power.
2. F Firms do have varying degrees of control over the market price in imperfect competition.
3. T
4. T
5. F Oligopolists are interdependent, i.e. a change in one firm's price or output will affect its competitors.
6. F The shape of the demand curve facing an oligopolist does depend on the responses of its rivals to a change in the price of its own output.
7. T
8. T
9. F Market share is a percentage measure. If one firm's percentage share of the market increases, other firms must experience a reduction in market share.
10. T

Multiple Choice

1. c	5. c	9. a	13. b	17. d
2. a	6. a	10. c	14. d	18. d
3. d	7. b	11. b	15. b	19. d
4. d	8. d	12. c	16. d	20. a

Problems and Applications

Exercise 1

1. c
2. a
3. **Table 10.1 Answer**

Firm	Sales	Market share
A	$ 60	30%
B	40	20
C	30	15
D	20	10
Top four firms	$150	75%
All other firms	50	25%
All firms	$200	100%

4. T

Exercise 2

1. 100 percent; 100 percent
2. 2,500 (= $25^2 + 25^2 + 25^2 + 25^2$); 9,412 (= $97^2 + 1^2 + 1^2 + 1^2$)
3. No. The second market would exhibit much more market power since firm E is the dominant firm and would effectively determine the price. By contrast, market power would be more diffused among the four equally sized firms in the first market.

4. d Both markets have a Herfindahl-Hirshman Index above 1800.

Exercise 3

1. 76 units
2. $37
3. Not change, MR
4. Reductions, increases

Exercise 4

1. The four firm concentration ratio is 92.6%, the sum of the shares of the four largest producers.
2. The strategy was, apparently, not to spend on advertising. The result was "... we lost a whole generation of cola drinkers .... ."
3. Their new strategy is to spend $15 million on advertising, the largest amount in their history, and to toss out a "... bunch of beverages targeted toward younger drinkers."
4. The article indicates that Pepsi and Coke "... have huge amounts of marketing muscle, financial resources, experience and bottling agreements, ..." which will deter new entrants.
5. Based on the information in the pie chart, the HHI is 3151.27 ($44.1^2 + 31.4^2 + 14.7^2 + 2.1^2 = 3151.27$)
6. Very likely, since Coke and Pepsi dominate the soft drink market. There are numerous opportunities for moves and countermoves by these oligopolists, and this is where game theory is very useful.

CHAPTER 11

Monopolistic Competition

Quick Review

- A market characterized as "monopolistic competition" has many firms and each firm has some market power. The firms are relatively independent and the barriers to entry are also characteristically low.
- Concentration ratios in these industries are relatively low and even then the firms must often contend with significant competition from foreign entrants.
- The market power possessed by monopolistically competitive firms is the direct result of product differentiation. Advertising is very important in creating brand loyalty.
- Firms in monopolistic competition use the same profit-maximizing rule ($MC = MR$) as firms in other markets. In the short run firms may earn economic profits, but low barriers to entry permit the entry of new firms with the consequent erosion of those profits. In the long run only normal profits can be earned.
- Because the demand curves of the firms slope downward, the long-run equilibrium will be one in which $P = LATC$, but will occur at a point to the left of the minimum of the $LATC$ curve. Thus there is production inefficiency ($P > \text{min } LATC$) and allocative inefficiency because the wrong mix of output is produced.
- Firms in monopolistic competition spend tremendous amounts on advertising aimed at increasing demand and hopefully reducing the price elasticity of demand for their output. Other forms of nonprice competition are also used.
- The presumption follows that nonprice competition leads to a less desirable use of society's resources.

Learning Objectives

After reading Chapter 11 and doing the following exercises, you should:

1. Be able to describe structural characteristics of monopolistic competition.
2. Know how firms in monopolistic competition achieve their market power.
3. Know why the demand curve faced by the firms in monopolistically competitive markets is downward-sloping.
4. Be able to tell why monopolistically competitive firms use the $MC = MR$ rule in making the production decision.
5. Be able to describe the process by which the economic profits are eroded away by the entry of new firms.
6. Be able to explain why the long-run equilibrium in monopolistic competition suffers from production *and* allocative inefficiency.
7. Understand the difference between price competition and nonprice competition and how it may lead to an undesirable use of resources.

Using Key Terms

Fill in the puzzle on the opposite page with the appropriate term from the list of Key Terms at the end of the chapter in the text.

Across

3. Features that make one product appear different from competing products in the same market.
5. Obstacles that make it difficult or impossible for new firms to enter a market.
6. The ability to alter the market price of a good or service.
7. The choice of the short-run rate of output.
8. The offer of goods at prices equal to their marginal cost.

Down

1. A market in which firms produce a similar product but each maintains some independent control of price.
2. The proportion of total industry output produced by the largest firms.
4. The difference between total revenue and total economic costs.

Puzzle 11.1

True or False: *Circle your choice and explain why any false statements are incorrect.*

T F 1. A monopolistically competitive firm confronts a downward-sloping demand curve and, as a result, has some market power.

T F 2. In monopolistic competition, changes in the output or price of any single firm will have no significant influence on the sales of other firms.

T F 3. In monopolistic competition, each firm competes with other firms offering identical substitutes.

T F 4. When marginal costs rise, monopolistically competitive firms do not change output or price.

T F 5. For a monopolistically competitive firm, low barriers to entry tend to push economic profits toward zero in the long run.

T F 6. As new firms enter a monopolistically competitive industry, the demand curve for individual firms will shift to the right.

T F 7. The monopolistically competitive firm charges prices at the minimum of the long-run average total cost curve in the long run.

T F 8. When compared to a perfectly competitive market, monopolistic competition tends to result in a lower output level and a higher price.

T F 9. Monopolistic competition results in allocative efficiency.

T F 10. Firms in a monopolistically competitive industry tend to advertise to increase brand loyalty and thus sales.

Multiple Choice: *Select the correct answer.*

_____ 1. One of the main differences between oligopoly and monopolistic competition is:
- (a) The amount of advertising that firms do.
- (b) The amount of nonprice competition that occurs.
- (c) The degree of interdependence among firms.
- (d) That the profit maximizing output level occurs where MR = MC.

_____ 2. One of the main similarities of perfect competition and monopolistic competition is:
- (a) That in the long run, price equals average total cost and marginal revenue equals marginal cost.
- (b) The amount of product differentiation.
- (c) The point on the long-run average total cost curve at which firms maximize profits.
- (d) All of the above.

_____ 3. A major difference between monopoly and monopolistic competition is:
- (a) One maximizes profits by setting MR equal to MC, and the other does not.
- (b) The number of firms.
- (c) One type of firm has market power, and the other does not.
- (d) One has a downward-sloping demand curve, and the other does not.

_____ 4. In monopolistic competition:
(a) Firms have market power.
(b) Entry is easy.
(c) A firm's demand curve is downward-sloping.
(d) All of the above.

_____ 5. "Product differentiation" refers to:
(a) Different prices for the same product in a certain market.
(b) The selling of identical products in different markets.
(c) Features that make one product appear different from competing products in the same market.
(d) The charging of different prices for the same product in different markets.

_____ 6. A monopolistically competitive firm maximizes profits or minimizes losses in the long run by producing where:
(a) MR = MC.
(b) The demand curve is tangent to the long-run average total cost curve.
(c) P = ATC.
(d) All of the above.

_____ 7. If more firms enter a monopolistically competitive market, we would expect:
(a) The demand curves facing existing firms to shift to the left and become more price inelastic.
(b) The demand curves facing existing firms to shift to the left and no change in price elasticity.
(c) The demand curves facing existing firms to shift to the left and become more price elastic.
(d) The demand curves facing existing firms to shift to the right and no change in price elasticity.

_____ 8. Exit from a market characterized by monopolistic competition:
(a) Can easily occur if firms are earning economic losses.
(b) Rarely occurs because each firm possesses significant market power.
(c) Rarely occurs because of federal regulations controlling the number of firms in the market.
(d) Rarely occurs because of strong brand name identification.

_____ 9. Entry into a market characterized by monopolistic competition:
(a) Is rare because firms have market power.
(b) Is frequent because barriers to entry are low.
(c) Occurs when a firm's demand is below its long-run average cost curve at all levels of output.
(d) Results from economies of scale.

_____ 10. Firms in a monopolistically competitive market will:
(a) Produce efficiently.
(b) Make zero economic profits in the long run.
(c) Use the profit-maximizing rule TC = TR.
(d) All of the above.

_____ 11. Compared to the outcome under a marginal cost pricing strategy, a monopolistically competitive firm will produce a:
(a) Lower output and charge a higher price.
(b) Greater output and charge a higher price.
(c) Lower output and charge a lower price.
(d) Greater output and charge a lower price.

_____ 12. Monopolistically competitive firms are productively inefficient because long-run equilibrium occurs at an output rate where:
(a) MC is greater than MR.
(b) Price is greater than MC.
(c) ATC is greater than the minimum ATC.
(d) Diseconomies of scale exist.

_____ 13. In monopolistic competition there is allocative inefficiency because:
(a) Price is greater than the minimum ATC.
(b) Production is not at the minimum ATC.
(c) Of excess capacity.
(d) Price is greater than MC.

_____ 14. A monopolistically competitive firm can raise its price somewhat without fear of great change in unit sales because of:
(a) Brand loyalty.
(b) Economies of scale.
(c) Perfectly elastic demand.
(d) Large market shares of firms in the market.

_____ 15. Advertising is:
(a) An efficient form of competition.
(b) Less important than price competition in oligopolistic and monopolistic competition.
(c) A major component of competition in perfectly competitive markets.
(d) A form of nonprice competition.

_____ 16. When firms enter a monopolistically competitive industry, *ceteris paribus*, the:
(a) Market price increases.
(b) Market price decreases.
(c) Market price remains unchanged.
(d) Change in market price is impossible to determine.

Select the letter of the diagram representing long-run equilibrium in Figure 11.1 that best matches the type of market named in questions 17-20. Use each diagram *only once*.

Figure 11.1 Long-run cost curves

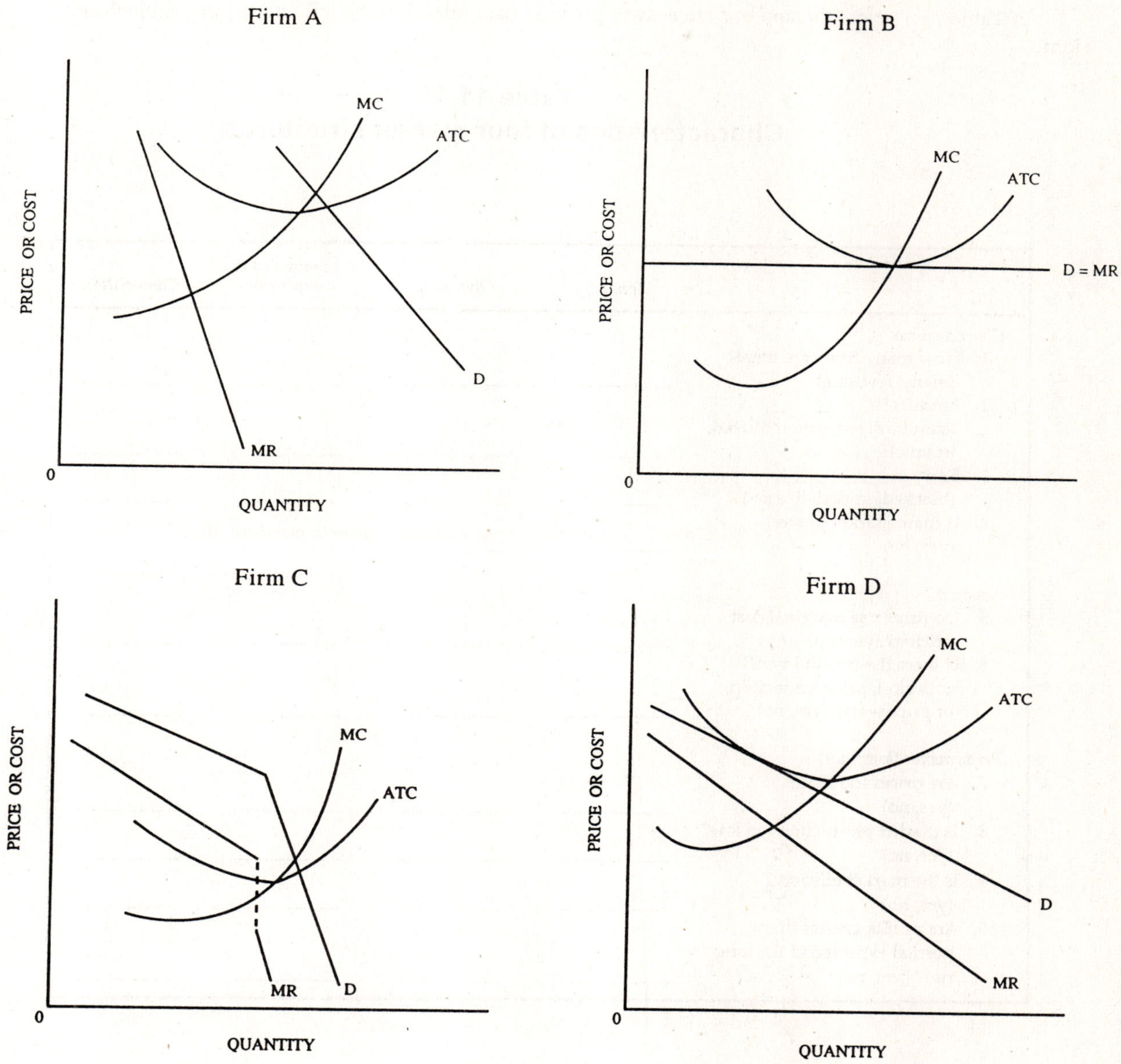

_____ 17. Perfect competition.

_____ 18. Oligopoly.

_____ 19. Monopolistic competition.

_____ 20. Monopoly.

Problems and Applications

Exercise 1

This exercise contrasts monopoly, oligopoly, monopolistic competition, and competition, and summarizes their differences.

In Table 11.1 select the appropriate answer given in parentheses at the left and fill in the blanks on the right.

Table 11.1
Characteristics of four market structures

	Monopoly	*Oligopoly*	*Monopolistic competition*	*Competition*
Characteristic				
1. How many firms are there? (many, few, one)	________	________	________	________
2. Product is________. (standardized, differentiated, unique)	________	________	________	________
3. Entry is ________. (blocked, impeded, easy)	________	________	________	________
4. Is there market power? (yes, no)	________	________	________	________
Conduct				
5. Do firms use marginal cost pricing? (yes, no)	________	________	________	________
6. Is there the possibility of collusion, price leadership, or price wars? (yes, no)	________	________	________	________
Performance (long run)				
7. Are prices too high? (yes, no)	________	________	________	________
8. Is market production too low? (yes, no)	________	________	________	________
9. Is the market efficient? (yes, no)	________	________	________	________
10. Are profits greater than normal expected in the long run? (yes, no)	________	________	________	________

Exercise 2

This exercise examines the characteristics of monopolistic competition using a graph.

Use Figure 11.2 to answer questions 1-6.

Figure 11.2

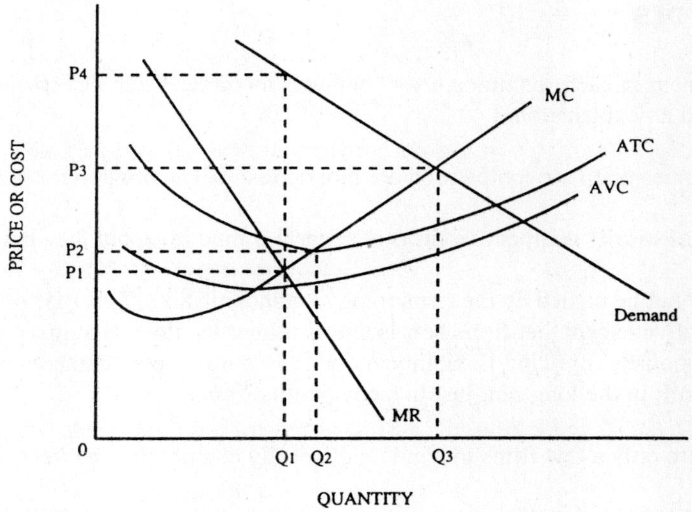

1. The profit-maximizing rate of output for a monopolistically competitive firm occurs where __________________.

2. According to Figure 11.2, the profit-maximizing rate of output is _____ units and the price is _____.

3. Does Figure 11.2 represent a short run or a long run situation? __________________

4. This firm is earning a (profit, loss) because at the profit-maximizing output level, the demand curve is above the _____________ curve.

5. In the long run, the average total cost curve will be tangent to the _______________ curve and economic profits will be _______________.

6. A perfectly competitive firm would maximize profits at an output of _____ and a price of _____.

Exercise 3

This exercise will use one of the articles in the text to show what kind of information to look for to determine whether a market is characterized by monopolistic competition.

Reread the article entitled "The Cola Wars: It's Not All Taste." Then answer the following questions.

1. Which passages address the market share held by Coke and Pepsi? ____

2. What form of nonprice competition do the two firms engage in? _______________________

3. Through their advertising campaigns, Pepsi and Coke hope to establish ________________ for each of their products.

4. Which phrase indicates that the advertising is successful? ______________________________
____

Common Errors

The first statement in each "common error" below is incorrect. Each incorrect statement is followed by a corrected version and an explanation.

1. Monopolies that face competition are monopolistically competitive. WRONG!

   Monopolistically competitive firms are nearly competitive, but they have brand loyalty. RIGHT!

   Do not be misled by the terminology "monopolistic." This type of industry is essentially competitive except that firms have some customer loyalty. That gives them a little ("monopolistic") pricing flexibility and a downward-sloping demand curve. But they still make zero profit in the long run, just like competitive firms.

2. There are only a few firms in a monopolistically competitive market. WRONG!

   There are many firms in a monopolistically competitive market. RIGHT!

   Again, don't let the word "monopolistic" fool you. Firms can easily enter or exit from a monopolistically competitive market. Each firm is likely to have excess capacity—which suggests there may be too many firms in a monopolistically competitive market. The restaurant business is a good example of a monopolistically competitive market.

3. Because price equals average cost in the long run in a monopolistically competitive firm, such firms must be efficient. WRONG!

   Because price equals average cost in the long run in a monopolistically competitive firm, profits are zero in the long run, but the firm is inefficient. RIGHT!

   Long-run profits are normal (zero economic profits) because competition forces prices to equal long-run average cost. The firm does not reach the *lowest* long-run average cost level, however, and so it is inefficient. The firm's demand curve touches the long-run average cost curve, but not at its lowest point.

•ANSWERS•

Using Key Terms

Across

3. product differentiation
5. barriers to entry
6. market power
7. production decision
8. marginal cost pricing

Down

1. monopolistic competition
2. concentration ratio
4. economic profit

True or False

1. T
2. T
3. F In monopolistic competition, each firm offers slightly different products.
4. F The MR curve for monopolistically competitive firms does not have a vertical segment because there is no significant interdependence between firms. As a consequence, a shift in MC will result in an intersection between MC and MR at a new output level.
5. T
6. F As new firms enter, individual firms will experience a decrease in the number of customers resulting in a shift in demand to the left.
7. F A monopolistically competitive firm will charge a price above the minimum ATC because of product differentiation.
8. T
9. F A monopolistically competitive firm will produce less than the allocatively efficient output level because of a downward sloping demand curve facing each firm.
10. T

Multiple Choice

1. c	5. c	9. b	13. d	17. b
2. a	6. d	10. b	14. a	18. c
3. b	7. c	11. a	15. d	19. d
4. d	8. a	12. c	16. b	20. a

Problems and Applications

Exercise 1

Table 11.1 Answer

	Monopoly	*Oligopoly*	*Monopolistic competition*	*Competition*
1.	one	few	many	many
2.	unique	standardized or differentiatiated	differentiated	standardized
3.	blocked	impeded	impeded or easy	easy
4.	yes	yes	yes	no
5.	no	no	no	yes
6.	no	yes	no	no
7.	yes	yes	yes	no
8.	yes	yes	yes	no
9.	no	no	no	yes
10.	yes	yes	no	no

Exercise 2

1. MC=MR
2. Q_1, P_4
3. Short run
4. Profit, ATC
5. Demand, zero
6. Q_3, P_3

Exercise 3

1. "The Coca-Cola Company produces about 40 percent . . . while Pepsi-Cola produces about 30 percent . . . With nearly 70 percent of the market between them, Pepsi and Coke wage fierce battles over market share."
2. Advertising
3. Brand loyalty
4. "Half of all soft drink consumers profess loyalty to either Coke or Pepsi."

PART 4 Regulatory Issues

CHAPTER 12

(De)Regulation of Business

Quick Review

- "Market failure" means that the market provides an inadequate output mix. To improve market outcomes where market failure occurs, the government intervenes in several ways.

- In situations of market power, the government has two possible methods of intervention. Antitrust laws address either the structure of the industry or its behavior. Regulation is focused specifically on industry behavior.

- The clearest case for intervention is in "natural monopolies," where a market is best served by a single firm because it alone can capture continuous economies of scale.

- In regulating natural monopolies, regulators may pursue three basic, but potentially conflicting, goals including price efficiency, production efficiency, and equity.

- Regulation itself may impose significant opportunity costs on the economy. Resources are used in devising and administering regulations. The firms in a regulated market use resources to comply with (or get around) regulations. Efficiency costs that result from bad decisions and incomplete information may worsen the mix of output.

- Railroads, telephone service, and airlines are industries in which deregulation has basically been completed. However, there are still many industries that are regulated and even some where regulation has increased.

- The question to be answered is always, "Do the benefits of the regulation exceed the cost of regulation?" Deregulation in practice seems to have served the consumer well. Prices are lower and output greater in the deregulated markets.

Learning Objectives

After reading Chapter 12 and doing the following exercises, you should:

1. Know several sources of market failure and several techniques of intervention.
2. Be able to distinguish social regulation from economic regulation.
3. Be able to demonstrate natural monopoly graphically and verbally.
4. Understand economies of scale.
5. Understand the potential conflict among the goals of price efficiency, production efficiency, and equity.
6. Know the difficulties associated with regulating the price, output, or profits of natural monopolies.
7. Understand the difficulty of devising regulations and why second-best solutions are a realistic goal.
8. Be able to distinguish between administrative, compliance, and efficiency costs of regulation.
9. Know the history of regulation and deregulation in the U.S. economy, and be able to cite some results of deregulation.

Using Key Terms

Fill in the puzzle on the opposite page with the appropriate term from the list of Key Terms at the end of the chapter in the text.

Across

3. The "free rider" problem is an issue when dealing with a ______ ______.
5. The market structure in Figure 12.1 in the text.
10. The use of high prices and profits on one product to subsidize low prices on another product.
11. Obstacles that make it difficult or impossible for new firms to enter a market.
13. An imperfectly competitive industry subject to potential entry if prices or profits increase.
14. Laws to prevent the abuse of market power.

Down

1. Occurs when the market mechanism results in a suboptimal outcome.
2. The decrease in minimum average costs because of an increase in the size of plant and equipment.
3. A form of nonprice competition to make a product appear different from competing products.
4. Government intervention that fails to improve economic outcomes.
6. The doctrine of nonintervention by government.
7. The goods and services that must be given up in order to obtain something else.
8. Equal to total revenue minus total economic profit.
9. The offer of goods at prices equal to their marginal cost.
12. Government intervention to alter the behavior of firms.

Puzzle 12.1

True or False: *Circle your choice and explain why any false statements are incorrect.*

T F 1. The costs associated with regulation are a source of government failure.

T F 2. The argument for regulation is that markets can generate imperfect outcomes, and the argument for deregulation is that government sometimes worsens market outcomes.

T F 3. Deregulation implies that government failure is worse than the market failure that regulation is designed to correct.

T F 4. Unregulated natural monopolies produce optimal rates of output.

T F 5. Economic regulation focuses on prices, production, and the conditions for industry entry or exit.

T F 6. Price regulation of a natural monopoly does not require a subsidy.

T F 7. Regulated monopolies that are allowed a specific profit rate have an incentive to hold down costs.

T F 8. In industries where governments regulate price, individual firms often engage in product differentiation.

T F 9. In the pursuit of profits, unregulated airlines are likely to increase expenditures on airport security.

T F 10. The marginal benefits of regulation should exceed the marginal costs of regulation if additional regulations are to be imposed.

Multiple Choice: *Select the correct answer.*

_____ 1. Which of the following is an example of government failure?
(a) Over-regulation resulting in wasted resources.
(b) Public goods.
(c) Externalities.
(d) All of the above.

_____ 2. Which of the following is an example of market failure?
(a) Inequities in the output mix and the distribution of income.
(b) Natural monopoly.
(c) Under production, from society's perspective.
(d) All of the above.

_____ 3. If government failure did not exist:
(a) Laissez faire would apply to all markets.
(b) Deregulation would be unnecessary.
(c) The invisible hand would be the most efficient and equitable way to run the economy.
(d) All markets would be regulated.

_____ 4. Government can intervene in the structure or behavior of a market. Which of the following correctly distinguishes between antitrust and regulation?
(a) Antitrust focuses on both, while regulation focuses mostly on behavior.
(b) Antitrust focuses on both, while regulation focuses mostly on structure.
(c) Regulation focuses on both, while antitrust focuses mostly on behavior.
(d) Regulation focuses on both, while antitrust focuses mostly on structure.

_____ 5. Natural monopolies:
(a) Always face downward-sloping long-run average total cost curves.
(b) Capture economies of scale over the entire market.
(c) Incur losses if they produce where price equals marginal cost.
(d) All of the above.

_____ 6. An unregulated natural monopoly is most likely to:
(a) Produce a lower output at a higher price than a perfectly competitive market.
(b) Price its output equal to marginal cost.
(c) Charge a lower price than if the same product were produced in a competitive market because of the monopoly's greater technical efficiency.
(d) Take advantage of the concept of marginal cost pricing.

_____ 7. Which of the following problems results from output regulation of a natural monopoly?
(a) Losses and bankruptcy for the natural monopoly.
(b) Loss of quality.
(c) Excess output.
(d) All of the above.

_____ 8. If the government regulated a natural monopolist to achieve price efficiency without subsidies or price discrimination, the monopolist would:
(a) Earn economic profits.
(b) Earn only normal profits.
(c) Have no incentive to stay in the market.
(d) Earn less of a profit than before, but still earn a profit.

_____ 9. Which of the following problems results from profit regulation of a natural monopoly?
(a) Production does not occur at a socially optimal rate.
(b) The firm has no incentive to strive for efficiency.
(c) There is an incentive to "pad costs."
(d) All of the above are problems.

_____ 10. The economic cost for a manufacturer to comply with the clean air law would be:
(a) The additional money required to buy an automobile with emissions control equipment.
(b) The resources that were used to produce the emissions control equipment.
(c) The best alternative goods and services forgone when the emissions control equipment is produced.
(d) All of the above.

_____ 11. The basic issue in regulatory policy is:
(a) Whether or not the benefits of government regulation exceed the costs.
(b) How to achieve second-best solutions in all markets.
(c) How to eliminate all natural monopolies.
(d) How to achieve profit regulation in all industries.

_____ 12. The case for deregulation of an industry rests on the argument that:
(a) The cost of market failure exceeds the cost of government failure.
(b) Regulations are more costly to implement than the market failure that is to be corrected.
(c) Regulation aids adaptation to market changes in tastes, costs, and technology.
(d) Antitrust intervention is less costly than regulation.

_____ 13. When market outcomes are improved after government regulation is enforced:
(a) Technical efficiency is being achieved.
(b) The net effect of government intervention on society in this case has been beneficial.
(c) Government intervention still may not be justified if the marginal costs of regulation are larger than the marginal benefits.
(d) All of the above.

_____ 14. If a natural monopoly was forced to break up into several small competing firms, economists would expect the:
(a) Costs of production to decrease because the new firms would be more efficient.
(b) Price charged by the competing firms to decrease because they would be more efficient.
(c) Price charged by the competing firms to increase because they would be less efficient.
(d) Total production in the industry to increase because the new firms would be more efficient.

_____ 15. The first major regulatory target in the United States was:
(a) Airlines.
(b) Railroads.
(c) Trucking firms.
(d) Telephone companies.

_____ 16. Deregulation of the trucking industry led to:
(a) A reduction in most truck rates.
(b) A significant increase in the number of trucking firms.
(c) The elimination of monopoly profits and increased quantity and variety of service.
(d) All of the above.

_____ 17. As a consequence of the deregulation of the telephone industry:
(a) Many telephone companies have abandoned the market.
(b) Long-distance phone rates have increased sharply.
(c) Local telephone rates have risen in the absence of cross-subsidization of local costs from long-distance profits.
(d) Long-distance users now subsidize local users of phone service to a greater extent than before deregulation.

_____ 18. Proponents of the deregulation of the electricity industry argued that deregulation was justified because:
(a) Other industries had been deregulated.
(b) Improvements in technology allowed easy transmission of electricity using satellite technology.
(c) Improvements in technology allowed easy transmission of electricity through the deregulated telephone system.
(d) Of the development of high-voltage transmission lines.

_____ 19. Deregulation of the airline industry has been followed by:
(a) Lower fares on shorter, less-traveled routes.
(b) Increased concentration in the airline industry.
(c) Higher average cost of service by surviving airlines.
(d) Reduced competition in most airline markets.

_____ 20. The electric utility industry became a target for deregulation when:
(a) The cost of constructing nuclear power plants declined.
(b) New technology allowed the transmission of power from region to region with insignificant power loss.
(c) Local utility companies began behaving like monopolies.
(d) All of the above.

Problems and Applications

Exercise 1

This exercise provides practice in identifying market imperfections, finding an appropriate form of government intervention, and recognizing the possible side effects of government intervention.

Table 12.1 lists market imperfections, means for the government to intervene, and some of the side effects of government policy.

Table 12.1
Market imperfections, government interventions, and side effects

Market imperfections	*Means of government intervention*	*Side effects of government policy*
I. Externalities	A. Taxes, subsidies, or transfers	1. Inefficiency (unnecessarily high costs)
II. Inequities	B. Regulation of prices, output, or entry	2. Shortages or surpluses
III. Natural monopoly	C. Antitrust activity	3. Lack of quality
IV. Nonexclusive goods	D. Provision of information	4. Inefficient government bureaucracy
V. Market power	E. Production of goods by the government	5. Dynamic inefficiencies
VI. Lack of information about tastes, costs, or prices		
VII. Lack of information about profitability or technology		

1. For each of the situations described in Table 12.2, choose the Roman numeral(s) for each market imperfection that applies, the letter(s) that represent appropriate action by the government, and the number(s) that indicate possible side effects of government involvement.

Table 12.2
Market imperfections and government intervention

Situation	Market imperfection	Government intervention	Possible side effects of government policy
1. Because of severe balance-of-trade deficits, the United States needs to export more goods abroad. If not, foreign exchange markets will be increasingly disrupted. However, many small American companies do not know enough about foreign markets to become exporters of goods and services.	________	________	________
2. It is not economical to have firms compete to provide sewage facilities for residential areas. Each house needs only one set of pipes and it is most efficient to attach all pipes from houses to one major sewer conduit.	________	________	________
3. Many workers at a firm find they are becoming nauseated in the workplace. Futhermore, the cancer rate among the employees appears to be very high. They cannot get management to study the problem because the firm can simply fire them and hire new employees.	________	________	________
4. Farmers are willing to use the latest techniques for growing crops. However, they have difficulty determining what the newest techniques are by themselves and the market does not undertake the continuous research process necessary to develop them.	________	________	________
5. If the farmers do not change continually to the latest disease-resistant seed varieties, it is likely that there will be a disastrous spread of disease that will threaten the economy's food supply. However, new varieties of grain are expensive to develop, and the private market would not undertake the continuous research process necessary to develop them.	________	________	________
6. At the beginning of World War II, the United States found that it was cut off from important suppliers of rubber, sugar, and hemp by the Japanese. The private market had not kept enough inventories of these goods on hand in case of war.	________	________	________
7. The St. Joe Mineral Company dumped taconite tailings filled with asbestos into the Great Lakes. While St. Joe suffered no bad side effects from this activity, many people who used the lakes began to suffer such effects.	________	________	________
8. Many older people are poor and as they age and become weaker are beset by various problems and cannot take care of themselves adequately. Private charities do not do enough to maintain a standard of care that society as a whole considers desirable.	________	________	________
9. It is very costly to run electrical lines into a house; thus, it is not economical to put more than one set of electric lines into a home. Electrical services are most economically provided by only one firm.	________	________	________
10. General Electric and Westinghouse decided to coordinate their activities and conspired to set the price of electronic equipment on which they were bidding.	________	________	________

Exercise 2

This exercise emphasizes the characteristics of a natural monopoly using a graph.

Use Figure 12.1 to answer questions 1-6.

Figure 12.1

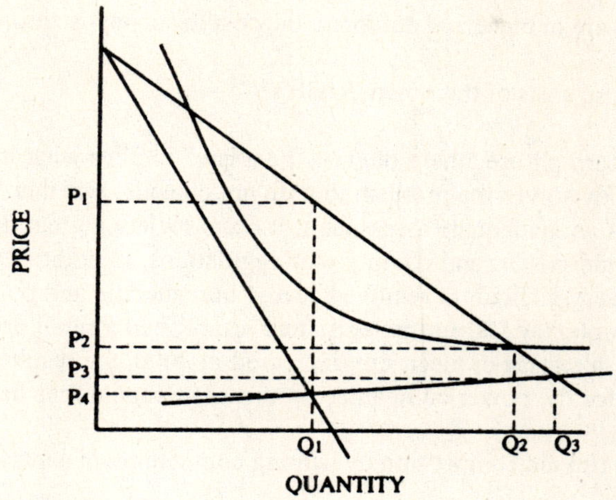

1. Label the ATC curve, the MC curve, the MR curve, and the demand curve in Figure 12.1.

2. What is the profit-maximizing price and output level for the unregulated natural monopolist in Figure 12.1? ________

3. At the unregulated output level, the natural monopolist (will, will not) earn an economic profit.

4. Regulation designed to achieve price efficiency would result in a price of _____ and an output level of _____.

5. At the output level in question 4, the natural monopoly will earn a (profit, loss) because ATC is (greater, less) than the price.

6. Profit regulation for the natural monopoly would result in a price of _____ and an output level of _____.

Exercise 3

This exercise focuses on market failure and government intervention.

Reread the In the News article "California Consumers Can Choose Power Company" in the text.

1. What passage indicates that deregulation in the electricity market has occurred? ____________
____

2. Which of the following forms of market failure justified the initial government intervention?
   (a) Externalities
   (b) Public good
   (c) Natural monopoly
   (d) Inequity

3. How are power companies responding to the deregulation?________________________________

Common Errors

The first statement in each "common error" below is incorrect. Each incorrect statement is followed by a corrected version and an explanation.

1. Once regulations are in place and enforced, the cost to society is zero. WRONG!

   Regulations impose costs of their own. RIGHT!

   The often-heard phrase "there ought to be a law" implies what is meant here. Many people believe that the law solves the problem, but do not consider whether the law itself causes other problems. This is an inadequate assessment. It costs society a great deal in the way of opportunity costs to devise, administer, and comply with regulations. In addition, once a regulation is in place, it's very, very difficult to remove because bureaucratic and political machinery works very slowly. For example, the California legislature established a retail price ceiling for electricity. When the wholesale price of electricity increased in 2000, the result was a shortage of electricity and bankruptcy for the power companies. In this case, regulations had their own costs.

2. The government can aid competition by helping competitors in a market to survive. WRONG!

   The government interferes with free entry and exit when helping competitors survive, and this interferes with competition. RIGHT!

   When the government prevents exit from the market, it is interfering with the contestability of the market. By not allowing inefficient firms to exit from the market, the government makes it more difficult for the more efficient firms to enter the market. Barriers to exit lead to barriers to entry, which interfere with the competitive process.

•ANSWERS•

Using Key Terms

Across

3. public good
5. natural monopoly
10. cross subsidization
11. barriers to entry
13. contestable market
14. antitrust

Down

1. market failure
2. economies of scale
3. product differentiation
4. government failure
6. laissez faire
7. opportunity cost
8. economic profit
9. marginal cost pricing
12. regulation

True or False

1. T
2. T
3. T
4. F Unregulated natural monopolies tend to produce less than optimal levels of output.
5. T
6. F Price regulation occurs where MC = demand which is below the firm's ATC, making a subsidy necessary.
7. F When a firm is allowed a specific profit rate, it has no incentive to keep costs in check.
8. T
9. F Airport security is a public good so deregulated airlines are likely to reduce expenditures on airport security.
10. T

Multiple Choice

1. a	5. d	9. d	13. c	17. c
2. d	6. a	10. c	14. c	18. d
3. b	7. b	11. a	15. b	19. b
4. a	8. c	12. b	16. d	20. b

Problems and Applications

Exercise 1

1. **Table 12.2 Answer**

Situation	*Market imperfections*	*Government interventions*	*Possible side effects of government policy*
1.	VI, VII	D	1, 4
2.	III, V	B or E	1, 2, 3, 4, 5
3.	I, IV	B, D	1, 2, 3, 4, 5
4.	VI, VII	D	1, 4, 5
5.	I, III, IV, VI, VII	A, D, E	1, 3, 4, 5
6.	I, IV	A, E	2, 4, 5
7.	I	A or B	1, 2, 4, 5
8.	II, IV	A	1, 4, 5
9.	III, V	B	1, 2, 3, 4, 5
10.	V	C	1, 2, 4, 5

Exercise 2

1. **Figure 12.1 Answer**

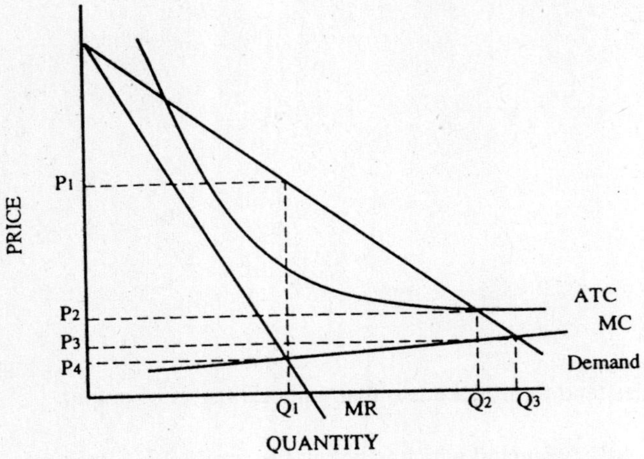

2. P_1, Q_1
3. Will
4. P_3,Q_3
5. Loss, greater
6. P_2,Q_2

Exercise 3

1. "Starting today, California becomes the largest state to let consumers pick their own electric company."
2. c
3. They are advertising in an effort to segment the market.

CHAPTER 13

Environmental Protection

Quick Review

- Nearly everyone is concerned about the environment and agrees that we ought to protect it. Air, water, and solid waste pollution result in both social and economic costs.
- External costs are the costs of a market transaction borne by a third party. Externalities create a divergence between social costs and private costs and lead to suboptimal market outcomes. In the case of externalities such as pollution, too much of the polluting good is produced.
- Most of the current pollution could be eliminated with known and available technology, but businesses and consumers are influenced by market incentives.
- Businesses are always attempting to maximize profits. In making the efficiency decision the firm chooses the least cost method of production.
- The existence of external costs means that a firm is able to avoid part of the costs of production by pushing some of the costs onto a third party. In this case, a private firm will not maximize social welfare and market failure will occur.
- To correct this failure the government must intervene by altering market incentives or bypassing the market and using direct controls.
- Market-based options to reduce pollution include emissions charges, higher user fees, "green" taxes, and pollution fines.
- Tradable pollution permits provide incentives for new, more cost-efficient technologies to be developed. Those with the highest marginal costs of pollution reduction purchase the right to pollute from those with the lowest marginal costs. As a result, the total resource cost of reducing pollution decreases.
- The direct-regulation (command and control) approach specifies mandatory pollution reductions *and* the specific technologies for achieving them.
- The optimal rate of pollution occurs when the marginal costs of cleaning up the environment are equal to the value of the marginal benefits from the clean up.

Learning Objectives

After reading Chapter 13 and doing the following exercises, you should:

1. Know the principal types and sources of pollution.
2. Understand how to apply the notion of opportunity cost to the pollution problem.
3. Understand how market forces influence the production and efficiency decisions for the producer.
4. Be able to distinguish between private costs and social costs.
5. Understand the term "externality," and how externalities arise.
6. Be able to show how taxes, emission charges, marketable pollution rights, and effluent charges can be used to control pollution.
7. Be able to show how regulation can be used to control pollution.
8. Understand the rationale for the market for pollution credits.
9. Understand how the optimal rate of pollution is determined and know why it is *not* zero.
10. Understand the international dimensions of the pollution problem.

Using Key Terms

Fill in the puzzle on the opposite page with the appropriate term from the list of Key Terms at the end of the chapter in the text.

Across

1. A fee imposed on polluters based on the quantity of pollution.
5. Occurs when government intervention fails to improve economic outcomes.
9. The most desired goods and services that are given up in order to obtain something else.
10. The costs of a market activity borne by a third party are referred to as ______ ______.

Down

2. Occurs when the marginal social benefit of pollution control equals its marginal social cost.
3. The total costs of all resources used in an economic activity.
4. The choice of a short-run rate of output using existing plant and equipment.
6. The choice of a production process that minimizes costs for any rate of output.
7. Occurs when the market mechanism results in a suboptimal outcome.
8. The resource costs borne by the specific producer.

Puzzle 13.1

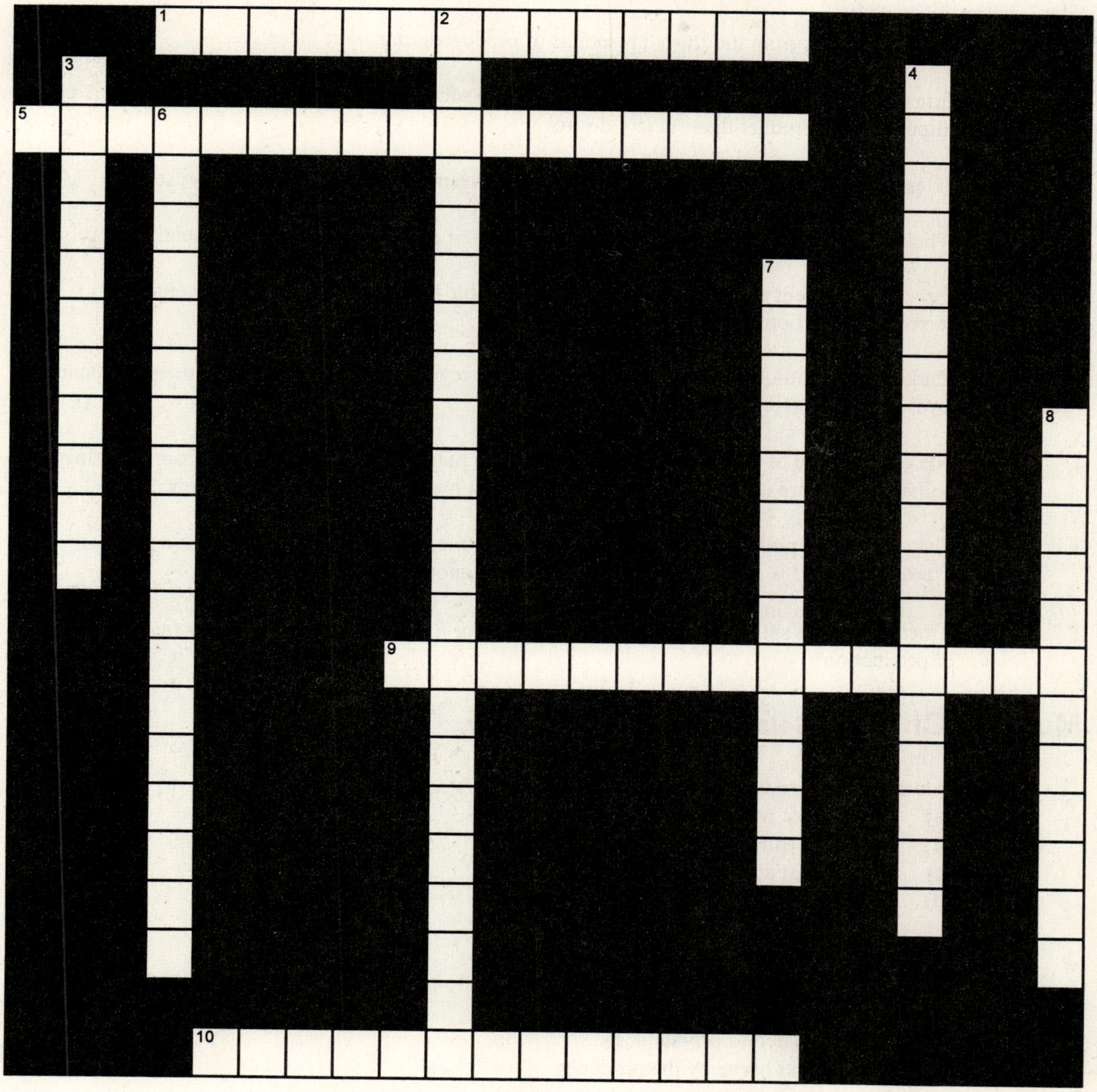

True or False: *Circle your choice and explain why any false statements are incorrect.*

T F 1. Pollution abatement imposes opportunity costs on society.

T F 2. Pollution results from the flawed response of producers to market incentives.

T F 3. Firms that are able to push part of their costs onto society by polluting will produce a greater output of their product than society desires.

T F 4. Externalities are a measure of the divergence between social costs and private costs.

T F 5. When externalities exist, firms will not allocate their resources to maximize social welfare.

T F 6. Direct government regulation is generally preferable to alteration of market incentives in correcting pollution problems.

T F 7. Marketable pollution permits rely on government regulation, not market incentives, to reduce the level of pollution.

T F 8. The optimal rate of pollution is attained when the marginal benefits received from lowering the pollution level are equal to the marginal costs that must be incurred to achieve it.

T F 9. The problem of pollution applies to market economies where the market fails as a result of externalities, but is not a problem in command economies without markets.

T F 10. An emission fee shifts marginal private costs closer to marginal social costs by raising the costs of production.

Multiple Choice: *Select the correct answer.*

_____ 1. In making the production decision, polluting firms equate marginal:
- (a) Social cost with marginal social benefits.
- (b) Revenue and private marginal costs.
- (c) Social cost and marginal revenue.
- (d) Private costs and marginal social costs.

_____ 2. Social costs:
- (a) Are less than private costs.
- (b) Include private costs.
- (c) Are unrelated to private costs.
- (d) Are always borne by the producer.

_____ 3. When social costs and private costs of consumption and production diverge, then inevitably:
- (a) Producers have an incentive to produce too little.
- (b) Consumers have an incentive to consume too little.
- (c) Both producers and consumers have an incentive to produce and consume too much.
- (d) External costs are zero.

_____ 4. When external costs result from the production of some good, the output level of that good tends to be:

(a) Larger than is desirable.
(b) Smaller than is desirable.
(c) Neither too small nor too large.
(d) Too small if the private costs exceed the external costs.

_____ 5. The market will overproduce goods that have external costs because:

(a) Producers experience lower costs than society.
(b) Producers experience higher costs than society.
(c) The government is not able to produce these goods.
(d) Producers cannot keep these goods from consumers who do not pay so they have to produce greater amounts.

_____ 6. A firm that dumps its waste products into our waterways will:

(a) Pay the full cost of production.
(b) Incur more than the full cost of production.
(c) Sell its product at a lower price than if it cleaned up its wastes.
(d) Cause the firm to internalize more of its costs.

_____ 7. Other things being equal, if a perfectly competitive firm is forced to switch to a more expensive, nonpolluting production process:

(a) The average cost curve will shift downward.
(b) The profit-maximizing level of output will be increased.
(c) The marginal cost curve will shift downward or to the right.
(d) Total profits will decrease.

_____ 8. When firms are allowed to pollute the environment without bearing the costs of polluting, then:

(a) Their marginal cost curve is too low.
(b) Their average variable cost curve is too low.
(c) Their average total cost curve is too low.
(d) All of the above.

_____ 9. Solution to the pollution-abatement problem involves:

(a) Eliminating the divergence between private costs and social costs.
(b) Compelling firms to consider all costs resulting from their production.
(c) Forcing polluters to pay all social costs.
(d) Doing all of the above.

_____ 10. If emission charges were affixed to all production and consumption activities:

(a) The relative price of highly polluting activities would increase.
(b) People would stop producing and consuming.
(c) Pollution would be eliminated.
(d) There would be no redistribution of income.

_____ 11. The purpose of an emission charge is to:

(a) Increase the difference between social and private costs.
(b) Externalize the costs of pollution.
(c) Reduce the socially optimal rate of output.
(d) Force polluters to consider externalities as a cost of production.

_____ 12. The primary purpose of tradable pollution permits is to:
(a) Reduce, but not eliminate, the level of pollution.
(b) Reduce the cost of pollution control.
(c) Reduce both the level of pollution and the cost of pollution control.
(d) Completely eliminate pollution.

_____ 13. The 1990 Clean Air Act relied on which of the following strategies to clean up the environment?
(a) Marketable pollution permits.
(b) "Command and control" approach to regulation.
(c) Subsidizing new pollution-control technologies.
(d) All of the above.

_____ 14. When there are external costs of production, then the social optimum occurs where marginal revenue equals:
(a) Private marginal cost.
(b) Social marginal cost.
(c) The minimum of the average cost curve.
(d) Social marginal benefit.

_____ 15. An optimal amount of pollution can be described as:
(a) The minimal amount technically possible.
(b) The amount that would result when polluting firms spend revenues on pollution-control equipment until they earn only normal profits.
(c) The amount for which a $1 increase in pollution-control expenditures creates $1 in additional social welfare.
(d) Zero.

_____ 16. A 5-cent container deposit on bottles:
(a) Decreases the price of recycled materials and thus encourages their use.
(b) Increases the price of recycled materials and thus discourages their use.
(c) Has no impact on the price of recycled materials.
(d) Increases the price of containers that do not use recycled materials.

_____ 17. The pursuit of a pollution-free environment is:
(a) The morally correct strategy and costs should not be a consideration.
(b) The economically correct strategy as long as benefits accrue to society.
(c) The economically correct strategy.
(d) Probably not in society's best interest, in view of the extremely high opportunity costs.

_____ 18. In cost-benefit analysis, the government should intervene as long as:
(a) Government corrects market failures without incurring resources costs.
(b) The value of government failure exceeds the value of market failure.
(c) Government's improvement of market outcomes exceeds costs of government intervention.
(d) Government corrects market failures in spite of government failure.

_____ 19. The costs of pollution control will:
(a) Always be borne entirely by the polluting producer.
(b) Always be passed on completely to the consumer.
(c) Be distributed between producer and consumer depending on factors like the price elasticity of demand.
(d) Be borne entirely by the taxpayers in the United States.

_____ 20. When human lives are involved, a cost-benefit ratio:
(a) Should have no bearing on decision making.
(b) Must be considered because it provides a measure of the opportunity costs of government policies.
(c) Is useless because human lives cannot be measured in dollars and cents.
(d) Is an indication that a policy should be implemented if it is a very high value.

Problems and Applications

Exercise 1

This exercise shows how to compute the optimal rate of pollution and will help with a problem in the text.

Table 13.1 indicates various levels of pollution that might be experienced in a lake near your home. It also contains information concerning the value of damages imposed on society by the pollution and the cost to society of cleaning the lake to particular levels. For example, the lake could be made pollution-free with an expenditure of $280,000. The question is: "Is it worth it?" Complete questions 1-7 to find out.

Table 13.1
Annual value of damages associated with polluted water and costs of reducing pollution

(1) Quantity of pollution (units of waste material per 100 cubic feet of water)	(2) Monetary value of damages (thousands of dollars)	(3) Marginal benefits of pollution abatement (thousands of dollars)	(4) Costs of treating polluted water (thousands of dollars)	(5) Marginal cost of pollution abatement (thousands of dollars)
6	$140	$ ---	$ 0	$ ---
5	100	40	5	5
4	70	______	15	______
3	45	______	30	______
2	25	______	50	______
1	10	______	100	______
0	0	______	280	______

1. Assume that without any controls, polluters will annually impose $140,000 of damages on the lake's users by generating 6 units of waste for every 100 cubic feet of water. To clean out the sixth unit of pollutants (that is, lower the quantity of pollution from 6 units to 5) costs $5,000. The value of the benefits gained is $40,000. Complete the rest of column 3.

2. Complete column 5 in Table 13.1 in the same way. The first calculation has been done for you.

3. Should the annual level of pollution be reduced from 6 units to 5? __________

4. Which of the following reasons explains why annual pollution should (or should not) be reduced from 6 to 5 units of pollution?
   (a) The optimal rate of pollution has been reached.
   (b) The marginal social benefits exceed the marginal social cost from reducing the pollution.
   (c) The marginal social costs exceed the marginal social benefits from reducing the pollution.

5. Should pollution be reduced annually from 5 units to 4? __________

6. What is the optimal rate of pollution? __________

7. Which of the following reasons explains why the lake should not be made free of pollution?
   (a) The optimal rate of pollution has been reached when the lake is free of pollution.
   (b) The marginal social costs incurred in eliminating the pollution would exceed the total social benefits achieved.
   (c) The marginal social costs incurred in eliminating all of the pollution would be less than the marginal social benefits achieved.
   (d) None of the above are the case.

Exercise 2

This exercise shows how externalities affect third parties. This exercise will help you complete the problems in the text.

A chemical plant and a plastics factory are located adjacent to the same stream. The chemical plant is located upstream. The downstream plastics factory requires pure water for its production process. Its basic supply is the stream that runs past both firms.

Figure 13.1
Markets for plastics and chemicals

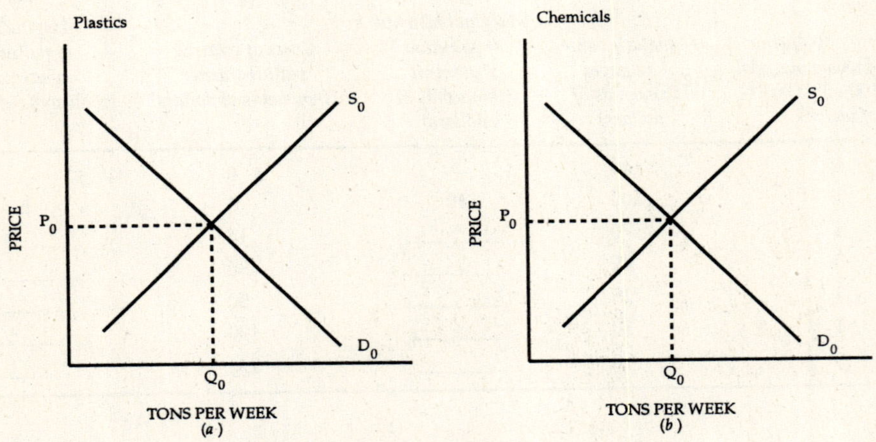

In Figure 13.1, diagrams *a* and *b*, S_0 and D_0 represent the supply and demand for plastics and chemicals, respectively. Assume that the economy is initially competitive and resources are allocated efficiently. Equilibrium price and quantity are P_0 and Q_0 in each case. But then the chemical producer decides to dump waste products into the stream rather than dispose of them with the costly process that had been used.

1. In Figure 13.1 diagram *b*, draw in a new supply curve for chemicals after the dumping in the stream begins. Label it S_1. (*Hint:* There are many ways to draw the curve.)

2. The pollution from the chemical plant forces the plastics manufacturer to use a costly water-purifying system. Draw a new supply curve for plastics in Figure 13.1 diagram *a*. Label it S_1. (There are many ways to draw this curve correctly.)

3. The effect of the decision to pollute on the quantity of chemicals sold is the same as if:
   (a) A new, improved technology were discovered.
   (b) Wages to its labor force were reduced.
   (c) The Social Security tax on employers had been abolished.
   (d) All of the above were the case.

4. As a result of the chemical plant's polluting activities:
   (a) The price of chemicals has risen.
   (b) The price of chemicals has fallen.
   (c) The price of plastics has not changed.
   (d) None of the above is the case.

5. As a result of the chemical plant's activities:
   (a) More chemicals are produced and sold than society desires.
   (b) More labor is used to produce chemicals than society desires.
   (c) More capital inputs are used to produce chemicals than society desires.
   (d) All of the above are the case.

6. The effect of the chemical firm's pollution is to:
   (a) Raise the price of plastics and reduce the quantity sold.
   (b) Lower the price of plastics and increase the quantity sold.
   (c) Raise the price of plastics and increase the quantity sold.
   (d) Do none of the above.

7. The impact of the pollution on the plastics industry in this example is, *ceteris paribus*, to:
   (a) Reduce the output of plastics below the level that society desires.
   (b) Reduce the employment possibilities in the plastics industry.
   (c) Raise the price of products made with plastics.
   (d) Do all of the above.

Exercise 3

This exercise shows the difference between private marginal costs and social marginal costs.

1. An iron-producing firm mines iron ore. Assume the iron ore industry is competitive. Table 13.2 depicts the private costs and social costs of the firm's iron production at each daily production rate. Complete Table 13.2.

Table 13.2 Costs of producing iron

Production rate (tons per day)	*Total private cost (dollars per day)*	*Private marginal cost (dollars per ton)*	*Total social cost (dollars per day)*	*Social marginal cost (dollars per ton)*
0	$ 0	$ ---	$ 0	$ ---
1	40	______	80	______
2	90	______	170	______
3	150	______	270	______
4	220	______	380	______
5	300	______	500	______
6	390	______	630	______
7	490	______	770	______
8	600	______	920	______
9	720	______	1,080	______
10	850	______	1,250	______
11	990	______	1,430	______
12	1,140	______	1,620	______

2. In Figure 13.2, the price of the iron in the competitive market is $140 per ton. Draw the private marginal cost curve and label it *PMC*. Draw the social marginal cost curve and label it *SMC*. Label the demand curve "Demand."

Figure 13.2

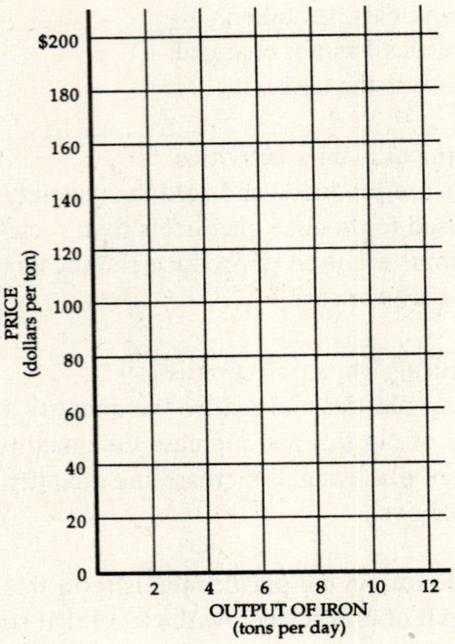

3. What is the profit-maximizing production rate for the firm if it considers only its private costs?
   (a) 5 tons per day.
   (b) 7 tons per day.
   (c) 9 tons per day.
   (d) 11 tons per day.

4. What is the profit-maximizing production rate if the firm is required to pay all social costs?
   (a) 5 tons per day.
   (b) 7 tons per day.
   (c) 9 tons per day.
   (d) 11 tons per day.

5. How much should the pollution (emission) fee be in order to induce the iron-producing firm to produce the socially optimal rate of output?
   (a) $4 per ton.
   (b) $40 per ton.
   (c) $100 per ton.
   (d) $50 per ton.

Exercise 4

The effects of pollution have become an increasingly important topic in the media. This exercise will use one of the articles in the text to show the kind of information to look for to identify the effects of pollution.

Reread the In the News article entitled "Dirty Air Can Shorten Your Life." Then answer the following questions.

1. What are the three general sources of pollution mentioned in the article?____________________
____

2. What phrase tells you that EPA standards do not guarantee healthy air to breathe?____________
____

3. How is the author implicitly measuring the cost of pollution in affected areas?________________
____

4. What phrase indicates that the effects of breathing polluted air are like those associated with smoking cigarettes?____

5. The effect of new and tougher standards on the polluting industries by the monitoring agency would cause the MC and ATC curves to shift (upward, downward).

Common Errors

The first statement in each "common error" below is incorrect. Each incorrect statement is followed by a corrected version and an explanation.

1. We should eliminate all pollution. WRONG!

   There is an optimal rate at which pollution can take place given the limited resources of our economy. RIGHT!

   Eliminating pollution involves some significant costs. Would it be practical to make sure that every cigarette butt on campus was picked up—even those that might have been flipped into the bushes? No, because the additional costs necessary to achieve a 100 percent pollution-free environment would exceed the additional benefits of doing so. We stop short of that 100 percent pollution-free level—at the point where the marginal social benefits equal the marginal social costs. It would be inefficient to do otherwise.

2. If business firms have a social conscience, they won't pollute. WRONG!

   Even if business firms have a social conscience, there will still be pollution. RIGHT!

   Firms produce goods and services to make profits. In so doing, they serve the rest of society by providing the goods and services society wants and jobs for millions of workers in the process. To avoid polluting, the firms would have to raise their own costs beyond what society could support, and firms would close down or never exist.

•ANSWERS•

Using Key Terms

Across

1. emission charge
5. government failure
9. opportunity cost
10. external costs

Down

2. optimal rate of pollution
3. social costs
4. production decision
6. efficiency decision
7. market failure
8. private costs

True or False

1. T
2. F Pollution is the result of the rational responses of producers to market incentives (i.e., private costs).
3. T
4. T
5. T
6. F Market incentives are typically more efficient than direct government regulation.
7. F Pollution permits rely on market incentives.
8. T
9. F Pollution also occurs as a result of government failure when government planners place a low priority on environmental quality.
10. T

Multiple Choice

1. b	5. a	9. d	13. a	17. d
2. b	6. c	10. a	14. b	18. c
3. c	7. d	11. d	15. c	19. c
4. a	8. d	12. b	16. a	20. b

Problems and Applications

Exercise 1

1. See Table 13.1 Answer, column 3.

Table 13.1 Answer

Quantity of pollution	*(3) Marginal benefits*	*(5) Marginal cost*
6	$ ---	$ ---
5	40	5
4	30	10
3	25	15
2	20	20
1	15	50
0	10	180

2. See Table 13.1 Answer, column 5.
3. Yes, because the marginal benefits are worth $40,000 annually, while the marginal costs are only $5,000 annually.
4. b
5. Yes
6. When pollution has been reduced to 2 parts per 100 cubic feet of water annually.
7. c

Exercise 2

1. See Figure 13.1 Answer, diagram *b*, line S_1.

Figure 13.1 Answer

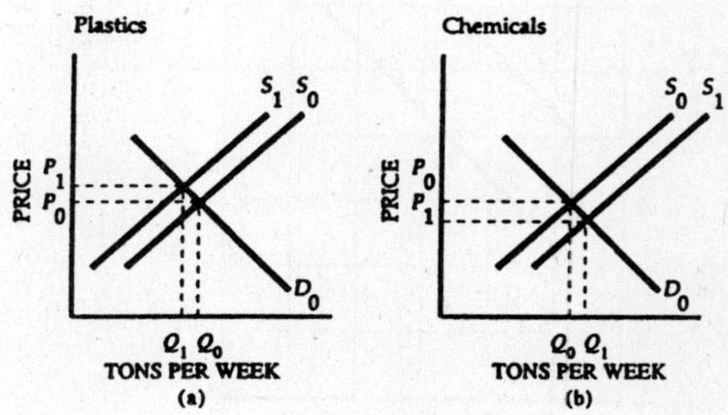

2. See Figure 13.1 Answer, diagram *a*, line S_1.

3. d 4. b 5. d 6. a 7. d

Exercise 3

1. **Table 13.2 Answer**

Production rate	*Private marginal cost*	*Social marginal cost*
0	$ ---	$ ---
1	40	80
2	50	90
3	60	100
4	70	110
5	80	120
6	90	130
7	100	140
8	110	150
9	120	160
10	130	170
11	140	180
12	150	190

2. **Figure 13.2 Answer**

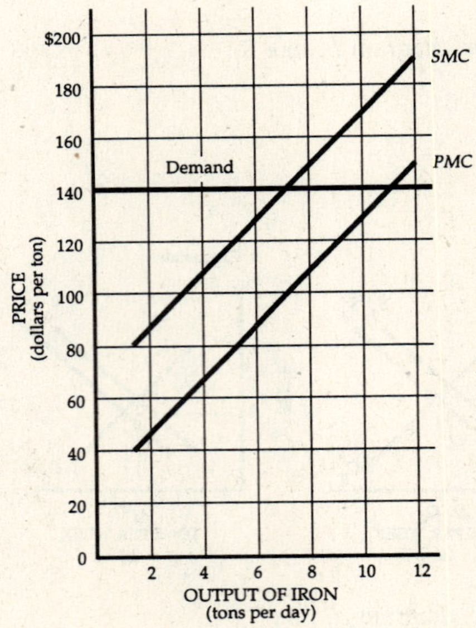

3. d 4. b 5. b

Exercise 4

1. Large particles, fine particles, gases
2. "This form of pollution is killing citizens even in areas that meet Environmental Protection Agency air quality standards. . ."
3. By estimating the probability of premature death due to breathing polluted air.
4. ". . . run a risk of premature death about one-sixth as great as if they had been smoking for 25 years."
5. Upward

CHAPTER 14

The Farm Problem

Quick Review

- There are 2 million farmers in the United States and even though some farms are very large, no one farmer has market power. As a result, the farming industry has many of the characteristics of a perfectly competitive market.

- Barriers to entry into the farming industry are low so anytime farmers are earning an economic profit new farmers are attracted to the market. This pushes long-run economic profit to zero.

- On the demand side, both price and income elasticities make it difficult for farmers. The price elasticity of agricultural goods is low because people only eat so much food regardless of a price decrease. Productivity advances, which are welcome in most other markets, result in much lower prices and farm incomes because of this low price elasticity of demand. A low income elasticity (low sensitivity of the demand for agricultural goods to changes in income) causes domestic demand to grow slowly even when the economy is growing.

- In addition, short-run price fluctuations because of supply changes are an issue for farmers. Sudden droughts, freezes, or blights shift the supply curve which, in turn, affects price. Time lags between when production decisions are made and when the harvest occurs also contribute to price changes.

- After World War II ended, demand for U.S. farm goods on the part of European countries decreased. At the same time, restrictions on international trade reduced demand while new technology caused an increase in supply for the agricultural industry. The result was a huge decrease in the price of farm goods.

- The U.S. government responded to the crisis with several programs, and assistance for farmers still exists today. Price supports are used to raise and stabilize farm prices, but the down side is that this creates a market surplus for the industry.

- Cost subsidies and supply restrictions are also used to increase farm prices, and direct income support aids farmers but does not change market price or output.

- Farm prices were severely impacted in the 1980s because of increased fuel and fertilizer costs and rising interest rates which reduced farm profits. The export of farm goods also decreased because the strength of the dollar made U.S. agricultural goods too expensive on the world market.

- Recently the government has taken steps to deregulate the farming industry. However, the Asian Crisis in 1997 and the economic slowdown in 2001 caused farmers to demand and get more government assistance. Essentially, U.S. farmers now expect the government to come to their aid which creates a situation of moral hazard.

Learning Objectives

After reading Chapter 14 and doing the following exercises, you should:

1. Know the dimensions and nature of the farm problem.
2. Understand the role of income and price elasticities in the farm problem.
3. Be able to relate the farm problem to forces on both the supply side and demand side of the market.
4. Understand the impact of supply- and demand-induced changes in prices of inputs on farm decision-making and profits.
5. Be able to describe several types of farm policies and their effects on the farming economy.
6. Be able to describe the causes and dimensions of the two great farm depressions.
7. Understand the direction and rationale of the efforts to deregulate farming.

Using Key Terms

Fill in the puzzle on the opposite page with the appropriate term from the list of Key Terms at the end of the chapter in the text.

Across

1. Income transfer paid to farmers for the difference between target and market prices.
3. Total revenue minus total economic costs.
7. Percentage change in quantity demanded divided by the percentage change in price.
10. The ability to change the market price of a good or service.
11. The implicit price paid by the government for surplus crops taken as collateral.
12. Land withdrawn from farm production in an effort to increase crop prices.

Down

2. Percentage change in quantity demanded divided by percentage change in income.
4. The relative price of farm products from 1910-1914.
5. An incentive to engage in undesirable behavior.
6. Obstacles that make it difficult or impossible for new producers to enter a market.
8. Equal to q_S minus q_D at a price of p_f in Figure 14.4 in the text.
9. Total revenue minus total cost.

Puzzle 14.1

True or False: *Circle your choice and explain why any false statements are incorrect.*

T F 1. Because the average corn farmer produces over 100,000 bushels of corn, that farmer has significant market power.

T F 2. Agricultural price-supports lead farmers to produce more goods than consumers want.

T F 3. When prices for farm commodities rise, total revenue will increase because the market demand for farm commodities is price inelastic.

T F 4. The demand for farmland reflects the present and future income-generating potential of the land.

T F 5. Price supports have lowered the price of farm products, increased consumption, and reduced production.

T F 6. Deficiency payments are designed to establish the same ratio of farm to nonfarm income as would parity prices.

T F 7. Direct income payments to farmers are less efficient at raising farm incomes than are price-support programs.

T F 8. When a large crop is produced by American farmers, farmers receive higher incomes because the price elasticity for agricultural products is low.

T F 9. The Farm Security Act of 2001 increased farm subsidies and created new subsidies for previously unsubsidized farm products.

T F 10. When the government continually bails out farmers during economic crises, rather than relying on the farmers themselves to manage their risks, the government has created a "moral hazard."

Multiple Choice: *Select the correct answer.*

_____ 1. If an agricultural market is perfectly competitive, then:
(a) A farmer is a price taker.
(b) A farmer uses price discrimination.
(c) The market demand curve is perfectly elastic.
(d) Each firm's demand curve is perfectly inelastic.

_____ 2. The Farm Security Act of 2001 created new subsidies for:
(a) Sugar growers.
(b) Hog operators.
(c) Horse breeders.
(d) All of the above.

_____ 3. Which of the following would result from a price-support program when the support price is set above the equilibrium price?
(a) The price paid by consumers would be higher.
(b) The consumption of the product would be reduced.
(c) Output would increase, *ceteris paribus.*
(d) All of the above would result.

_____ 4. When government subsidizes the purchase of irrigation water by farmers, the result is:
(a) Higher marginal costs of production.
(b) Lower fixed costs to farmers.
(c) Increased output because marginal costs are lower.
(d) Higher fixed costs to farmers.

_____ 5. Which of the following programs will raise farm incomes without generating market distortions?
(a) Set-aside programs.
(b) Direct income-support programs.
(c) Import restrictions.
(d) All of the above.

_____ 6. The primary intent of the 1996 Freedom to Farm Act was to:
(a) Make farmers more dependent on market forces.
(b) Increase prices paid to farmers.
(c) Increase set-aside acreage.
(d) All of the above.

_____ 7. Which of the following is consistent with farming as a competitive market?
(a) A small number of firms.
(b) Marginal revenue lower than price for each firm.
(c) Exit of small firms when profits are high for large firms.
(d) Zero economic profit in the long run.

_____ 8. When effective price floors are set for an agricultural market:
(a) Quantity demanded will be less than the equilibrium quantity, and price will be greater than the equilibrium price.
(b) Quantity demanded will be less than the equilibrium quantity, and price will be less than the equilibrium price.
(c) Quantity demanded will be greater than the equilibrium quantity, and price will be greater than the equilibrium price.
(d) Quantity demanded will be greater than the equilibrium quantity, and price will be less than the equilibrium price.

_____ 9. The surplus induced by farm price-support programs can be eliminated by all of the following *except*:
(a) Export sales.
(b) Reduced demand.
(c) Government purchases and stockpiling.
(d) Supply restrictions.

_____ 10. What impact did the "Asian crisis" have on U.S. agriculture beginning in 1998?
(a) Decreased farm exports to Asia.
(b) A decrease in grain prices.
(c) A decrease in employment in the U.S. farm equipment industry.
(d) All of the above.

_____ 11. Which of the following is *not* generally a characteristic of agriculture?
(a) Ease of entry and exit.
(b) Market power.
(c) Homogeneous products.
(d) Artificial restraints on prices.

_____ 12. Individual farmers view the demand curve they face for agricultural commodities as very price elastic, and:

(a) They are correct even though the market demand curve tends to be quite inelastic.
(b) They are correct, and the market demand curve is quite elastic as well.
(c) They are incorrect because the market demand curve tends to be price inelastic.
(d) They are incorrect because price and quantity demanded are inversely related in the product market.

_____ 13. Which of the following characterizes the price and income elasticities for farm products?

(a) When prices fall, consumers respond by buying a great deal more; when income increases, consumers respond by buying less.
(b) When prices and income fall, consumers respond by buying less.
(c) When prices fall, farmers get less revenue; when income rises, consumers do not change purchases much.
(d) All of the above are characteristic.

_____ 14. The government creates a "moral hazard" when it:

(a) Encourages the type of behavior that leads to an undesirable allocation of resources.
(b) Ignores the plight of a group suffering economic depravation, e.g. farmers during the third farm depression.
(c) Passes laws it knows can't be enforced.
(d) Doesn't provide the same level of moral leadership that it expects from U.S. citizens.

_____ 15. If the price of corn falls by 25 percent on world markets, causing American corn consumption to increase by 5 percent, *ceteris paribus*, the absolute value of the price elasticity of demand for corn in the United States would be:

(a) 0.25.
(b) 0.5.
(c) 5.0.
(d) 0.20.

_____ 16. If the price elasticity of corn is 0.4 and the price of corn falls by 10 percent, the income from corn for farmers will:

(a) Increase as quantity demanded increases.
(b) Decrease as quantity demanded increases.
(c) Increase as quantity demanded decreases.
(d) Decrease as quantity demanded decreases.

_____ 17. *Ceteris paribus*, when interest rates fall, land values:

(a) Increase because the profitability of land decreases.
(b) Increase because the profitability of land increases.
(c) Decrease because the profitability of land decreases.
(d) Decrease because the profitability of land increases.

_____ 18. If the market price of wheat is below the government's "loan rate":

(a) The Commodity Credit Corporation lends the farmer an amount equal to the loan rate times the farmer's wheat output and takes the farmer's wheat crop as collateral.
(b) The wheat farmer defaults on the loan but keeps the crop; the CCC keeps the money.
(c) The wheat farmer, in effect, "buys" the crop from the CCC.
(d) All of the above.

_____ 19. An advantage of set-aside programs over price-support programs is that they:

(a) Reduce the price of agricultural goods.
(b) Transfer more income to farmers.
(c) Raise the price of agricultural production but do not lead to a surplus of output.
(d) Affect the demand side as well as the supply side of the farm problem.

_____ 20. Which of the following agricultural programs reduces agricultural output, rather than increasing it?
(a) Direct income-support programs.
(b) Farm cost subsidies.
(c) Marketing orders.
(d) Export sales.

Problems and Applications

Exercise 1

This exercise shows the impact of farm subsidies on the market and consumers.

Figure 14.1 represents the agricultural market. Use this figure to answer questions 1-6.

Figure 14.1

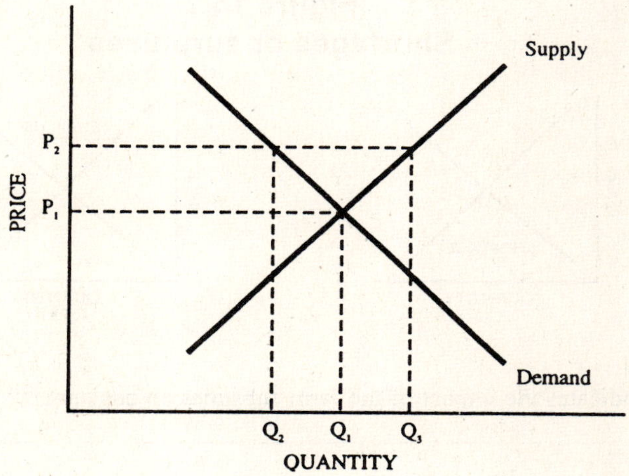

1. Without government intervention, the price of farm goods is determined by the intersection of ______________________________.

2. The equilibrium price is _____ and farmers supply farm goods equal to _____.

3. Individual farmers are price (makers, takers) and will always produce the level of output where price equals _________.

4. Government price supports would (increase, decrease) the price of farm goods and cause price to move to _____.

5. At the new price farmers would supply farm goods equal to _____.

6. The price support caused a (shortage, surplus) of output in the agricultural market equal to the distance ____________.

Exercise 2

Articles about agriculture often provide information about shortages or surpluses. This exercise will use one of the articles in the textbook to show the kind of information to look for to determine whether shortages or surpluses exist.

Reread the In the News article entitled "EU Farm Subsidies." Then answer the following questions.

1. The article indicates there are:
   (a) Shortages.
   (b) Surpluses.

2. Which passage in the article indicates the existence of the shortage or surplus? ______________
   ____

3. Which diagram in Figure 14.2 best represents the shortage or surplus mentioned in the article?
   _____

Figure 14.2
Shortages or surpluses

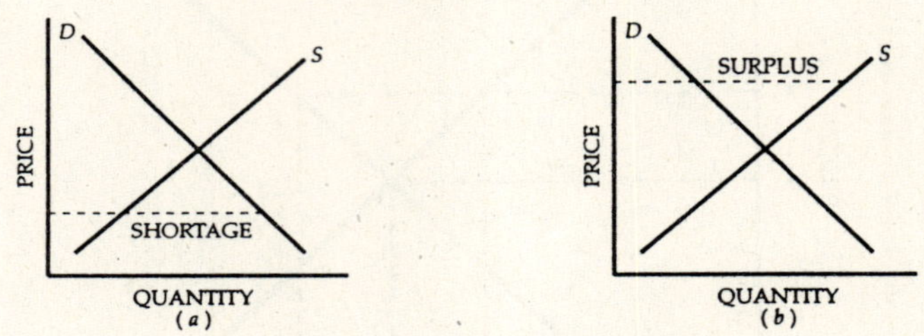

4. What phrase indicates the impact of the farm subsidies on consumers? ____________________
   ____

Common Errors

The first statement in each "common error" below is incorrect. Each incorrect statement is followed by a corrected version and an explanation.

1. Advances in farm productivity should be accompanied by improved profitability. WRONG!

   Competition translates improved productivity into lower prices, which can cause lower profitability. RIGHT!

   The spectacular increases in farm productivity that have occurred in the past decades have resulted in lower prices and lower incomes. Increases in supply coupled with price-inelastic and slow-growing demand have lowered rather than raised net farm income. Yet competition forces the adoption of the newest techniques of farming.

2. When there is a bumper crop, farm incomes will increase. WRONG!

   When there is a bumper crop, farm incomes are likely to decrease. RIGHT!

Because the demand for farm goods is price inelastic, a large percentage increase in output will cause an even larger percentage reduction in the price of farm goods.

•ANSWERS•

Using Key Terms

Across

1. deficiency payment
3. economic profit
7. price elasticity of demand
10. market power
11. loan rate
12. acreage set-aside

Down

2. income elasticity of demand
4. parity
5. moral hazard
6. barriers to entry
8. market surplus
9. profit

True or False

1. F Even though 100,000 bushels of corn is a large amount, that amount is insignificant relative to the total market output. As a result, the individual farmer has zero market power.
2. T
3. T
4. T
5. F Price supports have raised the price of farm products, reduced consumption, and encouraged production.
6. F Deficiency payments are payments made to farmers to make up the difference between target and market prices. Target prices may or may not be designed to reach parity.
7. F Direct income payments are more efficient because they do not cause market distortions, e.g., surpluses.
8. T
9. T
10. T

Multiple Choice

1.	a	5.	b	9.	b	13.	c	17.	b
2.	d	6.	a	10.	d	14.	a	18.	a
3.	d	7.	d	11.	b	15.	d	19.	c
4.	c	8.	a	12.	a	16.	b	20.	c

Problems and Applications

Exercise 1

1. Market supply and market demand
2. P_1, Q_1
3. Takers, MC
4. Increase, P_2
5. Q_3
6. Surplus, Q_3-Q_2

Exercise 2

1. b
2. The article says, ". . . governments also agree to purchase any surplus production."
3. Diagram b (surplus)
4. "All this protection costs the average EU consumer over $200 a year."

PART 5 Factor Markets: Basic Theory

CHAPTER 15

The Labor Market

Quick Review

- The motivation to work comes from a variety of social, psychological, and economic forces. The need to have income to purchase desired goods and services is, of course, very important. Working imposes opportunity costs on the worker because leisure time must be given up when one chooses to work.

- An increase in the wage rate motivates people to work more initially and the individual's supply curve of labor slopes upward to the right. At a point, higher wages allow people to work fewer hours and still earn the same income. When the income effects become greater than the substitution effects, the labor supply curve bends backward.

- The demand for labor is derived from the demand for the goods and services that the labor produces. The quantity of labor demanded will increase as the wage rate decreases. The marginal physical product (MPP) of labor is the change in total output because of an additional worker. The demand curve for labor is the marginal revenue product (MRP) curve; it combines the productivity of labor with the price of the output. The law of diminishing returns affects both MPP and MRP.

- The hiring decision requires that managers consider the contribution of labor to the firm's revenues (called its marginal revenue product) and what it costs to hire the labor. The marginal revenue product thus sets an upper limit to the wage that will be paid to labor. Labor should be hired until the marginal revenue product declines to the level of the wage rate. Increases in the productivity of labor and increases in the market price of the output will shift the demand for labor (MRP curve) to the right.

- The market equilibrium wage is determined by the intersection of the market supply and market demand curves. A minimum wage is set above the market equilibrium wage and causes the quantity of labor supplied to exceed the quantity of labor demanded. Unemployment is the inevitable result. Labor unions must exclude some workers from the market to achieve their goals, and the displaced workers depress wages in other markets.

- When choosing amongst alternative production processes (the efficiency decision), a producer must compare input costs and then choose the least-cost method of production. The most cost effective input is the one that produces the most output per dollar spent, not necessarily the cheapest one.

- It is sometimes difficult to determine the wages of certain individuals because their marginal revenue product is so difficult to calculate. In this situation opportunity wages, custom, power, tradition, and the like are used to determine the wage.

Learning Objectives

After reading Chapter 15 and doing the following exercises, you should:

1. Understand the labor-supply curve and its nonprice determinants.
2. Be able to apply the law of diminishing marginal utility to the labor market.
3. Know how people determine the number of hours they want to work.
4. Be able to explain the shape of the labor-supply curve using the income and substitution effects of wages.
5. Know how to calculate the elasticity of the market supply of labor.
6. Understand why the demand for factors of production is derived from the demand for goods and services.
7. Be able to derive the marginal revenue product curve and know why it slopes downward.
8. Understand how market supply and market demand interact to determine market wage rates when their nonprice determinants change.
9. Understand cost efficiency and how the efficiency decision is made.
10. Know that the "opportunity wage" reflects a worker's productivity in his or her best alternative employment, *ceteris paribus.*

Using Key Terms

Fill in the puzzle on the opposite page with the appropriate term from the list of Key Terms at the end of the chapter in the text.

Across

1. The choice of a production process for any given rate of output.
7. Determined by the intersection of the market supply and market demand for labor.
13. The percentage change in quantity of labor supplied divided by the percentage change in wage rate.
14. The willingness and ability to work specific amounts of time at alternative wage rates.
15. A specific combination of resources used to produce a good or service.

Down

2. The quantity of resources purchased by a firm depends on the firm's expected sales and output.
3. An increased wage rate causes people to work more hours.
4. The MPP of labor declines as the quantity of labor employed increases.
5. The change in total output because of one additional unit of input.
6. An increased wage rate allows people to reduce the hours worked without losing income.
8. The change in total revenue because of one additional unit of input.
9. The total quantity of labor that workers are willing and able to supply at alternative wage rates.
10. The MPP of an input divided by its price.
11. The highest wage an individual would earn in his or her best alternative job.
12. The quantity of labor employers are willing and able to hire at alternative wage rates.

Puzzle 15.1

True or False: *Circle your choice and explain why any false statements are incorrect.*

T F 1. The supply curve for labor bends backward when the substitution effect of wages exceeds the income effect of wages.

T F 2. For wages to be higher without sacrificing jobs, productivity must decrease.

T F 3. Higher wage rates are required to compensate for the increasing opportunity cost of labor.

T F 4. The value of additional income decreases as total income increases.

T F 5. The demand for labor is downward sloping because as more workers are hired their productivity increases.

T F 6. The concept of derived demand means that the demand for bricklayers, for example, is determined by the demand for new brick houses.

T F 7. The law of diminishing returns suggests that the fewer the number of workers employed, the more total output they can produce in a given time period, *ceteris paribus.*

T F 8. The intersection of the labor market supply and market demand curves establishes the minimum wage.

T F 9. The labor supply curve is equivalent to the marginal physical product multiplied times the selling price of the product being produced.

T F 10. If salary caps were placed on CEO wages below their opportunity wage, there would be a shortage of CEOs.

Multiple Choice: *Select the correct answer.*

_____ 1. The number of hours that a worker is willing to work is determined by the tradeoff between:
(a) Increasing marginal utility for income and decreasing marginal utility for leisure.
(b) Increasing marginal utility for leisure and decreasing marginal utility for income.
(c) Increasing total utility for leisure and decreasing total utility for income.
(d) Increasing marginal utility for both income and leisure.

_____ 2. The constraint that is *most* important in determining the tradeoff between leisure and work is:
(a) Income.
(b) Time.
(c) Available goods and services.
(d) Satisfaction from working.

_____ 3. If consumers wanted to increase wages and the number of jobs available for apple pickers, the best strategy would be to:
(a) Insist that the government establish a minimum wage for apple pickers.
(b) Boycott apples until wages increased.
(c) Buy more apples.
(d) Insist that the sellers raise the price of apples.

_____ 4. An upward-sloping labor-supply curve illustrates, *ceteris paribus*, that:
(a) The supply of labor and the wage rate are inversely related.
(b) The quantity supplied of labor and the hours of work per week are directly related.
(c) The quantity supplied of labor and the hours of work per week are inversely related.
(d) A greater quantity of labor would be supplied at higher wage rates.

_____ 5. The elasticity of labor supply does *not* depend on:
(a) The demand for labor.
(b) Income and wealth.
(c) The prices of consumer goods.
(d) Expectations for income or consumption.

_____ 6. If household income and wealth increases over time, the supply of labor will:
(a) Shift to the left.
(b) Shift to the right.
(c) Move up the curve to the right.
(d) Move down the curve to the left.

_____ 7. Determinants of the market supply of labor include:
(a) Tastes.
(b) Income and wealth.
(c) Expectations.
(d) All of the above.

_____ 8. A competitive firm should continue to hire workers until the:
(a) MRP is equal to demand.
(b) MPP is equal to the number of workers hired.
(c) MRP is equal to the market wage rate.
(d) MRP is equal to zero.

_____ 9. If Kendra's income effect outweighs her substitution effect, her labor supply curve will:
(a) Appear horizontal.
(b) Slope upward.
(c) Bend backward.
(d) Appear vertical.

_____ 10. Which of the following is true about the equilibrium market wage?
(a) All workers are satisfied with the wage.
(b) All employers are satisfied with the wage.
(c) There is no unemployment in this market at the equilibrium wage.
(d) All of the above are correct.

_____ 11. At the market equilibrium wage:
(a) *MRP* = wage rate.
(b) The ratio of the *MPP* of each factor to the factor's price is the same for all factors.
(c) The market demand curve for labor intersects the market supply curve of labor.
(d) All of the above.

_____ 12. The cost efficiency of labor is equal to:
(a) The marginal cost of output.
(b) The *MPP* of labor times the wage rate.
(c) The *MPP* of labor divided by the wage rate.
(d) The *MRP* of labor divided by the unit price of labor.

_____ 13. In order to calculate marginal revenue product, we need to know:
- (a) The change in total output and the change in quantity of labor.
- (b) The marginal physical product and the unit price of the factor.
- (c) The marginal revenue and the amount of the product produced.
- (d) The marginal revenue and the cost of the factor input.

_____ 14. The diminishing returns to a factor may be due to:
- (a) The declining utility of a good as we consume more of it.
- (b) Crowding or overuse of other factors as production is increased.
- (c) The decline in the demand curve for a product.
- (d) The decline in the marginal revenue curve for a product.

_____ 15. The efficiency decision involves choosing the input combination or process that:
- (a) Produces the greatest output.
- (b) Results in the lowest output per dollar of input.
- (c) Results in a given rate of output for the least cost.
- (d) Has the lowest ratio of *MPP* to input.

_____ 16. The marginal revenue product curve and marginal physical product curve have similar shapes:
- (a) Because marginal revenue product depends on marginal physical product.
- (b) Because the product demand curve slopes downward in accordance with the law of diminishing returns.
- (c) Because the law of demand and the law of diminishing returns are due to the same economic behavior.
- (d) For all of the above reasons.

_____ 17. Employment will definitely rise when:
- (a) Productivity and wages rise.
- (b) Productivity rises and wages fall.
- (c) Productivity falls and wages rise.
- (d) Productivity and wages fall.

_____ 18. A change in wages causes a:
- (a) Shift in the marginal revenue product curve for labor.
- (b) Shift in the marginal physical product curve for labor.
- (c) Shift in the derived demand curve for labor.
- (d) Movement along the labor-demand curve.

_____ 19. When the minimum wage is raised in a competitive market, *ceteris paribus*:
- (a) All workers are better off.
- (b) All workers are worse off.
- (c) Some workers are better off and some are worse off.
- (d) Workers are not affected by a minimum wage increase, only by decreases.

_____ 20. "Opportunity wage" is defined as:
- (a) The highest wage an individual would earn in his or her best alternative employment.
- (b) The value of goods or services that an individual can purchase with the income earned by working 1 hour.
- (c) The income equivalent of a volunteer worker.
- (d) The income a worker loses when he or she quits a job.

Problems and Applications

Exercise 1

This exercise shows how to determine the supply of labor. It provides practice in graphing labor supply and examines backward-bending supply curves, the substitution effect, and the income effect.

Suppose you came to school without any means of support and your advisor suggests that you take a job at the school. Your only task is to correct true-false examinations (the professors give you all of the answers to the exams), add up the scores, and calculate each student's grade. You can work as many hours as you wish because opportunities are plentiful.

Drawing Labor-Supply Curves

If the work were offered to you on a volunteer basis, you would not work at all. But at $2 an hour you might work 1 hour per day—just to see how well your classmates are doing. Only at $4 an hour would it be worthwhile to work many hours—perhaps 4 hours per day. At $8 an hour you would work 6 hours per day and at $16 an hour you would make it a full-time job of 8 hours per day. But at $32 an hour you would decide to spend more time at leisure and work only 6 hours per day.

1. Fill in column 2 of Table 15.1, your labor-supply schedule, using the information in the paragraph above.

Table 15.1
Supply of labor

(1) *Hourly wage (dollars per hour)*	(2) *Work effort (hours worked per day)*	(3) *Elasticity of supply*
$ 0	______	—
2	______	______
4	______	______
8	______	______
16	______	______
32	______	______

2. Graph the labor-supply curve in Figure 15.1. First label the axes for the graph and then draw the curve and label it. (The curve should pass through point *A*.)

Figure 15.1

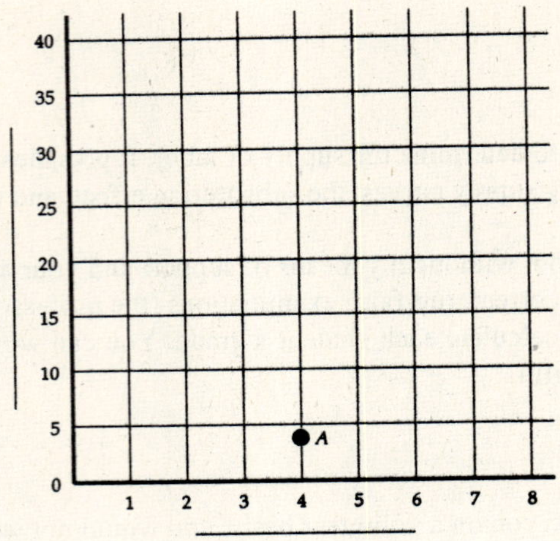

Backward-Bending Supply Curves

3. On the backward-bending segment of a supply curve, wage and quantity supplied are:
   (a) Directly (positively) related.
   (b) Inversely related.
   (c) Related by a horizontal line.
   (d) Related by a vertical line.

4. Which of the following circumstances might explain a backward-bending supply curve such as the one you have drawn in Figure 15.1?
   (a) You want to make a certain amount of income, and you want to spend the rest of your time sleeping and watching videos.
   (b) Because of the increased income you receive from an increase in your wage, you can increase your leisure without losing any income.
   (c) The marginal utility of each extra dollar falls as income rises.
   (d) All of the above might explain such a curve.

Substitution and Income Effects

5. An increase in wage rates:
   (a) Definitely increases hours worked through both the substitution and income effects.
   (b) Tends to increase hours worked through the substitution effect but may tend to decrease hours worked through the income effect.
   (c) Tends to increase hours worked through the substitution effect but definitely decreases hours worked through the income effect.
   (d) Tends to decrease hours worked through the substitution effect and may increase hours worked through the income effect.

6. On the backward-bending portion of the supply curve:
   (a) The income effect is greater than the substitution effect.
   (b) The substitution effect overpowers the income effect.
   (c) Both effects tend to decrease the quantity of labor supplied as a result of a wage increase.

7. In column 3 of Table 15.1, compute the elasticity of supply between each successive wage rate. Use the midpoint formula from the text.

Exercise 2

This exercise illustrates the relationship between marginal physical product and marginal revenue product for a company producing bottled water.

1. T F The marginal physical product (MPP) measures the change in total output that occurs when one additional worker is hired.

2. Which of the following formulas would provide a correct calculation of the marginal physical product?
   (a) Quantity / labor
   (b) Change in quantity /labor
   (c) Change in quantity / change in labor
   (d) Change in total revenue /change in labor

3. Calculate total revenue, marginal revenue product, and marginal physical product for Table 15.2.

Table 15.2
Marginal physical product and marginal revenue product

(1) Labor (workers per hour)	(2) Quantity produced (gallons per hour)	(3) Price (dollars per gallon)	(4) Total revenue (dollars per hour)	(5) Marginal revenue product (dollars per worker)	(6) Marginal physical product (gallons per worker)
0	0	$1	______	______	______
1	15	1	______	______	______
2	27	1	______	______	______
3	36	1	______	______	______
4	42	1	______	______	______
5	45	1	______	______	______
6	46	1	______	______	______

_____ 4. The law of diminishing returns implies that:
   (a) The marginal revenue declines as additional labor is employed in a given production process.
   (b) The marginal revenue product declines as additional labor is employed in a given production process.
   (c) The marginal physical product of labor increases as additional labor is employed in a given production process.
   (d) None of the above.

5. T F There are diminishing returns to labor with increased production in Table 15.2.

Exercise 3

This exercise provides experience in computing and graphing derived demand as well as determining the number of workers to hire.

1. You are the producer of a protein bar called EnerG, which sells for $1 per bar. You have to pay $6 an hour for labor. Complete Table 15.3.

Table 15.3 EnerG production, by labor hours

(1) Wage (dollars per hour)	*(2)* Labor (workers per hour)	*(3)* Quantity produced (bars per hour)	*(4)* Price (dollars per bar)	*(5)* Total revenue (dollars per bar)	*(6)* Marginal revenue product (dollars per worker)
6	0	0	$1	$______	$ ______
6	1	15	1	______	______
6	2	27	1	______	______
6	3	36	1	______	______
6	4	42	1	______	______
6	5	45	1	______	______
6	6	46	1	______	______

2. T F The demand curve for EnerG workers is found by plotting the marginal revenue product curve.

3. In Figure 15.2 draw the demand curve for labor from Table 15.3. Label it demand or MRP.

Figure 15.2

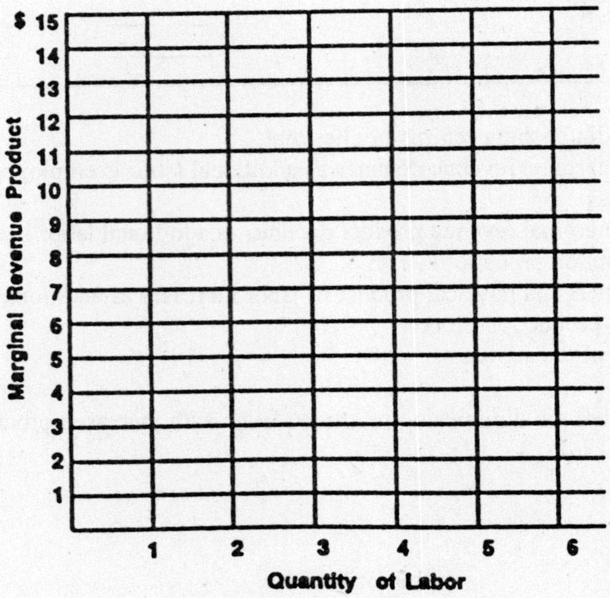

4. Draw a straight line at a wage of $6 in Figure 15.2 and label it wage rate.

5. How many workers are you willing to hire to produce EnerG bars? _________

6. How many EnerG bars will be produced per hour? __________

Exercise 4

This exercise examines the impact of a minimum wage on a labor market.

Figure 15.3

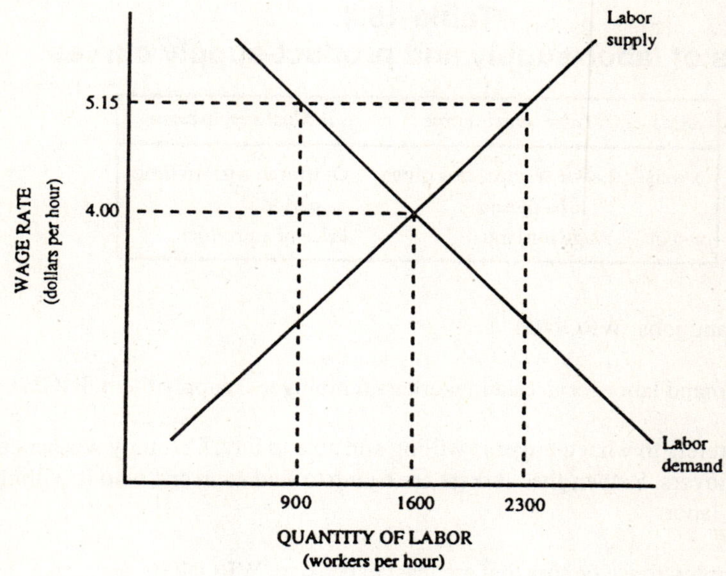

1. Figure 15.3 shows the labor market for unskilled workers. The equilibrium wage rate occurs at ______ per hour and at a quantity of _____ workers.

2. Now assume that the minimum wage is set at $5.15 per hour. The result of this government intervention is to create a (shortage, surplus) of labor.

3. At the new minimum wage _________ workers keep their jobs and _________ workers lose their jobs.

4. An increase in labor productivity in Figure 15.3 would cause the labor (supply, demand) curve to shift to the (left, right).

Common Errors

The first statement in each "common error" below is incorrect. Each incorrect statement is followed by a corrected version and an explanation.

1. People work because they have to. WRONG!

   Generally, people work in order to buy the goods and services they want. RIGHT!

People have flexibility in choosing the conditions under which they will work. What they *choose* to do reflects their utility of leisure compared with their utility of the goods and services they can buy with their income from work. If their needs for goods were satisfied, they might not work at all.

2. The labor-supply curve is the same as the supply curve of the products that labor produces. WRONG!

The labor-supply curve is a supply curve in a factor market, whereas a product supply curve applies to a product market. RIGHT!

Supply curves in different markets are not the same curves, although they may look the same. The chief difference is found on the axes, as shown in Table 15.4.

Table 15.4
Axes of labor-supply and product-supply curves

Axis	*Labor-supply curve*	*Product supply curve*
x-axis	Labor services in a given time period	Output in a given time period
y-axis	Wage for labor	Price of a product

3. Workers demand jobs. WRONG!

Employers demand labor services and workers (employees) supply them. RIGHT!

Demand refers to what a buyer is willing and able to buy. Certainly workers are not seeking to pay their employers. Rather, the workers are trying to find someone who is willing and able to pay them for their labor.

4. Employers employ those factors that are least expensive. WRONG!

Employers want to employ those factors that are most cost-effective. RIGHT!

If a factor is cheap, there may be a reason for it. It may not last long, may not work correctly, or may require heavier use of other factors of production—for example, maintenance workers. The marginal productivity of the cheap factor may therefore be low. An apparently more expensive factor might perform its proper function well and even save on the costs of other factors. The marginal productivity of the more expensive input would more than make up for its higher cost. Businesses would choose the more expensive factor of production.

5. Marginal revenue product is the same as marginal revenue. WRONG!

The marginal revenue product curve applies to the factor market, while the marginal revenue curve applies to the product market. RIGHT!

The formula for marginal revenue product is

$$\frac{\text{Change in total revenue}}{\text{Change in quantity of input}}$$

while that for marginal revenue is

$$\frac{\text{Change in total revenue}}{\text{Change in quantity of output}}$$

Marginal revenue shows changes in total revenue as a result of increased output and therefore is appropriate in analyzing what happens in the product market.

Marginal revenue product shows how total revenue changes as a result of the increased use of a factor and therefore is appropriate in analyzing what happens in the factor market. Both curves are derived from the demand curve in the product market. However, in order to find marginal revenue product, it is necessary also to know the relationship between the quantity of input and quantity of output. That is why the marginal physical product becomes important.

6. The law of diminishing returns means that average total costs will rise as a firm expands. WRONG!

   The law of diminishing returns applies only to changes in the use of one factor while all others remain constant. RIGHT!

   If a firm could expand all factors of production proportionately, there might be no decline in productivity at all, and thus no increase in average total cost. If the firm could do so without affecting factor prices, there would then be no change in unit costs either. The law of diminishing returns applies to changes of only one factor or group of factors, *ceteris paribus* (all other factors being held constant).

7. No one is hurt when companies are taxed except the companies themselves. WRONG!

   Part of the burden of taxes on a company may fall on the factors of production that a company employs. RIGHT!

   Remember that the demand for factors is derived from the product market. If the sales tax, for example, affects the demand curve for a product, it will affect the demand curve for the factors used to produce the product.

•ANSWERS•

Using Key Terms

Across

1. efficiency decision
7. equilibrium wage
13. elasticity of labor supply
14. labor supply
15. production process

Down

2. derived demand
3. substitution effect of wages
4. law of diminishing returns
5. marginal physical product
6. income effect of wages
8. marginal revenue product
9. market supply of labor
10. cost efficiency
11. opportunity wage
12. demand for labor

True or False

1. F The supply curve for labor bends backward when the income effect of wages exceeds the substitution effect of wages.
2. T
3. T
4. T
5. F The demand for labor is downward sloping due to diminishing marginal productivity caused by the fact that the amount of capital and space available to each worker decreases as more workers are hired.
6. T
7. F When fewer workers are hired total output is typically lower. It is also usually true, however, that when fewer workers are hired the MPP of the last worker increases.
8. F The intersection of supply and demand establishes the equilibrium wage. The minimum wage is typically set above the equilibrium wage by the government.
9. T
10. T

Multiple Choice

1.	b	5.	a	9.	c	13.	b	17.	b
2.	b	6.	a	10.	c	14.	b	18.	d
3.	c	7.	d	11.	d	15.	c	19.	c
4.	d	8.	c	12.	c	16.	a	20.	a

Problems and Applications

Exercise 1

1. See Table 15.1 Answer, column 2.

Table 15.1 Answer

(1) Hourly wage (dollars per hour)	(2) Work effort (hours worked per day)	(3) Elasticity of supply
$ 0	0	---
2	1	1.0
4	4	1.8
8	6	0.6
16	8	0.429
32	6	-0.429

2. **Figure 15.1 Answer**

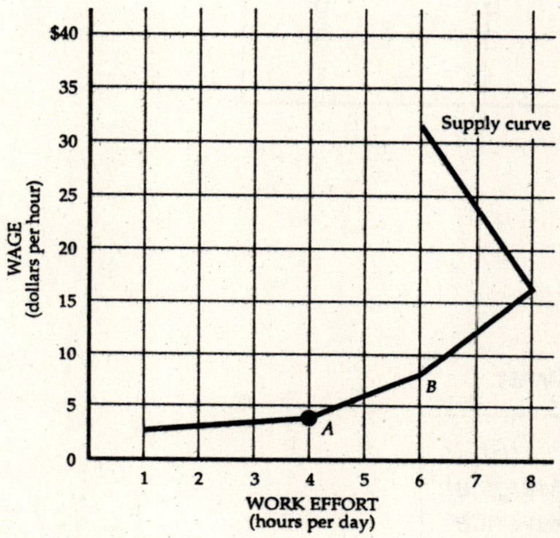

3. b 4. d 5. b 6. a

7. See Table 15.1 Answer, column 3. The formula for the elasticity of labor supply is

$$\frac{\text{Percentage change in quantity of labor supplied}}{\text{Percentage change in wage rate}}$$

The elasticity of labor supply can be estimated (just as the elasticity of demand was estimated) by using the following midpoint formula:

$$\frac{(L_2 - L_1) \div [1/2 \times (L_2 + L_1)]}{(W_2 - W_1) \div [1/2 \times (W_2 + W_1)]} = \frac{(6 - 8) \div [(1/2 \times (6 - 8)]}{(32 - 16) \div [(1/2 \times (32 - 16)]} = \frac{3}{7}$$

In the formula, L_1 is the amount of labor offered at the wage W_1 in period 1 and L_2 is the amount of labor offered at the wage W_2 in period 2. (*Note:* Elasticity is negative only on the backward-bending part of the supply curve.)

Exercise 2

1. T
2. c
3. **Table 15.2 Answer**

(1) Labor	(4) Total revenue	(5) Marginal revenue product	(6) Marginal physical product
0	----	----	----
1	$15	$15	15
2	27	12	12
3	36	9	9
4	42	6	6
5	45	3	3
6	46	1	1

4. b
5. T

Exercise 3

1. **Table 15.3 Answer**

(2) Labor	(5) Total revenue	(6) Marginal revenue product
0	$ 0	$ ----
1	15	15
2	27	12
3	36	9
4	42	6
5	45	3
6	46	1

2. T

3. **Figure 15.2 Answer**

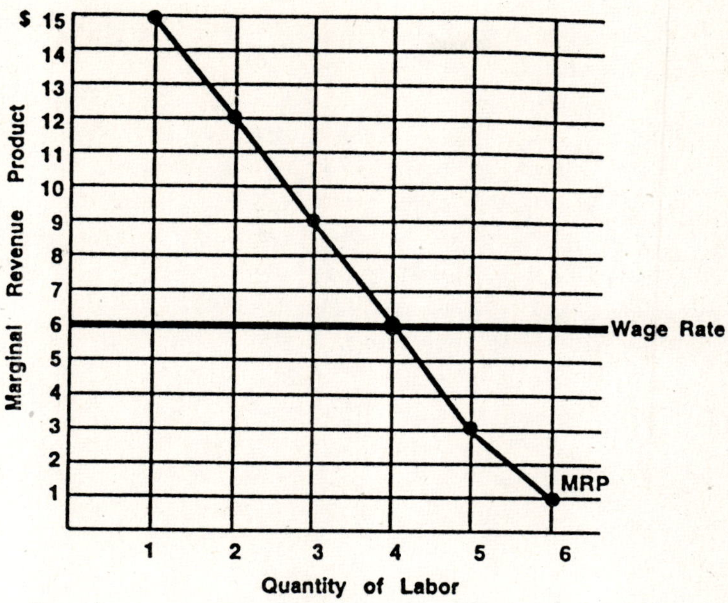

4. See Figure 15.2 Answer
5. 4 workers
6. 42 bars

Exercise 4

1. $4.00, 1600
2. Surplus
3. 900, 700
4. Demand, right

CHAPTER 16

Labor Unions

Quick Review

- The outcomes in the labor market, including the wage rate and the level of employment, can be distorted by market power on either the supply or demand side. Where the labor market is segmented by geographical, occupational, or industrial boundaries, market power may exist.
- Unions typically negotiate over a large number of objectives, but the most important is usually the wage rate. Unions tend to reduce the number of people they permit to be employed and to bargain for higher wages than would occur if the labor market were competitive. Union decisions are based on the collective interests of the members.
- The labor demand curve is downward sloping which means that additional labor can only be sold at a lower wage rate. The marginal wage is the change in total wages that results from employment of an extra unit of labor, and it lies below the labor demand curve.
- Unions establish the level of employment where the labor supply curve and the marginal wage rate are equated. The union wage is determined by the labor demand curve at the desired employment level.
- It is also possible for the firm to have market power such as a monopsonist or oligopolist. In this case, the more labor an employer seeks, the higher the wages will have to be. And when wages are raised for any worker, they must be raised for everyone. The marginal factor cost is therefore higher than the market wage rate.
- Monopsonists will attempt to equate marginal factor cost with marginal revenue product and then determine the wage rate from the labor supply curve. They will end up paying less than the competitive wage rate.
- In bilateral monopolies, where power exists on both sides of the labor market, unions and employers engage in collective bargaining to negotiate a final settlement.
- There is general agreement that unions have raised relative wages significantly and contributed to increased prices. Organized labor is also considered to be a potent political force.

Learning Objectives

After reading Chapter 16 and doing the following exercises, you should:

1. Understand the characteristics that are used to define the boundaries of labor markets.
2. Be able to demonstrate the meaning of the equilibrium wage rate.
3. Be able to describe the various types of labor buyers and suppliers.
4. Be familiar with the history of labor unions and their role in the economy.
5. Be able to define, compute, and graph the marginal wage curve and the demand curve for labor.
6. Be able to determine the optimal level of employment from a union point of view.
7. Know how to measure union power using the unionization ratio.
8. Be able to define, compute, and graph the marginal factor cost of labor and the supply curve of labor.
9. Be able to describe the monopsonist's desired equilibrium.
10. Understand how wages are determined in a market characterized by bilateral monopoly.
11. Be able to discuss the impact of unions in the U.S. economy.

Using Key Terms

Fill in the puzzle on the opposite page with the appropriate term from the list of Key Terms at the end of the chapter in the text.

Across

2. The change in total wages paid because of a one-unit increase in the quantity of labor employed.
5. A market with only one buyer and one seller.
10. The change in total costs because of a one-unit increase in the quantity of a factor employed.
11. A workplace in which all workers must join the union within 30 days after being employed.
12. The willingness and ability to work specific amounts of time at alternative wage rates.

Down

1. The quantity of labor employers are willing and able to hire at alternative wages.
2. The change in total revenue because of an additional unit of input.
3. Direct negotiations between employers and unions to determine labor market outcomes.
4. Output per unit of input.
6. The wage rate at which the quantity of labor supplied equals the quantity of labor demanded.
7. The percentage of the labor force belonging to a union.
8. The ability to alter the market price of a good or service.
9. A market in which there is only one buyer.

Puzzle 16.1

True or False: *Circle your choice and explain why any false statements are incorrect.*

T F 1. The equilibrium wage rate is the rate at which the quantity of labor demanded equals the quantity supplied.

T F 2. When determining the optimum level of employment, monopsonists will equate the marginal wage and the marginal revenue product.

T F 3. When determining the optimum level of employment, monopolists in the labor market will equate the marginal wage and the labor supply curve.

T F 4. The marginal wage curve lies below the labor-demand curve because all worker's wages are lowered when one more worker is hired.

T F 5. Unions do not need to control the labor supply in order to have market power.

T F 6. A craft union is a labor organization that represents workers in a particular industry.

T F 7. Union membership in the United States has risen steadily since the 1950s.

T F 8. A monopsony employer seeks to establish a wage rate that is lower than competitive standards.

T F 9. The collective bargaining process results in prices above the marginal revenue product curve.

T F 10. Unions are thought to be responsible for the rise in labor's share of national income and the rise in relative wages for unionized workers.

Multiple Choice: *Select the correct answer.*

_____ 1. Typical goals of a labor union in the United States include:
(a) Job security.
(b) Wages.
(c) Fringe benefits.
(d) All of the above.

_____ 2. The reason that a union may worry about having too many members is that:
(a) The union faces a downward-sloping marginal revenue product curve.
(b) It may be unable to control all of its members.
(c) It may not be able to reach optimal employment, at which the marginal labor cost curve intersects the demand curve.
(d) None of the above.

_____ 3. Total wages paid to labor are maximized when workers are hired up to the point where:
(a) The marginal wage is equal to the market wage.
(b) The demand for labor is equal to the marginal factor cost.
(c) The marginal wage equals zero.
(d) The market wage equals the marginal factor cost.

_____ 4. Unions must distinguish between the marginal wage and the market wage, but nonunion workers generally do not:
(a) Because the demand curve for labor from the union point of view slopes downward.
(b) Because for a nonunion worker who has no market power, the demand curve appears flat.
(c) Because for a nonunion worker who has no market power, the demand curve is the same as the marginal wage curve.
(d) For all of the above reasons.

_____ 5. From a union's perspective, the optimal level of employment is determined by the intersection of:
(a) The labor-demand curve and the labor-supply curve.
(b) The marginal wage curve and the labor-supply curve.
(c) The labor-demand curve and the marginal wage curve.
(d) The labor-demand curve and the marginal factor cost curve.

_____ 6. Assume a firm hires 10 workers at a wage rate of $15 per hour, but in order to hire the eleventh worker wages must fall to $14 per hour. What is the marginal wage of the eleventh worker?
(a) $154 per hour.
(b) $14 per hour.
(c) $4 per hour.
(d) $-1 per hour.

_____ 7. To be successful in changing wage rates and employment conditions, labor unions need to have control over only:
(a) Their own members.
(b) The supply of labor to the market.
(c) The *MRP* of employers.
(d) The production decision of employers.

_____ 8. An industrial union:
(a) Exerts market power by controlling the supply of labor to a particular industry.
(b) Exerts market power by controlling the supply of labor to a particular firm.
(c) Is an organization of workers with a particular skill.
(d) Is an organization of workers in a particular industry.

_____ 9. At a union-imposed level of employment:
(a) Employment is lower than at the competitive equilibrium.
(b) The marginal wage is negative.
(c) Employment and wages are both at the maximum possible levels.
(d) Employment would not be increased by reducing the wage rate.

_____ 10. A monopsonist must pay a higher wage rate to hire additional workers because:
(a) As a single seller in the market, it has market power.
(b) As a single buyer in the market, it faces an upward-sloping supply curve for labor.
(c) As a single seller in the market, it does not have to compete with other firms for customers.
(d) As a single buyer in the market, it faces a flat supply curve for labor.

_____ 11. The difference between a competitive labor market and a monopsonistic labor market is:
(a) That the monopsony will attempt to charge a higher wage than will be charged in a competitive market, *ceteris paribus.*
(b) That the monopsony will hire less labor than will be hired in a competitive market, *ceteris paribus.*
(c) That the shape of the marginal revenue product curve of a monopsony will differ from that of a competitive market.
(d) All of the above.

_____ 12. The marginal factor cost for labor is the:

(a) Net cost to a monopsonist of hiring an additional unit of labor.
(b) Net gain to a monopolist seller of labor if an additional unit of labor is hired.
(c) Demand for labor.
(d) Supply of labor.

_____ 13. A monopsonist pays $15 per hour for 10 workers. In order to hire an eleventh worker, the monopsonist must increase the wage rate to $16 per hour. What is the marginal factor cost of labor with eleven workers?

(a) $176 per hour.
(b) $26 per hour.
(c) $16 per hour.
(d) $15 per hour.

_____ 14. A profit-maximizing monopsonist will hire workers to the point where the marginal factor cost curve intersects the:

(a) Marginal wage curve.
(b) Equilibrium wage.
(c) Marginal revenue product curve.
(d) Labor-supply curve.

_____ 15. The buyer's profit-maximizing level of input use occurs at:

(a) Marginal wage = marginal factor cost.
(b) *MRP* = marginal wage.
(c) Marginal wage = zero.
(d) *MRP* = marginal factor cost.

_____ 16. A workplace that requires workers to become a member within thirty days of being hired by a firm is:

(a) A craft union.
(b) An industrial union.
(c) A union shop.
(d) The AFL-CIO.

_____ 17. Which of the following correctly assesses the impact of unions in the U.S. economy?

(a) Unions have been successful in raising both the relative wages and the absolute wages of their members.
(b) Union work rules have contributed to inflation because productivity increases have generally exceeded wage increases.
(c) The political power of unions has grown because the unionization ratio has grown at the same rate as the labor force.
(d) Unions have been successful at raising relative wages but not absolute wages.

_____ 18. The trend in the U.S. toward the merger of unions is driven by the labor movement's desire to:

(a) Increase representation.
(b) Increase financial support.
(c) Enhance their political power.
(d) All of the above.

_____ 19. In a bilateral monopoly, wages and employment are determined by:

(a) Negotiation.
(b) The intersection of market supply and demand.
(c) The intersection of marginal cost and marginal revenue product.
(d) The intersection of marginal wage and market demand.

_____ 20. Unions have had an adverse impact on the efficiency of U.S. firms by supporting which of the following types of legislation?
(a) Civil rights legislation.
(b) Tariffs and quotas.
(c) Health and education programs.
(d) All of the above.

Problems and Applications

Exercise 1

This exercise provides practice in calculating the marginal factor cost of labor (marginal wage) and the marginal revenue product of labor for a monopsony situation.

1. Suppose the data in Table 16.1 represent the wages, number of workers, and the price that you face when producing different amounts of Roaring Ripple, a new soft drink. Complete Table 16.1.

Table 16.1
Labor market with variable wage

(1) Labor (workers per hour)	(2) Wage (dollars per hour)	(3) Ripple (quarts per hour)	(4) Price (dollars per quart)	(5) TC (dollars per hour) (1) x (2)	(6) MFC (dollars per worker) ($\Delta TC/\Delta L$)	(7) TR (dollars per hour) (3) x (4)	(8) MRP (dollars per worker) ($\Delta TR/\Delta L$)
0	$1	0	$1	$_______	$ __	$_______	$ __
1	2	15	1	_______	_______	_______	_______
2	7	27	1	_______	_______	_______	_______
3	9	36	1	_______	_______	_______	_______

2. The amount of Roaring Ripple you will produce to maximize your profits is _________ ; the wage you will pay your workers is _________ ; the marginal cost of labor will be _________ ; the number of employees you will hire will be _________ .

3. T F For each new worker you hire, you must raise wages for all of the workers together, which means that the marginal cost of labor is different from the supply curve of labor.

4. T F The wage at which the marginal cost of labor curve intersects the marginal revenue product curve is the equilibrium wage rate.

Exercise 2

The differences in labor goals are the focus of this exercise.

Suppose that the supply and demand schedules in Table 16.2 apply to a particular labor market.

Table 16.2
Labor supply and demand

Wage rate (dollars per hour)	$14	13	12	11	10	9	8	7	6	5
Quantity of labor demanded (workers per hour)	0	1	2	3	4	5	6	7	8	9
Total wage bill (dollars per hour)	___	___	___	___	___	___	___	___	___	___
Marginal wage (dollars per worker)	___	___	___	___	___	___	___	___	___	___
Wage rate (dollars per hour)	$3	4	5	6	7					
Quantity of labor supplied (workers per hour)	1	3	5	7	9					
Total wage (dollars per hour)	___	___	___	___	___					
Marginal factor cost (dollars per worker)	___	___	___	___	___					

Figure 16.1

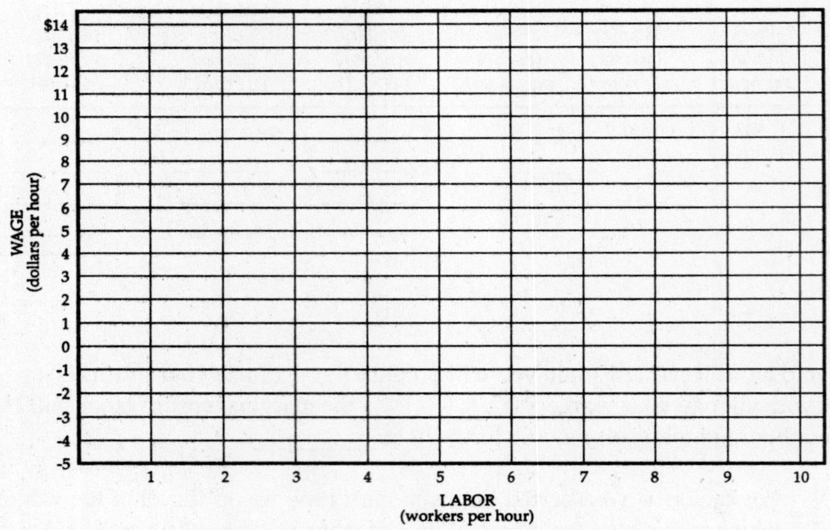

1. Compute the marginal wage and the marginal factor cost in the space provided in Table 16.2.

2. Graph the labor demand curve, the labor supply curve, marginal wage, and marginal factor cost in Figure 16.1.

3. The amount of labor hired in a competitive market would be ____________ workers at a wage of ________ per hour.

4. The amount of labor that a union would want hired if it acted as a monopolist would be ____________ workers at a wage of ________ per hour.

5. Suppose a union asks each member to contribute a certain percentage of income to the union. Therefore, when the wage bill is maximized the union maximizes the dues it receives. The amount of labor that would maximize union dues would be ____________ workers at a wage of ________ per hour.

6. Suppose the union wishes to maximize the number of employees that it has so that it can become a political force at the ballot box. The maximum amount of labor that such a union would be able to recruit would be ______ workers at a wage of _______ per hour.

7. The amount of labor hired by a monopsonist would be ___________ workers at a wage of ________ per hour.

The following are the names of the five types of labor market situations described in questions 3-7:

A. Competition (question 3)
B. Union monopolist (question 4)
C. Union dues maximizer (question 5)
D. Union vote maximizer (question 6)
E. Monopsony (question 7)

8. Each of the labor market situations listed above will result in a different wage-labor combination. Use the corresponding letter to label each wage-labor outcome in Figure 16.1.

9. Rank the above list of labor markets in order with respect to wage rates and then rank them with respect to total employment. When there is a tie, place the markets on the same line.

Table 16.3

(rank)	*Wage (highest to lowest)*	*(rank)*	*Amount of labor (lowest to highest)*
1.	____________	1.	____________
2.	____________	2.	____________
3.	____________	3.	____________
4.	____________	4.	____________
5.	____________	5.	____________

10. T F Market power, regardless of whether it is possessed by the buyer or the supplier, results in output equal to or lower than in a competitive labor market.

11. T F Market power, regardless of whether it is possessed by the buyer or the supplier, results in wage rates higher than those in a competitive labor market.

Exercise 3

Reread the *In the News* article titled "A Win for the Graduate(s)." Then answer the following questions.

1. Before the decision in the article, private universities had ____________________ power in the labor market for their own graduate students.

2. Now that graduate students are allowed to unionize, salaries should (increase, decrease, remain the same).

3. For a monopsonist, the marginal factor cost is (greater, less) than the wage rate because additional workers can be hired only if the wage rate for all workers (increases, decreases).

4. A monopsonist hires (more, fewer) workers at a (higher, lower) wage rate than would occur in a competitive market.

Common Errors

The first statement in each "common error" below is incorrect. Each incorrect statement is followed by a corrected version and an explanation.

1. The marginal cost of labor curve is the same as the marginal cost curve, and therefore it is also the supply curve for a firm. WRONG!

   The marginal cost of labor curve is derived from the supply of labor and is applicable only to the labor market, not to the product market. RIGHT!

   The marginal cost of labor is given by the formula

$$\frac{\text{Change in total wage cost}}{\text{Change in quantity of labor}}$$

   while the marginal cost curve is given by

$$\frac{\text{Change in total wage cost}}{\text{Change in quantity of product}}$$

   While the marginal cost of labor applies only to labor costs in the labor market, the marginal cost curve applies to all costs in the product market.

2. In bilateral monopoly the optimal level of employment occurs where the marginal cost of labor curve intersects the marginal wage curve. WRONG!

   In bilateral monopoly, it is possible to determine the limits between which the labor employment and wage levels will fall but not the precise optimal levels. RIGHT!

   The buyer wishes to buy labor at the point where the marginal cost of labor curve intersects the labor-demand curve. Only through negotiation can a compromise be worked out. The final outcome reflects the relative market power of supplier and buyer.

3. Powerful unions can get whatever wage they want. WRONG!

   Powerful unions are limited by the demand for labor. RIGHT!

   If unions make and receive exorbitant wage demands, they may find the union membership dwindling as more employees are laid off. Frequently, unions moderate wage demands in order to prevent employers from going out of business, foreign competition from undercutting prices, and non-unionized workers from becoming attractive to employers. All of these considerations reflect the law of demand.

•ANSWERS•

Using Key Terms

Across

2. marginal wage
5. bilateral monopoly
10. marginal factor cost
11. union shop
12. labor supply

Down

1. demand for labor
2. marginal revenue product
3. collective bargaining
4. productivity
6. equilibrium wage
7. unionization ratio
8. market power
9. monopsony

True or False

1. T
2. F Monopsonists will equate marginal factor cost and marginal revenue product.
3. T
4. T
5. F To maintain higher than equilibrium wages labor supply must be reduced.
6. F A craft union represents workers with specific skills.
7. F The unionization rate in the United States has been in steady decline for more than 40 years.
8. T
9. F The marginal revenue curve sets an upper limit for wages because it measures the value of each worker to the firm.
10. T

Multiple Choice

1. d	5. b	9. a	13. b	17. a
2. a	6. c	10. b	14. c	18. d
3. c	7. b	11. b	15. d	19. a
4. d	8. d	12. a	16. c	20. b

Problems and Applications

Exercise 1

1. **Table 16.1 Answer**

(1) Labor	*(2) Wage*	*(5) TC*	*(6) MFC*	*(7) TR*	*(8) MRP*
0	$1	$ 0	$ ---	$ 0	$ ---
1	2	2	2	15	15
2	7	14	12	27	12
3	9	27	13	36	9

2. 27 quarts per hour; $7 per hour; $12 per hour; 2 employees per hour
3. T
4. F

Exercise 2

1. **Table 16.2 Answer**

Wage rate (dollars per hour)	$14	13	12	11	10	9	8	7	6	5
Quantity of labor demanded (workers per hour)	0	1	2	3	4	5	6	7	8	9
Total wage bill (dollars per hour)	0	13	24	33	40	45	48	49	48	45
Marginal wage (dollars per worker)	—	13	11	9	7	5	3	1	-1	-3

Wage rate (dollars per hour)	$3	4	5	6	7
Quantity of labor supplied (workers per hour)	1	3	5	7	9
Total wage (dollars per hour)	$3	12	25	42	63
Marginal factor cost (dollars per worker)	3	4.5	6.5	8.5	10.5

2. **Figure 16.1 Answer**

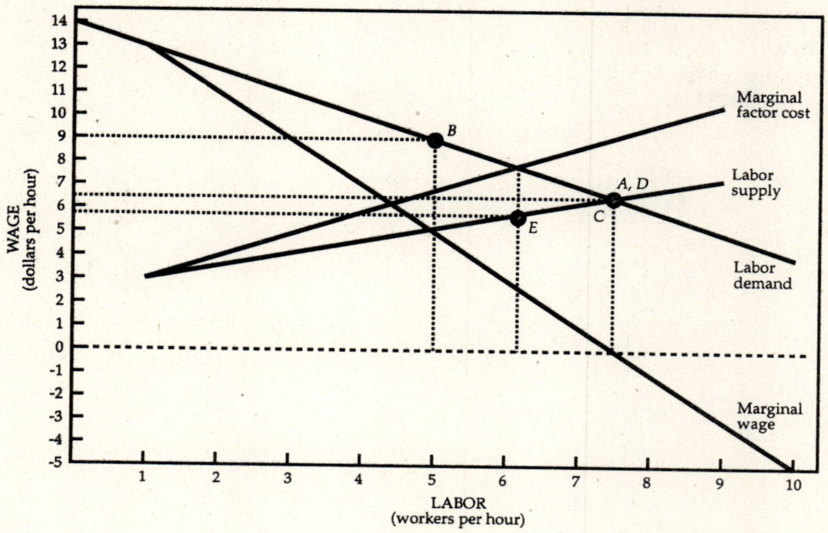

Note: When demand falls below the price at which workers are willing and able to work, there can be no greater employment. So the dues-maximizing and wage bill-maximizing unions will push employment to the competitive level. However, more inelastic demand can mean that wage bill-maximizing unions would produce less than the competitive level at a higher wage.

3. 7 (Labor supply and labor demand intersect at 7.5 workers.); $6.50
4. 5; $9.00
5. 7; $6.50. The wage bill is maximized where the marginal wage intersects the *x*-axis. But the equilibrium amount of labor, where labor supply equals labor demand, tells us the maximum number of workers which could be hired.
6. 7; $6.50
7. 6; $5.75. Remember that a monopsonist forces the wage down to the supply curve from which the wage is read.
8. See the letters marking the points in Figure 16.1 Answer.

9. **Table 16.3 Answer**

(rank)	Wage (highest to lowest)	(rank)	Amount of labor (lowest to highest)
1.	Union monopolist	1.	Union monopolist
2.	Competition	2.	Monopsony
	Union dues maximizer	3.	Competition
	Union vote maximizer		Union vote maximizer
3.	Monopsony		Union dues maximizer

10. T
11. F Monopsony results in a lower price than the competitive price.

Exercise 3

1. Monopsony
2. Increased
3. Greater, increases
4. Fewer, lower

CHAPTER 17

Financial Markets

Quick Review

- Financial markets assist the economy in its search for the optimal mix of output by helping to mobilize savings, manage risk, and signal desired resource allocations.

- Financial markets bring together those who wish to save more than they spend (the savers) and those who wish to spend more than they save (the borrowers). This is vital to the process of "spreading the risk" of failure over a large number of individuals.

- Three distinct financial markets, the stock market, the bond market, and the futures market aid in financial intermediation through which risk spreading occurs. Financial intermediaries also reduce the costs of information and search, and in doing so, they make the financial markets more efficient.

- Financial intermediaries discount future dollars by the opportunity cost of money or the market interest rate. Higher interest rates and a longer time until future payment will cause a decrease in the present discounted value of a future payment. Risk also has an impact on the expected value of future payments.

- The stock market allows firms to raise capital by selling ownership in the corporation. Changing expectations regarding the future profitability of particular corporations and the future course of the economy are important determinants of the price of a stock.

- Debt instruments, called bonds, are bought and sold in the bond market. Each bond is essentially an IOU which states the principal amount, interest, and terms on which the debt must be repaid. While the initial purchasers lend directly to the borrower, the bonds are also traded in a secondary market. Bond yields are inversely related to bond prices.

- Changes in investors' expectations concerning future interest rates and the borrowers' potential ability to pay interest and repay principal will affect the supply and demand for bonds.

- Venture capitalists provide initial funding for entrepreneurial ventures. If the project is a success, they reap profits; if not, they experience losses.

Learning Objectives

After reading Chapter 17 and doing the following exercises, you should:

1. Understand the primary function of financial markets.
2. Understand how financial markets increase efficiency.
3. Know what present discounted value means and how to calculate it.
4. Know that risk has an impact on the expected value of future payments.
5. Understand how companies raise funds through the stock market and the bond market.
6. Know some of the determinants of the demand for and supply of stocks and bonds, and know how changes in those determinants affect stock and bond prices.
7. Be able to explain why bond yields are inversely related to bond prices.
8. Understand the role of venture capitalists.

Using Key Terms

Fill in the puzzle on the opposite page with the appropriate term from the list of Key Terms at the end of the chapter in the text.

Across

1. The probable value of a future payment, including the risk of nonpayment.
6. A limited liability form of business.
8. Amount of corporate profit paid out for each share of stock.
10. The ability of an asset to be converted to cash.
11. The rate of return on a bond.
13. An increase in the market value of an asset.
14. The first sale to the general public of stock in a corporation.
15. The price of a stock share divided by earnings per share.

Down

2. The value today of future payments, adjusted for interest accrual.
3. An IOU issued by corporations and government agencies.
4. An institution that brings savers and dissavers together.
5. Failure to make scheduled payments of interest or principal on a bond.
6. Shares of ownership in a corporation.
7. Corporate profits not paid out in dividends.
9. The difference in rates of return on risky and safe investments.
12. The face value of a bond.

Puzzle 17.1

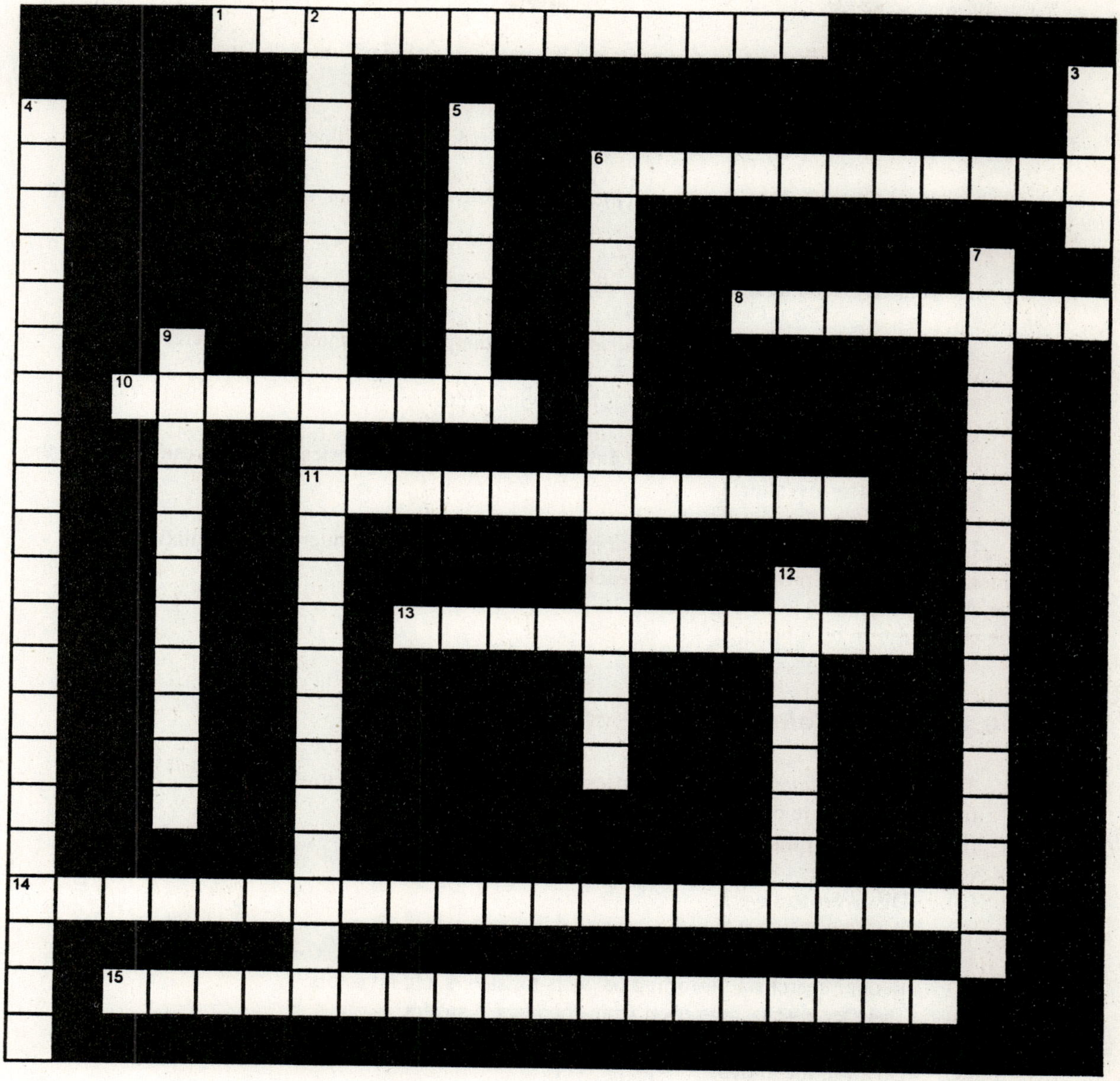

True or False: *Circle your choice and explain why any false statements are incorrect.*

T F 1. Financial intermediaries change the mix of output by transferring purchasing power from dissavers to savers.

T F 2. If the opportunity cost of money was zero, the expected value of future dollars would be equal to their present value.

T F 3. A risk premium compensates people who invest in risky ventures that succeed.

T F 4. One reason present dollars are worth more than future dollars is that income-earning investment opportunities exist.

T F 5. The present discounted value of a future payment will increase when interest rates increase.

T F 6. Stock prices will increase, *ceteris paribus*, when the prevailing interest rate increases.

T F 7. When a corporation issues a bond, it is borrowing funds.

T F 8. External shocks to the stock market have little impact on stock prices since investors look at the long run when investing.

T F 9. The present value of a future payment is discounted by potential interest accumulation.

T F 10. As bond prices increase, bond yields also increase.

Multiple Choice: *Select the correct answer.*

_____ 1. The function of financial intermediaries is to transfer purchasing power from:
- (a) Dissavers to consumers.
- (b) Savers to dissavers.
- (c) Consumers to savers.
- (d) Dissavers to savers.

_____ 2. Financial intermediaries:
- (a) Reduce search and information costs for savers and investors.
- (b) Transfer purchasing power from spenders to savers.
- (c) Concentrate investment risk.
- (d) Do all of the above.

_____ 3. Present dollars are worth more than future dollars because:
- (a) Income-earning investment opportunities exist.
- (b) There is always a chance that you may not receive the future dollars.
- (c) Of the opportunity cost of money.
- (d) All of the above.

_____ 4. The term present discounted value means the:
- (a) Future value of today's dollars.
- (b) Value today of future payments adjusted for inflation.
- (c) Value today of future payments adjusted for interest accrual.
- (d) Value today of future payments adjusted for risk.

_____ 5. Higher interest rates:

(a) Reflect a higher opportunity cost of money.
(b) Raise the future value of current dollars.
(c) Lower the present value of future payments.
(d) All of the above.

_____ 6. The present discounted value of a future payment will increase when the:

(a) Risk of non-payment decreases.
(b) Interest rate increases.
(c) Future payment is further into the future.
(d) Opportunity cost of money decreases.

_____ 7. The possibility of non-payment is taken into account in the calculation of the:

(a) Present discounted value.
(b) Future discounted value.
(c) Expected value.
(d) Profits.

_____ 8. The term expected value means:

(a) The future value of a current payment.
(b) The present value of a future payment.
(c) The probable value of a future payment.
(d) The difference in the rates of return on risky and safe investments.

_____ 9. Suppose Bill has a 40 percent chance of not collecting $5,000 in 4 years. If the interest rate is 12 percent, the expected value of the future payment is closest to:

(a) $1,907.
(b) $3,000.
(c) $3,178.
(d) $4,721.

_____ 10. A motivation for holding stocks is:

(a) To receive interest payments on the firm's debt.
(b) To receive potential capital gains.
(c) To have a direct role in the operation of the corporation.
(d) All of the above.

_____ 11. The purpose of an initial public offering is to:

(a) Raise funds for investment and growth by selling shares of the company to the public.
(b) Change the membership of the Board of Directors.
(c) Borrow funds for investment and growth.
(d) See if there is a demand for a company's new product.

_____ 12. Which of the following determines the price of a stock?

(a) The amount of stock that people are willing and able to purchase.
(b) The amount of stock that people offer for sale.
(c) Expectations of future earnings.
(d) All of the above.

_____ 13. The price of a stock will increase, *ceteris paribus*, when:
(a) When there is a shortage of the stock at the current price.
(b) The demand for the stock increases.
(c) The supply of the stock decreases.
(d) All of the above.

_____ 14. The expected rate of return for an IPO must take into consideration the:
(a) Risk factor.
(b) Time value of money.
(c) Interest rate.
(d) All of the above.

_____ 15. You purchase shares in Acme gadget company for $20 per share. There is an 80 percent chance the company will earn $1 profit per share in 8 years. The expected rate of return is closest to:
(a) 2.7 percent.
(b) 2.2 percent.
(c) 5.0 percent.
(d) 8.0 percent.

_____ 16. When investors expect greater future profits from a company, the:
(a) Demand for the company's bonds increases.
(b) Price of the company's bonds increases.
(c) Yield on the company's bonds decreases.
(d) All of the above occur.

_____ 17. When the interest rate rises:
(a) The demand for loanable funds falls and the supply of loanable funds falls.
(b) The demand for loanable funds rises and the supply of loanable funds rises.
(c) The demand for loanable funds falls and the supply of loanable funds rises.
(d) The quantity of loanable funds demanded falls and the quantity of loanable funds supplied rises.

_____ 18. The present value of $100,000 to be received every year for 3 years when the discount rate is 10 percent is:
(a) $300,000.
(b) $248,742.
(c) $133,100.
(d) $330,000.

_____ 19. As the interest rate increases, the opportunity cost of money:
(a) Increases for both lender and borrower.
(b) Increases for the borrower but not the lender.
(c) Decreases for both lender and borrower.
(d) Decreases for the borrower but not the lender.

_____ 20. As the interest rate increases, *ceteris paribus*, the tradeoff between present and future consumption:
(a) Is not affected.
(b) Encourages present consumption.
(c) Changes in favor of future consumption.
(d) Makes it less appealing to sacrifice present consumption.

Problems and Applications

Exercise 1

This exercise shows how to compute the present discounted value of an investment. It also shows how important the interest rate and length of time until payment are in the present value calculation.

1. Suppose you own 1,000 acres of forest land. Next year you could have the trees cut down for lumber and receive $1,320,000 (after taxes and all other expenses). The interest rate is 10 percent. Find the present discounted value of your 1,000 acres of forest land. __________

2. Suppose interest rates rose to 20 percent. What would the present discounted value of cutting down the forest for lumber be at the 20 percent interest rate if the cost and profit were the same as at 10 percent? __________

3. Suppose interest rates are at the original 10 percent. What would the present discounted value of cutting down the forest for lumber be if you had to wait two years to receive $1,320,000?

   ____

4. T F When the interest rate rises, the present value of an investment rises.

5. T F The longer one has to wait for a future payment, the less present value it has.

Exercise 2

This exercise uses the loanable funds market to determine the market interest rate and investment.

1. The supply and demand of loanable funds are shown in Figure 17.1. If the supply of loanable funds is S_1, then the equilibrium interest rate is _____ percent.

Figure 17.1
Investment demand, and the supply of loanable funds

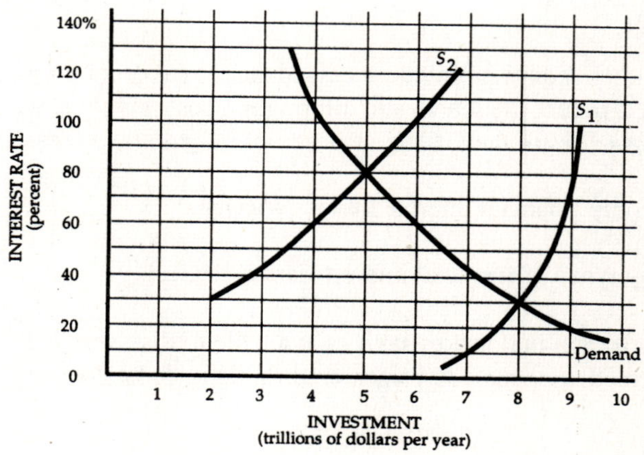

2. At the equilibrium interest rate, the level of investment would equal $_____ trillion.

3. If the supply of loanable funds shifts to S_2, this represents a(an) (increase, decrease) in loanable funds.

4. The equilibrium interest rate would (increase, decrease) to _____ percent and the level of investment would (increase, decrease) to $_____ trillion.

5. One reason for the shift in loanable funds in Figure 17.1 might be the (increase, decrease) in savings by consumers.

Exercise 3

The media often carry information about the amount of money won in lotteries. The reality is often different than what is reported.

Reread pages 356 through 357 in the text about the Powerball lottery winners. Then answer the following questions.

1. What was the advertised amount of the payoff from the winning lottery? ________________

2. When discounted at 4.87%, what was the present value of the payout? ________________

3. What would happen to the present value of the payout if it were discounted at an interest rate greater than 4.87%? ________________________

4. How many payments was the winner of the lottery to receive? __________

5. If the payoff was made in ten annual installments instead of the number above, what would have happened to the present value of the winnings? ________________________

Common Errors

The first statement in each "common error" below is incorrect. Each incorrect statement is followed by a corrected version and an explanation.

1. The primary function of financial intermediaries is to provide checking accounts for customers. WRONG!

   The primary function of financial intermediaries is to transfer income from savers to spenders. RIGHT!

   Financial intermediaries provide access to the savings pool for government and the business sector. They also reduce the search and information costs involved with lending and investment opportunities. As a result they change the mix of output and increase market efficiency.

2. Banks are the only financial intermediaries. WRONG!

   There are many types of financial intermediaries. RIGHT!

   Any organization that makes savings available to dissavers is a financial intermediary. Financial intermediaries include banks, credit unions, federal savings banks, and insurance companies.

3. As bond prices rise, the rate of return or current yield also rises. WRONG!

   As bond prices rise, the rate of return or current yield falls. RIGHT!

The rate of interest earned on a bond, or the coupon rate, is stated on the bond certificate and does not change. The current yield represents the rate of return on a bond. It is calculated as the annual interest payment divided by the bond price. The price of a bond in the secondary bond market varies based on changes in expectations and opportunity cost. If the annual interest payment stays constant and the bond price increases, the rate of return or current yield falls.

•ANSWERS•

Using Key Terms

Across

1. expected value
6. corporation
8. dividend
10. liquidity
11. current yield
13. capital gain
14. initial public offering
15. price earnings ratio

Down

2. present discounted value
3. bond
4. financial intermediary
5. default
6. corporate stock
7. retained earnings
9. risk premium
12. par value

True or False

1. F Financial intermediaries change the mix of output by transferring purchasing power from savers to dissavers.
2. F The expected value calculation takes into account the possibility of not getting the future payment. Whenever this is a possibility, future dollars will be worth less than current dollars.
3. T
4. T
5. T
6. F Stock prices will decrease when the prevailing interest rate increases because the opportunity cost of holding stocks will increase, making stocks a less desirable investment option (i.e., the demand for stocks will decrease).
7. T
8. F External shocks, such as a war, can and do have an impact on stock prices by affecting confidence and future expectations.
9. T
10. F Bond prices and yields move in opposite directions.

Multiple Choice

1. b	5. d	9. a	13. d	17. c
2. a	6. a	10. b	14. d	18. b
3. d	7. c	11. a	15. b	19. a
4. c	8. c	12. d	16. d	20. c

Problems and Applications

Exercise 1

1. $\$1{,}320{,}000/(1.10)^1 = \$1{,}200{,}000$
2. $\$1{,}320{,}000/(1.20)^1 = \$1{,}100{,}000$
3. $\$1{,}320{,}000/(1.10)^2 = \$1{,}090{,}909$
4. F
5. T

Exercise 2

1. 30 percent
2. $8 trillion
3. Decrease
4. Increase, 80 percent, decrease, $5 trillion
5. Decrease

Exercise 3

1. The advertised amount was $295 million.
2. $165.6 million.
3. If discounted at more than 4.87%, the present discounted value would be less than $165.6 million.
4. The text says that the payments were to be made as 25 annual installments.
5. Ten annual installments would raise the present discounted value.

PART 6 Distributional Issues

CHAPTER 18

Taxes: Equity vs. Efficiency

Quick Review

- The distribution of income is a major concern of public policy because income determines, to a large extent, who receives the goods and services in our society. Income is a flow and is measured over time; wealth is a stock of purchasing power and is measured at a point in time.
- The size distribution of income concentrates on the way income is distributed among income-receiving units, such as households. The Lorenz curve is a graph that compares the actual distribution of income to a distribution of income in which everyone receives the same income.
- The distribution of income in the United States is definitely not equal across all groups. The top 20 percent of households receives almost half of all income.
- Taxes are used to transfer command of resources from the private sector to the public sector and to redistribute income from the rich to the poor. The impact of taxes on the economy is not always easy to determine, and there appears to be a tradeoff between society's goals of equity and efficiency.
- Provisions in the tax law, called "loopholes," allow individuals to reduce the amount of income subject to tax. The loopholes also result in horizontal and vertical inequities. Economists use the nominal tax rate and the effective tax rate to analyze the tax system.
- The Tax Reform Act of 1986 closed loopholes, reduced marginal tax rates, reduced the number of tax brackets, increased the tax burden of corporations relative to individuals, and provided tax relief for the poor. The revisions in 1990 and 1993 added a fourth bracket, a new marginal tax rate and a surcharge.
- The Bush tax cuts of 2001 reduced marginal tax rates and also created tax incentives for education, marriage, and saving.
- State and local governments raise money through sales and property taxes. Both are regressive because low-income families spend a greater percentage of their income on housing and basic consumption goods than do high-income families. The payroll tax is also regressive.
- Tax incidence refers to the actual burden of the tax. Many argue that the burden of a payroll tax falls to the employees because employers reduce wages to compensate for their share of the tax.

- Income is distributed unequally in the United States. Some believe more should be transferred from those with higher incomes to those with lower incomes. Others argue that such a redistribution of income would damage the incentives to produce.

- There is debate about replacing the current tax structure with a flat tax. This would simplify the tax system, but it would also reduce the government's ability to alter the mix of output.

Learning Objectives

After reading Chapter 18 and doing the following exercises, you should:

1. Be able to distinguish between wealth and income.
2. Understand the size distribution of income and be able to interpret a Lorenz curve.
3. Be aware of the impact of taxes and transfers on the distribution of income.
4. Understand the principles of horizontal and vertical equity.
5. Be able to distinguish the marginal, nominal, and effective tax rates.
6. Understand the impact of tax "loopholes."
7. Be able to distinguish arguments for equality from arguments for equity.
8. Know the major reforms in the Tax Reform Act of 1986 and the changes in 1990, 1993, and 2001.
9. Be able to distinguish among progressive, regressive, and proportional taxes.
10. Recognize that the most serious potential cost of greater equality would be damaged incentives.
11. Be aware of the arguments for and against the proposed "flat tax."

Using Key Terms

Fill in the puzzle on the opposite page with the appropriate term from the list of Key Terms at the end of the chapter in the text.

Across

4. The percentage change in the quantity supplied divided by the percentage change in tax rates.
7. A tax system in which tax rates rise as incomes rise.
14. Taxes paid divided by total income.
15. Taxes paid divided by taxable income.
16. The proportion of total income received by a particular group.
17. The change in total revenue associated with one additional unit of input.
20. The idea that people with higher incomes should pay more taxes.
21. A tax system in which tax rates fall as incomes rise.

Down

1. The tax rate imposed on the last dollar of income.
2. The way total personal income is divided among households.
3. People with equal incomes should pay equal taxes.
5. Distribution of the real burden of a tax.
6. A graph that contrasts complete equality with the actual distribution of income.
7. Income received by households before taxes.
8. Goods and services received directly, without payment in a market transaction.
9. A mathematical summary of inequality based on the Lorenz curve.
10. A situation in which the market mechanism prevents optimal outcomes.
11. A situation in which government intervention fails to improve market outcomes.
12. A single-rate tax system.
13. Payments to individuals for which no current goods or services are exchanged.
18. The amount of income directly subject to nominal tax rates.
19. The market value of assets.

Puzzle 18.1

True or False: *Circle your choice and explain why any false statements are incorrect.*

T F 1. Marginal tax rates must increase as income increases for a tax to be progressive, *ceteris paribus.*

T F 2. When people believe that the market's answer to the FOR WHOM question is suboptimal, taxes can be used as a policy lever to address the problem.

T F 3. A flat tax rate would take the same dollar amount from each taxpayer.

T F 4. The efficiency issue in taxation refers to the negative impact of higher marginal tax rates on the incentive to produce and work.

T F 5. Fewer workers are employed and the net wage is reduced when a payroll tax is imposed.

T F 6. The nominal tax rate refers to the taxes actually paid as a percentage of total income.

T F 7. Greater income equality has only positive impacts on an economy.

T F 8. The Bush tax cuts (2001-2010) reduced the marginal tax rates which should increase the incentive to work and produce.

T F 9. The federal income tax is a proportional tax.

T F 10. Government failure results when government intervention fails to improve market outcomes.

Multiple Choice: *Select the correct answer.*

_____ 1. The distribution of income is basically the answer to:
(a) The WHAT question for society.
(b) The HOW question for society.
(c) The FOR WHOM question for society.
(d) None of the above.

_____ 2. Which of the following is typically a regressive tax?
(a) A sales tax.
(b) A property tax.
(c) The Social Security tax.
(d) All of the above.

_____ 3. When people believe that the market's answer to the FOR WHOM question is suboptimal:
(a) Market failure exists.
(b) Taxes can be used as a policy to address the problem.
(c) The government has an obligation to change the market outcome.
(d) All of the above are correct.

_____ 4. Suppose that in 2001, Ms. Gonzales had a taxable income of $100,000. Assume that the marginal tax rates are 10% of the first $10,000, 20% of the income in excess of $10,000 up to $60,000, and 30% of any income over $60,000. Ms. Gonzales' tax bill was:
(a) $23,000.
(b) $18,000.
(c) $10,000.
(d) $30,000.

_____ 5. If income is distributed unequally, the:
(a) Lorenz curve would be a straight line.
(b) Line of equality sags below the Lorenz curve.
(c) Lorenz curve sags below the line of equality.
(d) Gini coefficient would be greater than zero.

_____ 6. The U.S. tax system results in a slight reduction in inequality of after-tax income because:
(a) Of the progressive nature of state and local taxes.
(b) Of the progressive nature of the federal income tax.
(c) The rich have fewer available loopholes than the poor.
(d) The poor receive such generous welfare benefits.

_____ 7. Government attempts to create a more equitable income distribution by increasing marginal tax rates may:
(a) Reduce output.
(b) Increase unemployment.
(c) Reduce government tax receipts.
(d) All of the above.

_____ 8. The argument *in favor* of greater equality of income distribution in the United States hinges on:
(a) The idea that greater equality does not affect incentives.
(b) The idea that low-income earners would be more willing and able participants in the economy if income were distributed more equally.
(c) The idea that those with high incomes wield greater political power and strengthen the democratic process.
(d) All of the above.

_____ 9. In making comparisons of income among countries, care must be exercised because:
(a) In poor countries much of what is produced does not pass through markets and thus does not get counted in the nation's income.
(b) In countries such as Sweden and Great Britain, the government provides more goods and services directly than in the United States.
(c) In-kind benefits should be included in real income in all countries.
(d) All of the above are true.

_____ 10. The tax elasticity of labor supply measures the:
(a) Response of workers to a change in the tax rate.
(b) Response of workers to a change in prices.
(c) Change in the amount of taxes workers must pay when tax rates change.
(d) Response of employers to a change in the tax rate.

Use the following information to answer questions 11-12. The tax schedule is hypothetical to keep the calculations simple.

Suppose an individual has total income of $150,000, has taxable income of $100,000, and pays taxes of $10,000.

_____ 11. This individual's __________ tax rate is 6.7 percent.
(a) Effective.
(b) Nominal.
(c) Marginal.
(d) Incidence.

_____ 12. This individual's __________ tax rate is 10 percent.
(a) Marginal.
(b) Effective.
(c) Nominal.
(d) Incidence.

_____ 13. The principle of taxation that says people with equal incomes should pay equal taxes is called:
(a) Vertical equity.
(b) Horizontal equity.
(c) Progressive.
(d) Regressive.

_____ 14. Transfer payments are an appropriate mechanism for correcting:
(a) Market power.
(b) Government failure.
(c) Natural monopoly.
(d) Inequity.

_____ 15. Food stamps, public housing, and subsidized public education are examples of:
(a) Free goods.
(b) "In-kind" benefits or income.
(c) Tax expenditures.
(d) Money incomes.

_____ 16. If the tax elasticity of supply is negative 0.7 and tax rates increase by 21 percent, the quantity of labor supplied would:
(a) Increase by 14.7 percent.
(b) Decrease by 14.7 percent.
(c) Increase by 30 percent.
(d) Decrease by 30 percent.

_____ 17. The flat tax:
(a) Reduces the government's ability to alter the mix of output.
(b) Encourages economic activity through deductions and credits.
(c) Includes many tax brackets.
(d) All of the above.

_____ 18. By instituting a sales tax, a tax plan would:
(a) Be more progressive since it takes a larger fraction of income as income falls.
(b) Increase horizontal equity.
(c) Increase vertical equity.
(d) Shift the Lorenz curve for after-tax income away from the line of equality.

_____ 19. A tax is progressive if it takes a:
(a) Larger number of dollars as income rises.
(b) Larger number of dollars as income falls.
(c) Smaller fraction of income as income falls.
(d) Smaller fraction of income as income rises.

_____ 20. New loopholes in the personal income tax law tend to:
(a) Make the system more regressive.
(b) Increase horizontal equity.
(c) Increase the tax base.
(d) All of the above.

Problems and Applications

Exercise 1

This exercise will help you understand the Lorenz curve.

1. Complete column 3 in Table 18.1 using the data from column 2. Then draw a Lorenz curve based on column 3 in Figure 18.1.

Table 18.1
Size distribution of personal income, by household income group

(1) Quintile of income recipients (households)	*(2) Percent of total household income received*	*(3) Percent of income received (cumulative)*
Lowest fifth	3.8%	______%
Second fifth	9.6	______
Third fifth	16.0	______
Fourth fifth	24.2	______
Highest fifth	46.3	______

Figure 18.1
Lorenz curve

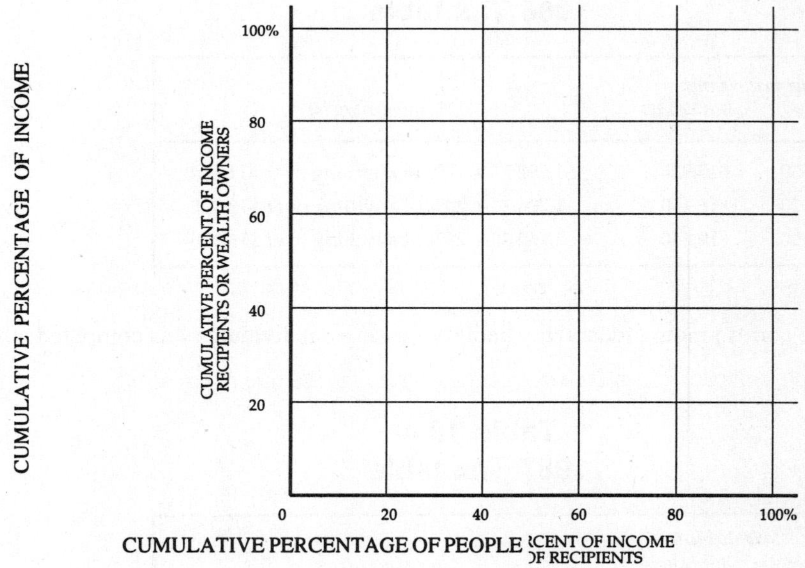

2. According to the information given in Table 18.1, income was distributed (equally, unequally).

3. Draw the line of absolute equality in Figure 18.1 and label it. Shade in the area between the Lorenz curve and the line of equality. The shaded area is a measure of the degree of ________ .

4. In Figure 18.1 draw a second Lorenz curve that indicates the distribution of wealth for the same year. Use the hypothetical data from Table 18.2. Calculate column 3 first.

Table 18.2
Size distribution of wealth, by wealth-holding group

(1) *Quintile of wealth owners*	(2) *Wealth owned*	(3) *Wealth owned (cumulative)*
Lowest fifth	0.5%	________%
Second fifth	5.0	________
Third fifth	12.0	________
Fourth fifth	20.0	________
Highest fifth	62.5	________

5. Although the data in Table 18.2 are hypothetical, they do actually indicate the direction of inequality of wealth ownership relative to the distribution of income. Wealth is (more, less) equally distributed than income.

Exercise 2

This exercise will use the tax reform legislation for the 1987 tax year to show how to determine the impact of a tax change on vertical and horizontal equity.

For the 1986 tax year the federal tax liability for single individuals was computed on the basis of the schedule shown in Table 18.3.

Table 18.3
1986 Tax table

If your taxable income *Is above:*	*But below:*	*Then your tax is:*
$11,650	$13,920	$1,297.70 + 18% of anything over $11,650
13,920	16,190	1,706.30 + 20% of anything over $13,920
16,190	19,640	2,160.30 + 23% of anything over $16,190

For the 1987 tax year the corresponding federal tax liability for single individuals was computed with the schedule found in Table 18.4.

Table 18.4
1987 Tax table

If your taxable income *Is above:*	*But below:*	*Then your tax is:*
$ 1,800	$16,800	$ 198.00 + 15% of anything over $ 1,800
16,800	27,000	2,448.00 + 28% of anything over $16,800

1. What would the marginal tax rates be for a single taxpayer with a taxable income of $17,000 in 1986? __________ In 1987? __________ On the basis of this information, does it appear that the tax reform of the Reagan administration increased work incentives for single taxpayers with a taxable income of $17,000? __________

2. For the three taxpayers listed in Table 18.5, compute the taxable income, taxes in the years 1986 and 1987, and difference in taxes for the two years.

Table 18.5
Taxable income and tax computations

Taxpayer	*Gross income*	*Exemptions and deductions*	*Taxable income*	*1986 Tax*	*1987 Tax*	*Difference*
1	$30,000	$18,000	$_____	$_____	$_____	$_____
2	30,000	13,000	_____	_____	_____	_____
3	50,000	38,000	_____	_____	_____	_____

3. On the basis of Table 18.5 did the tax reform package lower taxes for single taxpayers in the taxable income range of $12,000 to $17,000? __________

4. In Table 18.6 rank each taxpayer on the basis of the effective tax rate. Then complete the table by filling in the nominal, effective, and marginal tax rates for each taxpayer.

Table 18.6
Rankings for 1987

Rank	*Tax payer*	*Nominal tax rate*	*Effective tax rate*	*Marginal tax rate*
1	_____ (highest)	_______%	_______%	_______%
2	_____ (middle)	_______	_______	_______
3	_____ (lowest)	_______	_______	_______

5. How should horizontal equity be determined?
   (a) The two taxpayers with the same nominal incomes should be compared for their marginal tax rates.
   (b) The two taxpayers with the same nominal incomes should be compared for their effective tax rates.
   (c) The effective tax rate of the taxpayer with the highest nominal income should be compared with the effective tax rates of taxpayers with lower nominal incomes.
   (d) The marginal tax rate of the taxpayer with the highest nominal income should be compared with the marginal tax rates of taxpayers with lower nominal incomes.

6. How should vertical equity be determined?
   (a) The two taxpayers with the same nominal incomes should be compared for their marginal tax rates.
   (b) The two taxpayers with the same nominal incomes should be compared for their effective tax rates.
   (c) The effective tax rates of the taxpayer with the highest nominal income should be compared with the effective tax rates of taxpayers with lower nominal incomes.
   (d) The marginal tax rate of the taxpayer with the highest nominal income should be compared with the marginal tax rates of taxpayers with lower nominal incomes.

7. T F For single taxpayers with taxable incomes between $12,000 and $17,000, the tax-reform package reduced vertical equity from 1986 to 1987. (See last column in Table 18.5)

Exercise 3

Around April 15 of every year many articles appear which discuss changes in the tax laws from the previous year. This exercise will use one of the cartoons in the text to show the kind of information to look for to identify and classify changes in the tax system.

Look at the cartoon on page 387 in the text. Then answer the following questions.

1. What word indicates a change in policy has occurred or has been proposed?_______________

2. What three words indicate a change in horizontal or vertical equity resulting from the change?

   ____

3. The change in equity indicated in the article concerns:
   (a) Vertical equity.
   (b) Horizontal equity.

Common Errors

The first statement in each "common error" below is incorrect. Each incorrect statement is followed by a corrected version and an explanation.

1. Income and wealth are the same thing. WRONG!

   Income and wealth mean distinctly different things. RIGHT!

   The distinction between income and wealth is critical to sound economic analysis. Income is a flow and has a time dimension. For example, one states one's income in dollars *per year.* Wealth is a stock and is measured at a point in time; for example, you may say you have $5,000 in your savings account *today.* Some people with apparently great wealth may have very little income, as in the case of someone who owns land known to contain oil. On the other hand, someone who has much income may have little wealth; some famous entertainers earn large incomes, save little (accumulate no wealth), and wind up in bankruptcy. Of course, wealth and income may go hand in hand: the incomes of some oil magnates flow *from* their wealth. But clearly the two terms imply different things about one's economic well-being and command over goods and services.

2. Equity and equality of income distribution mean the same thing. WRONG!

   Equity and equality of income distribution mean different things. RIGHT!

   Many arguments over the division of the income pie, whether at the national level, the corporate level, or the university level, are laced with the terms "equity" and "equality" used interchangeably. They are *not* interchangeable. Equality of income distribution means that each person has an equal share. Equity of income distribution implies something about fairness. In a free society some will surely be more productive than others at doing what society wants done. The brain surgeon's services have greater value than the hairdresser's. The surgeon's income will exceed that of the hairdresser—that is, they'll be unequal. But is that inequitable? This is a matter of judgment. It's safe to say, however, that if one were not allowed to keep some of the rewards for being more productive than average, our economy would suffer. An equitable distribution of income in our society will require some inequality. How much? There is no sure answer to that question, only a series of compromises.

•ANSWERS•

Using Key Terms

Across

4. tax elasticity of supply
7. progressive tax
14. effective tax rate
15. nominal tax rate
16. income share
17. marginal revenue product
20. vertical equity
21. regressive tax

Down

1. marginal tax rate
2. size distribution of income
3. horizontal equity
5. tax incidence
6. Lorenz curve
7. personal income
8. in-kind income
9. Gini coefficient
10. market failure
11. government failure
12. flat tax
13. income transfers
18. tax base
19. wealth

True or False

1. T
2. T
3. F A flat tax takes the same percentage of income from each taxpayer.
4. T
5. T
6. F The nominal tax rate refers to the taxes actually paid as a percentage of taxable income.
7. F Greater income equality can have negative impacts on work incentives and efficiency.
8. T
9. F The federal income tax is a progressive tax.
10. T

Multiple Choice

1. c	5. c	9. d	13. b	17. a
2. d	6. b	10. a	14. d	18. d
3. d	7. d	11. a	15. b	19. c
4. a	8. b	12. c	16. b	20. a

Problems and Applications

Exercise 1

1. **Table 18.1 Answer**

(1) *Quintile of income recipients (households)*	*(3)* *Percent of income received (cumulative)*
Lowest fifth	3.8%
Second fifth	13.4
Third fifth	29.4
Fourth fifth	53.6
Highest fifth	99.9

See Figure 18.1 Answer.

Figure 18.1 Answer

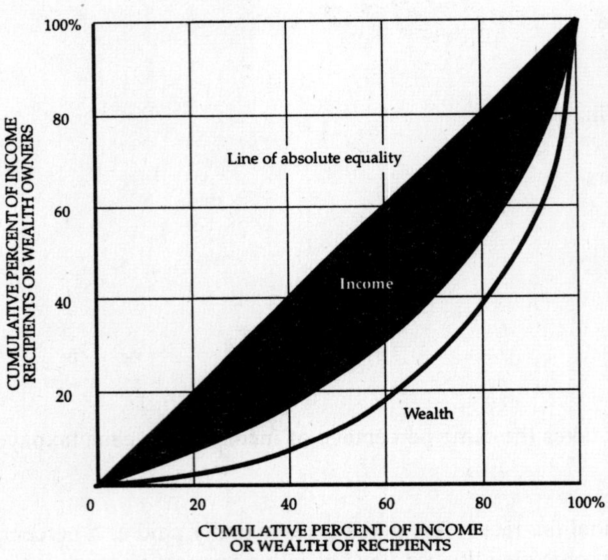

2. Unequally
3. See line of absolute equality and shaded area in Figure 18.1 Answer; inequality.

4. **Table 18.2 Answer**

(1) Quintile of wealth owners	(3) Wealth owned (cumulative)
Lowest fifth	0.5%
Second fifth	5.5
Third fifth	17.5
Fourth fifth	37.5
Highest fifth	100.0

See Figure 18.1 Answer.

5. Less

Exercise 2

1. 23 percent for 1986 (the percentage used in the formula is the marginal tax rate); 28 percent for 1987; no

2. **Table 18.5 Answer**

Taxpayer	Taxable income	1986 Tax	1987 Tax	Difference
1	$12,000	$1,360.70	$1,728	$367.30
2	17,000	2,346.60	2,504	157.40
3	12,000	1,360.70	1,728	367.30

3. No

4. **Table 18.6 Answer**

Rank	Tax payer	Nominal tax rate	Effective tax rate	Marginal tax rate
1	2	14.7% (=2,504/17,000)	8.4% (=2,504/30,000)	28%
2	1	14.4% (=1,728/12,000)	5.8% (=1,728/30,000)	15
3	3	14.4% (=1,728/12,000)	3.5% (=1,728/50,000)	15

5. b
6. c
7. T The difference in total taxes paid was greater at a $12,000 taxable income than it was at a $17,000 taxable income, as shown in the last column of Table 18.5 Answer.

Exercise 3

1. "it," when referring to some generic policy that has changed
2. "favors the rich"
3. a

CHAPTER 19

Transfer Payments: Welfare and Social Security

Quick Review

- Approximately half of every U.S. tax dollar is spent on income transfers, payments for which no current goods or services are exchanged. Most of the transfer payments received by poor families are in the form of "in-kind" transfers such as food stamps, medical aid, and housing assistance. Other transfer payments, such as Social Security, are cash transfers.

- Welfare programs are means-tested and require some type of income eligibility test, while social insurance programs offer event-conditioned benefits. They insure people against events such as old age or unemployment.

- All income transfers result in a redistribution of income, but not all income transfers go to the poor.

- Welfare benefits perpetuate dependence, since they do not increase human capital or job opportunities, and welfare benefits may *worsen* the poverty problem by discouraging recipients from working. Because of how welfare benefits are calculated, a person might be worse off if he or she enters into the labor market.

- Modifications of existing programs have taken this into account by adjusting the marginal tax rate on earned income. The basic problem is that low marginal tax rates encourage more work effort, but make more people eligible for welfare. High marginal tax rates discourage work effort, but make fewer people eligible for welfare.

- The Social Security program faces the same work disincentives as the welfare program. The program provides income for older people who do not work, but it imposes high marginal tax rates on those who do work. Because of the way the program is designed, people retire earlier than they would otherwise. The result is a decrease in total output for the economy.

- The economic issue with Social Security has to do with costs versus benefits. If the work test was eliminated, the economic cost of the Social Security program could be reduced. This would do away with the work disincentive and total output would increase. Others say Social Security should operate like a private retirement plan where people make a contribution to their own pension plan.

Learning Objectives

After reading Chapter 19 and doing the following exercises, you should:

1. Know the impact of transfer payments in the United States.
2. Be able to distinguish between cash transfers and "in-kind" transfers.
3. Understand the role of human capital and derived demand in the poverty dilemma.
4. Know what the basic government welfare programs are, which level of government administers them, and who is eligible for the various programs.
5. Be able to describe the work disincentive that results from the welfare program and Social Security.
6. Understand how welfare eligibility changes as income increases.
7. Be able to describe how a welfare recipient's real income changes as money income increases.
8. Know some of the recent initiatives to reform the welfare system and Social Security.

Using Key Terms

Fill in the puzzle on the opposite page with the appropriate term from the list of Key Terms at the end of the chapter in the text.

Across

1. The income level at which welfare eligibility ceases.
10. The percentage of income transfers that goes to the intended recipients and purposes.
11. An incentive to engage in undesirable behavior.
12. Payment to individuals for which no good or service is exchanged.
13. Means-tested income transfer programs.
14. The percentage of base wages paid out in benefits is the _______ _______ rate.

Down

2. The _______ _______ _______ _______ is the percentage of the working-age population working or seeking employment.
3. Income transfers of direct cash payments.
4. The tax rate imposed on the last dollar of income.
5. Direct transfers of goods and services rather than cash.
6. Occurs when the market mechanism results in a suboptimal outcome.
7. The willingness and ability to work specific amounts of time at alternative wage rates.
8. The shortfall between actual income and the poverty threshold.
9. Programs that provide event-conditioned income transfers.
10. The percentage change in quantity of labor supplied divided by the percentage change in tax rates is the _______ _______ of labor supply.

Puzzle 19.1

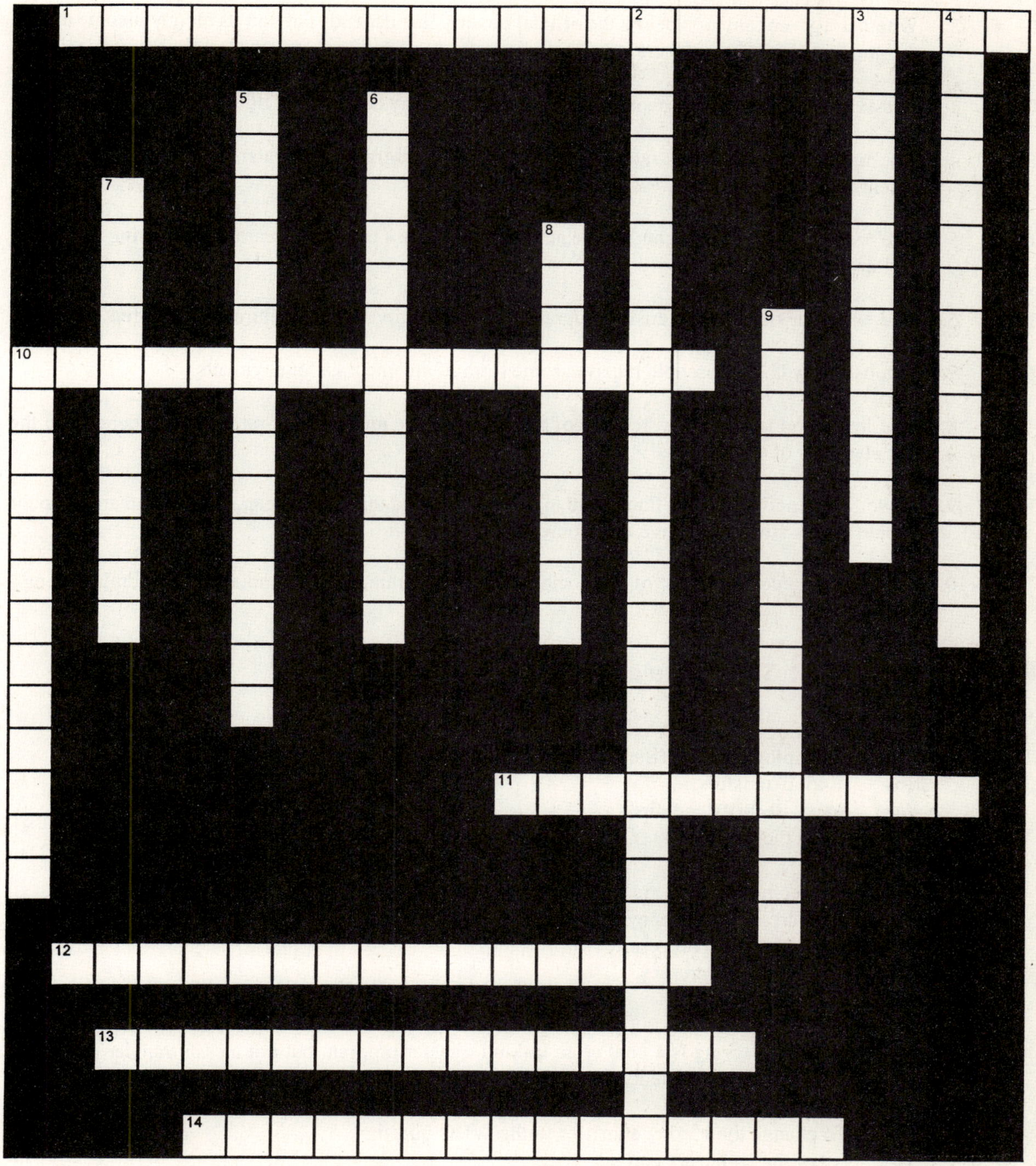

True or False: *Circle your choice and explain why any false statements are incorrect.*

T F 1. The Social Security payments received by retired persons are an in-kind transfer payment.

T F 2. Whether a given family is below the official poverty line depends only on its money income and the number of family members.

T F 3. The availability of welfare benefits shifts the labor supply curve to the right.

T F 4. The higher the marginal tax rate of any given welfare program, the greater the damage to the work incentives of recipients, *ceteris paribus*.

T F 5. The break-even level of income is the amount of income a person can earn before losing all welfare benefits.

T F 6. The existence of income transfer programs suggests a government failure has occurred.

T F 7. Almost every U.S. household receives some form of income transfer payments.

T F 8. The impact on labor supply because of a decrease in the marginal tax rate does not depend on the tax elasticity of supply.

T F 9. If welfare benefits for each household in poverty equaled the poverty gap, people who are not poor would have a strong incentive to become poor.

T F 10. The primary economic cost of the Social Security program is the financial cost of administering the program.

Multiple Choice: *Select the correct answer.*

_____ 1. Transfer payments include:
- (a) Unemployment benefits for the unemployed.
- (b) In-kind transfers.
- (c) Social Security benefits.
- (d) All of the above.

_____ 2. Increased income transfers are undesirable because:
- (a) They create dependency.
- (b) Work disincentives result.
- (c) Total output decreases.
- (d) All of the above.

_____ 3. Which of the following is a goal of an in-kind transfer program but not a cash transfer program?
- (a) To insure that recipients get the type of aid intended.
- (b) Equity.
- (c) To change the market's answer to the WHO question.
- (d) All of the above are correct.

_____ 4. Medicaid and food stamps are received by:
- (a) Anyone who applies.
- (b) Only the elderly.
- (c) Only the poor.
- (d) Mostly upper income households in the U.S. due to inequities in the system.

_____ 5. Social insurance programs:
- (a) Are event conditional.
- (b) Insure people against specific problems, e.g. unemployment.
- (c) Are not welfare programs.
- (d) All of the above are correct.

_____ 6. Income-transfer programs can:
- (a) Change the answer to the WHAT to produce question.
- (b) Change the answer to the FOR WHOM to produce question.
- (c) Result in reduced output.
- (d) All of the above are correct.

_____ 7. If welfare benefits for each household in poverty equaled the poverty gap:
- (a) The effective marginal tax rate for welfare recipients would be 100 percent.
- (b) People who are not poor would have a strong incentive to become poor.
- (c) Poverty would be eliminated.
- (d) All of the above would occur.

_____ 8. Suppose a poverty program provides a basic benefit of $3,000, and a marginal tax rate of 0.50. The break-even level of income is:
- (a) $6,000.
- (b) $1,500.
- (c) $4,500.
- (d) $9,000.

_____ 9. The official poverty index is based on:
- (a) Family size.
- (b) Cash income.
- (c) Age of the household head.
- (d) All of the above.

_____ 10. A good reason for excluding in-kind transfers from income calculations is:
- (a) That the more poor there are, the more jobs there will be for bureaucrats.
- (b) That people would be forced above the poverty line by consuming things like medical services.
- (c) That it is impossible to place a value on most of the services provided.
- (d) All of the above.

Use the following welfare benefit formula to answer the following questions.
Welfare Benefit = Maximum benefit - 0.60 [Wages - (work expenses + child care costs)]

_____ 11. Based on the information given above, the marginal tax rate is:
- (a) Zero percent.
- (b) 0.40 percent.
- (c) 0.60 percent.
- (d) 100 percent.

_____ 12. Suppose that Mr. Henry works 1200 hours per year at a wage of $8 per hour, has child care expenses of $1600 per year and work expenses of $1400. If Mr. Henry's state has a maximum welfare benefit of $8000 per year, based on the welfare formula given above, Mr. Henry's welfare benefit will be:
- (a) Zero. His income has exceeded the limit.
- (b) $4,040.
- (c) $1,400.
- (d) $6,600.

_____ 13. Social security benefits paid by the federal government:
- (a) Are income transfers financed by taxes on workers and employers.
- (b) Are classified as in-kind benefits.
- (c) Have no effect on the decision regarding for whom output is to be produced.
- (d) All of the above.

_____ 14. Which of the following programs does *not* provide in-kind benefits?
- (a) The food stamp program.
- (b) The housing assistance program.
- (c) Temporary Aid to Needy Families (TANF).
- (d) Medicaid.

_____ 15. When authorities choose to "disregard" income earned by welfare recipients, they are:
- (a) Intentionally helping the welfare recipient cheat.
- (b) Attempting to improve work incentives.
- (c) Looking out for their own jobs because the more income they disregard, the more poor there will be.
- (d) Being arbitrary in their administration of the program.

_____ 16. Higher marginal tax rates in welfare programs will:
- (a) Decrease the incentive to work.
- (b) Decrease total welfare costs.
- (c) Reduce the number of people on welfare.
- (d) Do all of the above.

_____ 17. The Social Security program tends to:
- (a) Increase work incentives for both older and younger workers.
- (b) Increase work incentives for older workers but not younger workers.
- (c) Decrease work incentives for both older and younger workers.
- (d) Decrease work incentives for older workers but not younger workers.

_____ 18. If the Social Security program is privatized:
- (a) Work disincentives for younger workers will be reduced.
- (b) Income inequalities would increase.
- (c) Another kind of public transfer program may have to be implemented for those elderly who made bad investments.
- (d) All of the above could occur.

_____ 19. The primary economic cost of the Social Security program is the:
- (a) Financial costs of administering the program.
- (b) Reduction in total output the program causes because of work disincentives.
- (c) Redistribution of income from younger to older workers.
- (d) Benefits paid.

_____ 20. The primary benefit of the Social Security program is the:
- (a) Increased work incentives for older workers.
- (b) More equitable distribution of income that results.
- (c) Jobs created by the additional spending.
- (d) All of the above are benefits.

Problems and Applications

Exercise 1

This exercise examines welfare benefits and the marginal tax rate on benefits.

Assume the welfare benefit is calculated as:

Benefit = maximum benefit - wages

1. Every additional dollar of wages (increases, reduces) welfare benefits by the same amount.

2. T F In this case there is a disincentive to work because the marginal tax rate is 100 percent.

3. Now assume the welfare benefit formula changes to:

   Benefit = maximum benefit - 0.4(wages)

   What is the marginal tax rate? _____________

4. A decrease in the marginal tax rate will encourage (more, less) work effort and make (more, fewer) people eligible for welfare.

5. Use the formula in question 3. Assume the maximum benefit is $12,000. If a welfare recipient earns $5,000 in a part-time job, his or her total income will be _______________.

6. The break-even level of income is the amount of income a person can earn before losing (some, all) welfare benefits.

7. The break-even level of income in question 5 is _______________.

Exercise 2

This exercise focuses on the Social Security program.

1. The Social Security program is a __________ transfer program because it sends checks to recipients.

2. T F The primary economic cost of the Social Security program is benefits it pays to retired workers.

3. Assume a person is entitled to a maximum award of $12,000 in Social Security benefits. But this person continues to work upon reaching retirement age and earns $10,000 per year. Given the following benefit formula:

   Benefit amount = maximum award - 0.60(wage - $6000)

   What is the Social Security benefit for this individual? _______________

4. What is the total income for this individual? _______________

Common Errors

The first statement in each "common error" below is incorrect. Each incorrect statement is followed by a corrected version and an explanation.

1. The federal government runs the welfare system. WRONG!

   The welfare system consists of programs administered by federal, state, and local governments. RIGHT!

   It's true that the federal government is heavily involved in the welfare system, but state and local governments are involved as well. As a matter of fact, the benefits that a poor person may receive vary from state to state. The differentials in benefits have been the reason for the migration of some poor people from low-benefit states to high-benefit states. The federal government is trying to reduce its role in this area, however.

2. Welfare recipients are typically minority families headed by able-bodied males. WRONG!

   There is no average welfare recipient. RIGHT!

   The stereotype of the welfare recipient seems firmly entrenched in the minds of American taxpayers. The poor are a very heterogeneous group, however, with many more whites than minority-group members. Most work when they can find employment. Some work all year long and are still poor.

•ANSWERS•

Using Key Terms

Across

1. break-even level of income
10. target efficiency
11. moral hazard
12. transfer payment
13. welfare programs
14. wage replacement

Down

2. labor force participation rate
3. cash transfers
4. marginal tax rate
5. in-kind transfers
6. market failure
7. labor supply
8. poverty gap
9. social insurance
10. tax elasticity

True or False

1. F They are a cash transfer payment.
2. T
3. F The availability of welfare benefits reduces the incentive to work, thus shifting the labor supply curve to the left.
4. T
5. T
6. F The existence of income transfer programs suggests that market failure has occurred. The program is intended to help correct the market failure.
7. T
8. F Whether a person chooses to work more hours due to a decrease in the marginal tax rate depends to a large extent on the tax elasticity of supply.
9. T
10. F The primary economic cost of the Social Security program is the reduction in total output the program causes because of work disincentives.

Multiple Choice

1.	d	5.	d	9.	d	13.	a	17.	c
2.	d	6.	d	10.	b	14.	c	18.	d
3.	a	7.	d	11.	c	15.	b	19.	b
4.	c	8.	a	12.	b	16.	d	20.	b

Problems and Applications

Exercise 1

1. Reduces
2. T
3. 40 percent
4. More, more
5. \$12,000 - 0.4(\$5,000) = \$12,000 - \$2000 = \$10,000 \$10,000 + \$5,000 = \$15,000
6. All
7. \$12,000/0.4 = \$30,000

Exercise 2

1. Cash
2. F The primary economic cost is the decrease in total output because workers retire early.
3. \$12,000 - 0.6(\$10,000 - \$6000) = \$12,000 - 0.6(\$4000) = \$12,000 - \$2400 = \$9600
4. \$10,000 + \$9600 = \$19,600

PART 7 International Economics

CHAPTER 20

International Trade

Quick Review

- The trade balance for any country is the difference between its exports and imports. Since the mid-1970s, the United States has experienced a trade deficit.
- Without trade, each country's consumption possibilities are limited to its production possibilities. With trade, a country may concentrate its resources on the goods it produces relatively efficiently. Trade allows for specialization and increases total world output. For each country, consumption possibilities will exceed production possibilities.
- For trade to be mutually beneficial, each country must exploit its comparative advantage. Comparative advantage is based on relative efficiency in production. If Country A produces a specific good, and in doing so gives up less in terms of other goods than Country B gives up to produce the same good, then Country A has a comparative advantage. Comparative advantage relies on a comparison of relative opportunity costs.
- For trade to be mutually beneficial, the terms of trade—the rate at which one good is exchanged for another—must lie between the opportunity costs for each of the individual countries. The closer the terms of trade are to the slope of a country's production-possibilities curve, the fewer benefits it receives, and vice versa.
- Not everyone benefits from trade. Those involved in import competing industries will object to trade because they may lose jobs to foreign producers. Other arguments against free trade include concerns about national security, dumping, and protection of infant industries. Those engaged in export industries will favor trade because jobs and profits are likely to increase.
- There are several different types of trade barriers. An embargo prohibits the trade of certain goods. Tariffs discourage imports by making the goods more expensive. Quotas set a limit on the quantity of a particular good that may be imported. Nontariff barriers can also restrict trade.
- The World Trade Organization (WTO) polices world trade and looks for trade agreement violations. Regional pacts, such as NAFTA and the EU, are designed to reduce trade barriers.

Learning Objectives

After reading Chapter 20 and doing the following exercises, you should:

1. Know some basic facts about U.S. trade patterns.
2. Understand the macroeconomic impact of international trade.
3. Understand why specialization and trade increase both production possibilities and consumption possibilities.
4. Be able to explain comparative advantage using opportunity costs.
5. Know how to determine the limits to the terms of trade.
6. Be able to calculate the gains from specialization and trade at given terms of trade.
7. Be able to show how trade allows a country to consume beyond its production-possibilities curve.
8. Recognize the sources of pressure that result in restricted trade.
9. Know some of the arguments used by those wishing to restrict trade.
10. Be able to discuss tariff and nontariff barriers to trade.
11. Be able to discuss the reasons for the rise of regional trading arrangements.

Using Key Terms

Fill in the puzzle on the opposite page with the appropriate term from the list of Key Terms at the end of the chapter in the text.

Across

2. Alternative combinations of goods and services that can be produced with available resources and technology.
3. Alternative combinations of goods and services that a country can consume.
5. The ability to produce a good at a lower opportunity cost than another country.
9. A negative trade balance.
11. The sale of goods in export markets at prices below domestic prices.
13. A limit on the quantity of a good that may be imported.
14. The most desired goods and services that are foregone in order to obtain something else.
15. A tax imposed on imported goods.
16. The amount of good A given up for good B in trade.

Down

1. An agreement to reduce the volume of trade in a specific good.
4. Determined by the intersection of market demand and market supply.
6. The ability of a country to produce a good with fewer resources than other countries.
7. A prohibition on exports or imports.
8. The amount by which exports exceed imports.
10. Goods and services sold to foreign buyers.
12. Goods and services purchased from foreign sources.

Puzzle 20.1

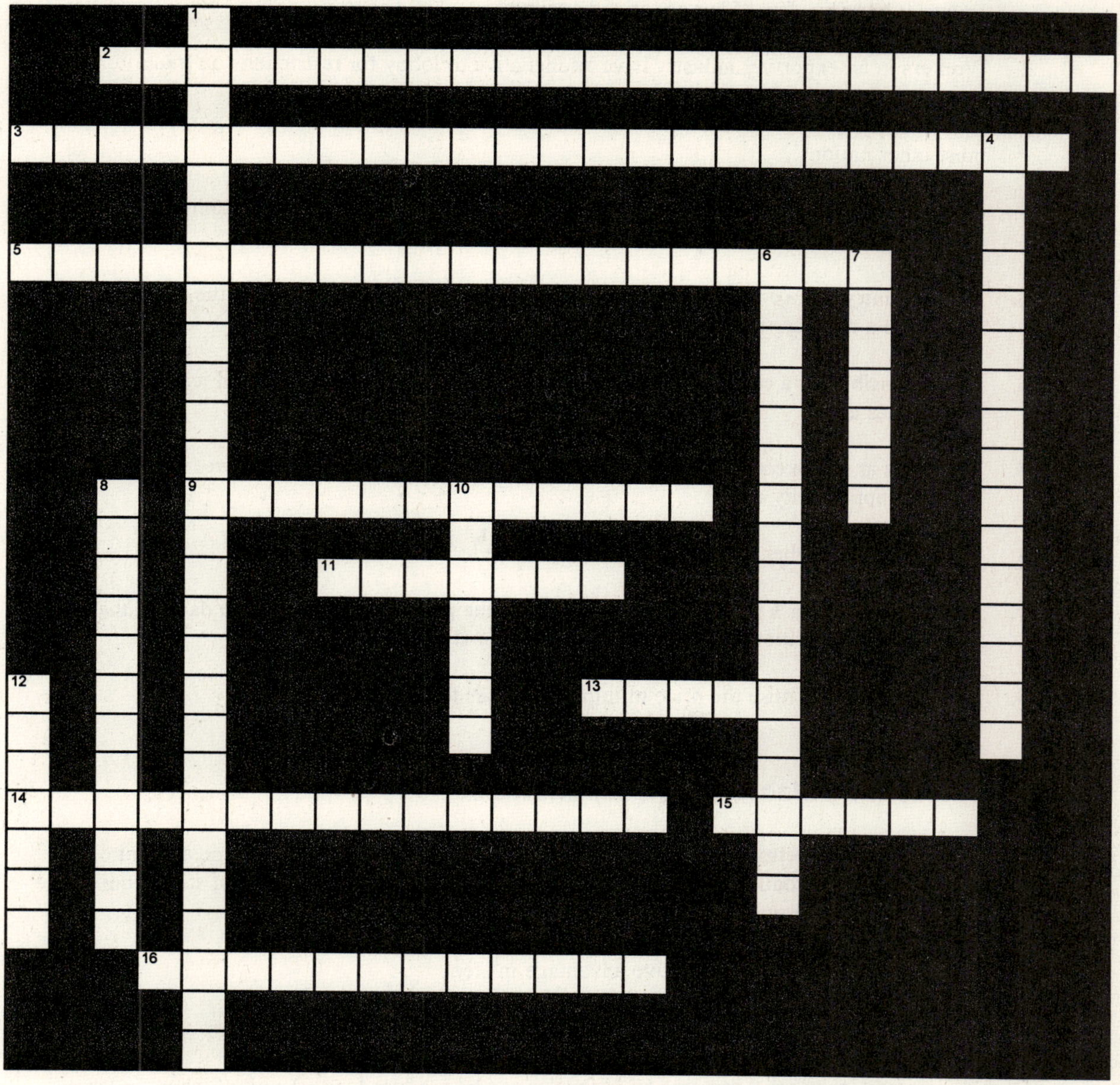

True or False: *Circle your choice and explain why any false statements are incorrect.*

T F 1. The United States buys large quantities of goods and services from other countries but foreign countries buy very few of our goods and services.

T F 2. Workers in an exporting industry have an incentive to lobby for restrictions on trade.

T F 3. The United States relies less on foreign trade, as measured by the ratio of exports to GDP, than most other nations.

T F 4. Comparative advantage refers to the ability to produce output with fewer resources than any other country.

T F 5. If one country has a comparative advantage in producing one of two goods, the other country must have a comparative advantage in the other good.

T F 6. It is impossible for a country to consume a mix of goods and services beyond its production-possibilities curve.

T F 7. The terms at which countries will trade one good for another will occur between their respective domestic opportunity costs.

T F 8. Everybody wins when countries specialize and trade.

T F 9. From the consumer's point of view, quotas have the potential to inflict more damage than do tariffs because additional imports are not available at any price.

T F 10. Tariffs and quotas raise the price of imported goods to consumers.

Multiple Choice: *Select the correct answer.*

_____ 1. Suppose the production of 1 ton of steel in the United States requires the same amount of resources as the production of 100 metric tons of wheat. In Canada, 2 tons of steel requires the same amount of resources as 200 metric tons of wheat. This means that:
(a) Neither country has a comparative advantage.
(b) Canada has the comparative advantage in steel.
(c) The United States has an absolute advantage in steel.
(d) The United States has the comparative advantage in steel.

_____ 2. In Germany, suppose 6 cameras or 4 bicycles can be produced with 1 unit of labor. In Japan, suppose 9 cameras or 5 bicycles can be produced with 1 unit of labor. Therefore:
(a) Japan has an absolute advantage in the production of both goods.
(b) Japan has a comparative advantage in the production of both goods.
(c) Germany has a comparative advantage in the production of cameras.
(d) Japan has a comparative advantage in the production of bicycles.

_____ 3. If a country is completely self-reliant in producing goods for its own consumption needs, then:
(a) It is consuming more than it could with trade.
(b) Its consumption possibilities will equal its production possibilities.
(c) It is promoting specialization.
(d) It will achieve a higher standard of living by exporting.

_____ 4. The expansion of world output as a result of trade is mainly due to the effects of:
(a) Higher trade barriers.
(b) Improved terms of trade.
(c) Specialization according to comparative advantage.
(d) Specialization according to absolute advantage.

_____ 5. When one country can produce a given amount of a good using fewer inputs than any other country:
(a) It has an absolute advantage in producing the good.
(b) It has a comparative advantage in producing the good.
(c) Specialization will definitely increase worldwide consumption possibilities.
(d) All of the above.

_____ 6. "Terms of trade" refers to:
(a) The opportunity costs incurred in trade.
(b) The rate at which goods are exchanged.
(c) The degree to which one country has an absolute advantage.
(d) Which country pays the transportation costs when trade occurs.

_____ 7. To say that a country has a comparative advantage in the production of wine is to say that:
(a) It can produce wine with fewer resources than any other country can.
(b) Its opportunity cost of producing wine is greater than any other country's.
(c) Its opportunity cost of producing wine is lower than any other country's.
(d) The relative price of wine is higher in that country than in any other.

_____ 8. America's tariffs on foreign goods result in:
(a) Lower domestic prices than those that would prevail in their absence.
(b) A stimulus to efficient American firms that are not protected.
(c) Higher employment and output in protected industries than would otherwise be the case.
(d) A more efficient allocation of resources than would occur in their absence.

_____ 9. A principal objective of GATT is to:
(a) Reduce barriers to trade.
(b) Settle domestic tax disputes internationally.
(c) Equalize income tax structures in various countries.
(d) Protect domestic producers from foreign competition.

_____ 10. World output of goods and services increases with specialization because:
(a) The world's resources are being used more efficiently.
(b) Each country's production possibilities curve is shifted outward.
(c) Each country's workers are able to produce more than they could before specialization.
(d) All of the above are correct.

_____ 11. Suppose the production of 12 tons of copper in the United States requires the same amount of resources as the production of 1 ton of aluminum. In Mexico, 12 tons of copper requires the same amount of resources as 2 tons of aluminum. This means that:
(a) Mexico has an absolute advantage in producing copper.
(b) The United States has a comparative advantage in producing copper.
(c) The United States has an absolute advantage in producing aluminum.
(d) All of the above.

Suppose the production possibilities of Japan and the U.S. are given in Table 20.1. Use Table 20.1 to answer questions 12 and 13.

Table 20.1
Output per worker day in the United States and Japan

Country	*TV sets (per day)*	*Bicycles (per day)*
Japan	2	10
United States	1	8

_____ 12. Which of the following statements is true?
(a) The United States has an absolute advantage in the production of bicycles.
(b) Japan has an absolute advantage in the production of bicycles only.
(c) Japan has an absolute advantage in the production of TV sets only.
(d) Japan has an absolute advantage in the production of both bicycles and TV sets.

_____ 13. Suppose the terms of trade are established in such a way that 1 TV set equals 5 bicycles. Which of the following statements would be true?
(a) These terms of trade provide gains for the United States, but Japan is worse off.
(b) These terms of trade provide gains for Japan, but the United States is worse off.
(c) These terms of trade provide gains for the United States, and Japan is no worse off.
(d) These terms of trade provide gains for Japan, and the United States is no worse off.

_____ 14. As a result of specialization and trade, total world output of goods and services:
(a) Decreases along with consumption levels.
(b) Increases along with consumption levels.
(c) Decreases, but consumption levels increase.
(d) Increases, but consumption levels decrease.

_____ 15. "Dumping" is said to occur when:
(a) Foreign producers sell more of a particular good in the United States than domestic producers sell.
(b) Foreign producers sell their goods in the United States at prices lower than the U.S. average cost of production.
(c) Foreign producers sell their goods in the United States at prices lower than those prevailing in their own countries.
(d) The foreign countries have trade surpluses and the United States has a trade deficit.

_____ 16. What should happen to the equilibrium price and quantity in a market as a result of a tariff on imports?
(a) Equilibrium price and quantity should both go up.
(b) Equilibrium price should go up, and equilibrium quantity should go down.
(c) Equilibrium price should go down, and equilibrium quantity should go up.
(d) Equilibrium price and quantity should both go down.

_____ 17. With regard to international trade, the market mechanism:
(a) Provides a profit incentive to producers who specialize in the goods and services for which a comparative advantage exists.
(b) Provides a profit incentive to producers who trade in the goods and services for which a comparative advantage exists.
(c) Determines the terms of trade.
(d) Does all of the above.

_____ 18. International trade:
(a) Lowers prices to consumers.
(b) Alters the mix of domestic production.
(c) Redistributes income toward export industries.
(d) All of the above.

_____ 19. Suppose that Brazil has a comparative advantage in coffee and Mexico has a comparative advantage in tomatoes. Which of the following groups would be worse off if these two countries specialize and trade?
(a) Brazilian tomato producers.
(b) Brazilian coffee producers.
(c) Mexican tomato producers.
(d) Everyone is better off when specialization and trade take place.

_____ 20. If we add together all the gains from specialization and trade and then subtract all the losses, the net result would be:
(a) Zero; the gains and losses would cancel out.
(b) Positive; a net gain for the world and each country.
(c) Negative; a net loss for the world and each country.
(d) Impossible to tell; the net result could be zero, positive, or negative.

Problems and Applications

Exercise 1

This exercise shows how trade leads to gains by all trading partners through specialization and comparative advantage.

Suppose that Japan has 20 laborers in total and that the United States has 40 laborers. Suppose their production possibilities are given in Table 20.2. (*Be careful:* The table tells you that a worker in Japan can produce 2 TV sets per day *or* 10 bicycles per day, *not* two TV sets *and* 10 bicycles!)

Table 20.2
Output per worker day in the United States and Japan

Country	*TV sets (per day)*	*Bicycles (per day)*
Japan	2	10
United States	1	8

1. Draw the production-possibilities curves for each country in Figure 20.1. Assume constant costs of production.

Figure 20.1

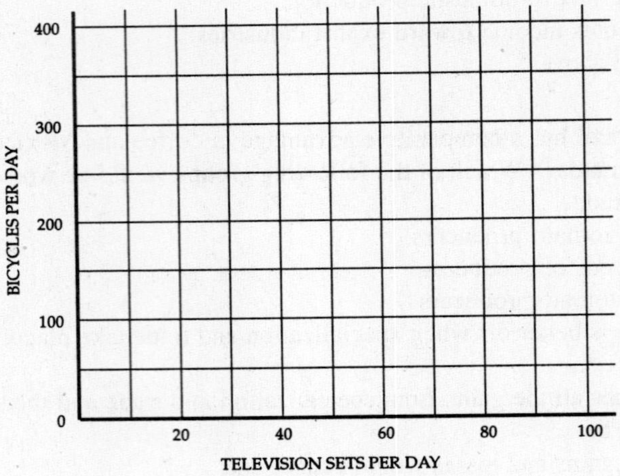

2. Suppose that before trade, Japan uses 12 laborers to produce bicycles and 8 laborers to produce television sets; suppose also that in the United States 20 workers produce bicycles and 20 produce television sets. Complete Table 20.3.

Table 20.3
Output produced and consumed without trade

Country	*TV sets (per day)*	*Bicycles (per day)*
Japan	____	____
United States	____	____
Total	____	____

3. Before trade, the total output of television sets is __________ ; of bicycles, __________ .

4. What is the opportunity cost of 1 television set in Japan? __________ In the United States? __________

5. What is the opportunity cost of 1 bicycle in Japan? __________ In the United States? __________

6. If Japan and the United States specialize according to their respective comparative advantages, Japan will produce __________ and the United States will produce __________ . They will do so because the opportunity cost of bicycles in terms of television sets is (lower, higher) in the United States than in Japan, and the opportunity cost of television sets in terms of bicycles is (lower, higher) in Japan than in the United States.

7. After specialization, the total output of television sets is __________ and the total output of bicycles is __________ . (*Hint:* Assume 20 Japanese produce only TV sets, and 40 Americans produce only bicycles.)

8. This output represents an increase of __________ bicycles and __________ television sets over the pre-specialization output. (*Hint:* Compare answers to questions 3 and 7.)

Exercise 2

This exercise will help you understand how the terms of trade are determined. Refer to Exercise 1 for the data.

If Japan and the United States are to benefit from the increased production, trade must take place. The Japanese will be willing to trade television sets for bicycles as long as they get back more bicycles than they could get in their own country.

1. The terms of trade will be between 1 television set equals __________ bicycles and 1 television set equals __________ bicycles.

2. If the terms of trade were 4 bicycles equals one television set:
   (a) Neither country would buy bicycles, but both would buy TV sets.
   (b) Neither country would buy TV sets, but both would buy bicycles.
   (c) Both countries would buy bicycles and TV sets.

3. Suppose that the two countries agree that the terms of trade will be 6 bicycles equals 1 television set. Let Japan export 20 television sets per day to the United States. Complete Table 20.4. Assume that Japan produces 40 television sets per day and the United States produces 320 bicycles.

Table 20.4
Consumption combination after trade

Country	*TV sets (per day)*	*Bicycles (per day)*
Japan	_____	_____
United States	_____	_____
Total	40	320

4. As a result of specialization and trade, the United States has the same quantity of television sets and __________ more bicycles per day. (Compare Tables 20.3 and 20.4.)

5. As a result of specialization and trade, Japan has the same number of bicycles and __________ more television sets per day.

Now suppose that at the exchange rate of 6 bicycles to 1 TV set, Japan would like to export 10 TV sets and import 60 bicycles per day. Suppose also that the United States desires to export 90 bicycles and import 15 television sets per day.

6. At these terms of trade there is a (shortage, surplus) of television sets.

7. At these terms of trade there is a (shortage, surplus) of bicycles.

8. Which of the following terms of trade would be more likely to result from this situation?
   (a) 5 bicycles equal 1 television set.
   (b) 6 bicycles equal 1 television set.
   (c) 7 bicycles equal 1 television set.

Exercise 3

When protection is provided to producers of a particular product, consumers of that product are harmed because they must pay higher prices than in the absence of protection. In addition, the effects of the protection in one market spill over into related factor and product markets, thus distorting both production and consumption patterns. This exercise will help you to discover how this occurs.

Reread the World View article entitled "Sugar Quota a Sour Deal," and then answer the following questions.

1. What was the estimated overall cost to U.S. consumers in 2001 due to the quota on sugar?
____

2. If the U.S. sugar quota was abolished, which of the following would be the most likely equilibrium world price for sugar, *ceteris paribus*?
   (a) 7 cents per pound.
   (b) 15 cents per pound.
   (c) 22 cents per pound.
   (d) 24 cents per pound.

3. If the sugar quota was abolished, what would you predict to happen to the number of sugar producers in the United States?______________________________

4. Suppose the next best use of land used to produce sugar beets in the U.S. was to produce wheat. What would you predict to happen to the price of wheat in the U.S. market, *ceteris paribus*, if the sugar quota was abolished?______________________________

5. If the sugar quota was abolished, what would you predict to happen to the marginal revenue product of labor and the level of employment of labor in the Caribbean sugar industry, *ceteris paribus*?______________________________

Common Errors

The first statement in each "common error" below is incorrect. Each incorrect statement is followed by a corrected version and an explanation.

1. A country must have an *absolute advantage* in order to gain from trade with another country. WRONG!

   A country must have a *comparative advantage* in order to gain from trade with another country. RIGHT!

   Mutually advantageous trade requires only that the opportunity costs of producing goods differ between the two countries, *ceteris paribus*. Another way of stating this is that the production-possibilities curves of the two countries must have different slopes. The two circumstances noted above are indicated in Figure 20.2 below.

Figure 20.2

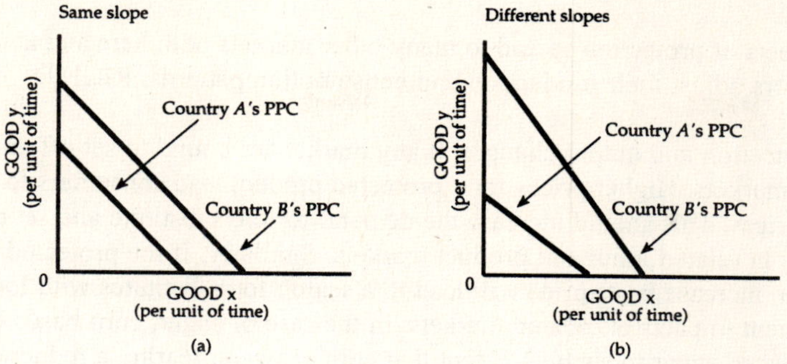

In diagram (a), in which country B has an absolute advantage over country A, the production-possibilities curves have the same slope; thus mutually advantageous trade *is not* possible. In diagram (b), each country has a comparative advantage because the production-possibilities curves of the two countries have different slopes; thus mutually advantageous trade *is* possible.

2. Foreign trade costs a country jobs. WRONG!

   Although jobs may be lost, new ones will be created by the opportunities opened up with trade. RIGHT!

   When countries specialize and trade according to the law of comparative advantage, some particular workers and firms may be hurt by imports, but the economy as a whole gains by trade. More output per resource input will be attainable. Because the economy is able to reach full employment with trade as well as without trade, there is no reason to assume there will be fewer jobs.

3. A country is well off only as long as it exports more than it imports. WRONG!

   Countries may, at times, be well off when they experience a trade surplus; they may also be well off when they have a trade deficit. RIGHT!

   Both trade deficits and trade surpluses can be problems if either situation persists for a long period of time. Trade surpluses mean that a country is giving more of its limited, precious resources in trade than it is acquiring from other countries. The currencies of deficit countries tend to depreciate, which means they will be unable to buy as many foreign goods with a unit of currency.

4. Countries tend to enter into trade to get things they cannot produce themselves. WRONG!

   Countries very often trade for things they could produce themselves. RIGHT!

   Be careful! Countries often trade for things they could produce themselves because the relative costs of domestic production would be prohibitive. Take baskets as an example. Producers in the U.S. could certainly produce baskets if they really wanted to. The technique is not difficult to learn and the materials are abundant. But baskets do not lend themselves to machine production, and hand labor is expensive here. The cost in terms of goods forgone would be tremendous. (So would the price of the baskets.) We're better off specializing in something like computers, where we have a comparative advantage, and trading for baskets, where we clearly do not have a comparative advantage.

5. The effects of protection affect only workers in the protected industry and the domestic consumers of the protected commodity. WRONG!

The effects of protection spread to many other markets both here and abroad as producers and consumers adjust their production and consumption patterns. RIGHT!

Protection and output changes in any market are bound to set off additional changes in related markets. Higher prices for a protected product lead consumers to seek out substitutes with lower prices. This should increase the demand for the substitute and set off a host of other changes in related input and product markets. Similarly, if the protected commodity is used as an input, an increase in its price will lead to a search for substitutes with lower prices and have consequent impacts on related markets. In the case of sugar, corn based high-fructose corn syrup has replaced sugar to such an extent that corn growers, fearing a reduction in the demand for their output, now lobby their congressional delegations to maintain the sugar quota! Similar impacts can be expected in the markets of foreign producers.

•ANSWERS•

Using Key Terms

Across

2. production possibilities
3. consumption possibilities
5. comparative advantage
9. trade deficit
11. dumping
13. quota
14. opportunity cost
15. tariff
16. terms of trade

Down

1. voluntary restraint agreement
4. equilibrium price
6. absolute advantage
7. embargo
8. trade surplus
10. exports
12. imports

True or False

1. F Approximately 11 percent of U.S. GDP is exported. In dollar terms, the U.S. is the world's largest exporter of goods and services.
2. F Workers in an exporting industry typically benefit from trade so they would not lobby for trade restrictions.
3. T
4. F Comparative advantage refers to the ability to produce output at a smaller opportunity cost than another country, i.e., giving up fewer alternative goods and services.
5. T

6. F With specialization and free trade it is possible for a country to consume a mix of goods and services beyond its production-possibilities curve although it is never possible for a country to produce beyond its production-possibilities curve.

7. T

8. F Although countries as a whole benefit from specialization and free trade, there are always individuals and groups that may lose, e.g. import-competing firms.

9. T

10. T

Multiple Choice

1.	a	5.	a	9.	a	13.	c	17.	d
2.	a	6.	b	10.	a	14.	b	18.	d
3.	b	7.	c	11.	b	15.	c	19.	a
4.	c	8.	c	12.	d	16.	b	20.	b

Problems and Applications

Exercise 1

1. **Figure 20.1 Answer**

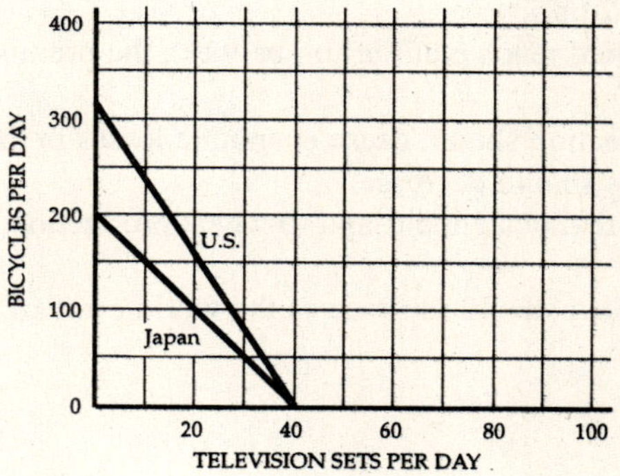

2. **Table 20.3 Answer**

Country	*TV sets*	*Bicycles*
Japan	16	120
United States	20	160
Total	36	280

3. 36; 280
4. 5 bicycles; 8 bicycles
5. 1/5 television set; 1/8 television set
6. Television sets; bicycles; lower; lower
7. 40; 320
8. 40; 4

Exercise 2

1. 5; 8
2. a
3. **Table 20.4 Answer**

Country	*TV sets*	*Bicycles*
Japan	20	120
United States	20	200
Total	40	320

4. 40
5. 4
6. Shortage, The Japanese wish to export fewer (10) TV sets than Americans want to import (15).
7. Surplus, The Americans wish to export more (90) bicycles than the Japanese want to import (60).
8. c The shortage of TV sets will cause their price to increase.

Exercise 3

1. The estimated cost to U.S. consumers due to the price difference between the U.S. market and the world market was $2 billion.
2. b The market should reach equilibrium between the previous world price and the protected U.S. price.
3. The absence of protection should cause economic losses in the U.S. sugar industry and the number of producers should decrease.
4. As sugar producers reallocate their land to wheat production, the market price of wheat should fall.
5. Their marginal product should increase as the world price of sugar rises; the level of employment should increase.

CHAPTER 21

International Finance

Quick Review

- All of the trade between nations must somehow be financed. Since each country has its own money and in order to facilitate trade, markets for foreign exchange have developed.
- When goods are traded between countries, there is an exchange of currency. The exchange rate is the price of one currency in terms of another currency.
- A currency will appreciate or depreciate in value based on the supply and demand for the currency. Factors that shift the foreign exchange supply or demand include changes in relative incomes, relative prices, and interest rates.
- If a nation's currency appreciates, its goods become more expensive for foreigners and it exports less, *ceteris paribus*. The opposite is true if the currency depreciates.
- The balance of payments is an accounting statement of a country's international economic transactions. It is composed of the trade balance, the capital-account balance, and the current-account balance.
- Countries resist exchange rate movements because any change in the exchange rate automatically alters the price of all exports and imports. These changes complicate the conduct of domestic monetary and fiscal policy.
- Under a fixed exchange rate system, the value of a currency does not change because of shifts in the supply or demand for the foreign exchange. In this case balance of payments deficits or surpluses occur because of the excess demand or excess supply of foreign exchange.
- To maintain fixed rates, governments must intervene. Intervention requires a country to accumulate reserves (foreign currencies, gold, etc.) sometimes and to release reserves at other times.
- A flexible exchange rate system does not require government intervention because the exchange rate automatically adjusts to the equilibrium rate. But a totally flexible system can result in many changes. To avoid this problem a system of "managed rates" has evolved in which governments still intervene, but now with the idea of reducing, rather than eliminating, fluctuations.

Learning Objectives

After reading Chapter 21 and doing the following exercises, you should:

1. Understand that an exchange rate is the price of a currency.
2. Know the forces that operate on the demand side of the foreign exchange market.
3. Know the forces that operate on the supply side of the foreign exchange market.
4. Understand how supply and demand interact to determine the equilibrium exchange rate.
5. Understand the essentials of balance-of-payments accounting.
6. Be able to demonstrate graphically the forces that cause a currency to appreciate or depreciate.
7. Understand why there is resistance to exchange-rate changes.
8. Be able to describe several exchange-rate systems and their consequences.
9. Understand the macroeconomic and microeconomic consequences of exchange-rate movements.
10. Be able to describe a balance-of-payments problem.
11. Be aware of the recent history of currency bailouts.

Using Key Terms

Fill in the puzzle on the opposite page with the appropriate term from the list of Key Terms at the end of the chapter in the text.

Across

2. Places where foreign currencies are bought and sold.
4. The amount by which the quantity demanded exceeds the quantity supplied.
6. A system in which governments intervene in foreign-exchange markets to limit exchange-rate fluctuations.
8. Stocks of gold held by a government to purchase foreign exchange.
9. A rise in the price of a currency relative to another.
10. The price of one currency in terms of another currency.
11. A fall in the price of one currency relative to another.
13. A mechanism for fixing the exchange rate.
14. The price at which the quantity demanded equals the quantity supplied.
15. An excess demand for domestic currency at current exchange rates.

Down

1. An excess demand for foreign currency at current exchange rates.
2. Holdings of foreign exchange by official government agencies.
3. Floating exchange rates.
5. A summary record of a country's international economic transactions.
7. An abrupt depreciation of a currency whose value was fixed or managed by the government.
12. A situation in which the value of imports exceeds the value of exports.

Puzzle 21.1

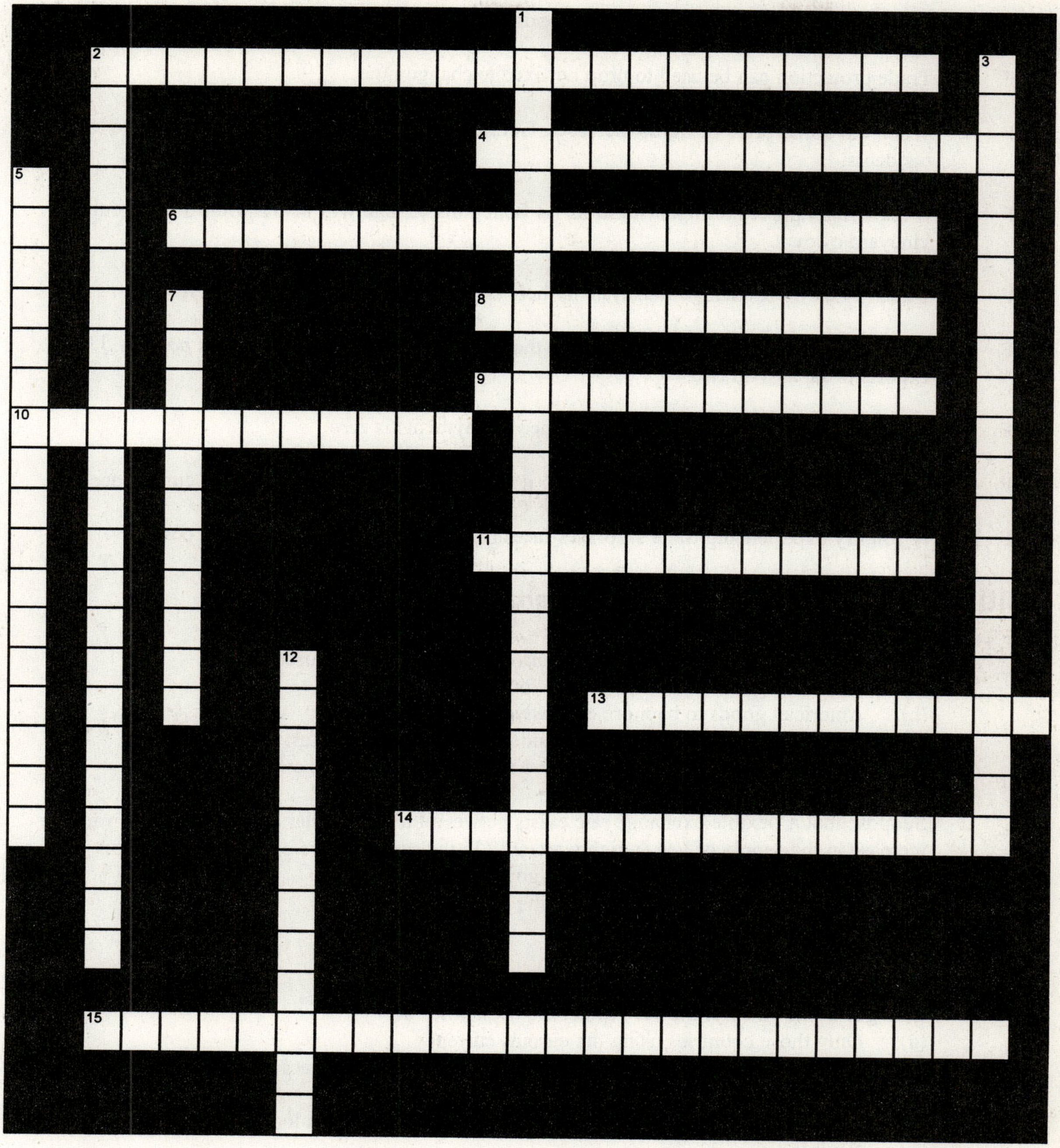

True or False: *Circle your choice and explain why any false statements are incorrect.*

T F 1. The U.S. demand for Swiss francs represents a supply of dollars to the foreign-exchange market.

T F 2. Increased foreign travel by Americans tends to cause the dollar to appreciate, *ceteris paribus*.

T F 3. Trade protection can be used to prop up fixed exchange rates.

T F 4. When the dollar price of Euros increases, German machinery becomes more expensive to U.S. residents.

T F 5. If the dollar appreciates against the Swiss franc, this change will be harmful to California vineyard owners.

T F 6. Under a flexible-exchange-rate system, there is no need for foreign-exchange reserves.

T F 7. If the U.S. price level rises more rapidly than the Japanese price level, *ceteris paribus,* U.S. exports to Japan will rise.

T F 8. When exchange rates are fixed, the balance of payments is zero.

T F 9. If there is a deficit in the capital account, it must be offset by a surplus in the current account.

T F 10. A country experiencing trade surpluses faces higher foreign debt and interest costs.

Multiple Choice: *Select the correct answer.*

_____ 1. An increase in the dollar price of other currencies will tend to cause:
- (a) American goods to be cheaper for foreigners.
- (b) American goods to be more expensive for foreigners.
- (c) Foreign goods to be cheaper to residents of the United States.
- (d) Foreign goods to be more expensive to residents of foreign countries.

_____ 2. Suppose that a flexible exchange rate exists between the U.S. dollar and the Japanese yen. An increase in the supply of yen (a rightward shift in the supply curve of yen) will tend to:
- (a) Increase U.S. imports of Japanese goods.
- (b) Push the U.S. balance of trade in the direction of a surplus.
- (c) Lower the yen price of the dollar.
- (d) Raise the dollar price of the yen.

_____ 3. Changes in the value of the euro affect the economies of:
- (a) Only those countries using the euro as currency.
- (b) All European countries but there would no significant impact on countries outside Europe.
- (c) Potentially the entire world.
- (d) There would be no significant impact on any economies as long as exchange rates are flexible.

_____ 4. If the exchange rate between U.S. dollars and Japanese yen changes from $1 = 100 yen to $1 = 90 yen:
- (a) All Japanese producers and consumers will lose.
- (b) U.S. auto producers and autoworkers will lose.
- (c) U.S. consumers of Japanese TV sets will gain.
- (d) Japanese tourists to the U.S. will gain.

_____ 5. A country will experience a reduction in its balance-of-payments deficit, *ceteris paribus,* if:
(a) Its level of GDP rises relative to foreign levels of GDP.
(b) Its prices fall relative to foreign price levels, *ceteris paribus.*
(c) The domestic price of the foreign currency falls.
(d) It lowers its tariffs.

_____ 6. A result of the Asian Crisis of 1997-98 was:
(a) A general increase in the value of the U.S. dollar in relation to Southeast Asian currencies.
(b) A major decrease in the level of U.S. exports to Southeast Asia.
(c) Political unrest in many Southeast Asian countries.
(d) All of the above.

_____ 7. Greater volatility of floating exchange rates results in:
(a) Greater costs because of uncertainty.
(b) Balance-of-payments instability.
(c) Smaller market shortages and surpluses of currencies.
(d) Depletion of foreign reserves.

_____ 8. Which of the following changes will tend to cause a shift in the domestic demand curve for foreign currencies?
(a) Changes in domestic incomes, *ceteris paribus.*
(b) Changes in domestic prices of goods, *ceteris paribus.*
(c) Changes in consumer taste for foreign goods, *ceteris paribus.*
(d) All of the above.

_____ 9. An increase in the U.S. trade deficit could be caused by:
(a) A depreciation of the dollar in terms of other currencies.
(b) An appreciation of the dollar in terms of other currencies.
(c) The imposition of a tariff on imported goods.
(d) An increase in the capital-account deficit.

_____ 10. In a floating-exchange-rate system, the capital-account balance equals:
(a) The negative of the current-account balance.
(b) Foreign purchases of U.S. assets minus U.S. purchases of foreign assets.
(c) The balance of payments minus the sum of the trade balance, the services balance, and unilateral transfers.
(d) All of the above.

_____ 11. American citizens planning a vacation abroad would welcome:
(a) Appreciation of the dollar.
(b) Depreciation of the dollar.
(c) Devaluation of the dollar.
(d) Evaluation of the dollar.

_____ 12. A change in the exchange rate for a country's currency alters the prices of:
(a) Exports only.
(b) Imports only.
(c) Both exports and imports.
(d) Only domestic goods and services.

_____ 13. In a floating exchange-rate regime, the overall "balance" of the balance of payments must be:
(a) Equal to zero.
(b) Positive if exports of goods and services exceed imports of goods and services.
(c) Positive if the capital account is in surplus.
(d) Negative if the current account is in deficit.

_____ 14. When exchange rates are flexible, they are:
(a) Determined by proclamation of the monetary authorities of a country.
(b) Determined by the relative levels of gold reserves.
(c) Permitted to vary with changes in supply and demand in the foreign exchange market.
(d) Determined by the provisions of the Bretton Woods agreement.

_____ 15. If the U.S. dollar depreciates, the United States should experience in the long run, a:
(a) Lower inflation rate.
(b) Smaller deficit on the U.S. trade balance.
(c) Larger deficit on the U.S. current account.
(d) Larger deficit on the U.S. capital account.

_____ 16. The major drawback to a system of managed exchange rates is that:
(a) A country's efforts to manage exchange-rate movements may arouse suspicion and retaliation.
(b) A country's efforts to affect changes in exchange rates are almost totally ineffective.
(c) Government efforts to alter exchange rates usually result in violent disruptions of the domestic economy.
(d) It requires enormous gold reserves.

_____ 17. If French speculators believed the yen was going to appreciate against the dollar, they would:
(a) Purchase francs.
(b) Purchase dollars.
(c) Purchase yen.
(d) Sell yen.

_____ 18. Suppose that at the prevailing yen-dollar exchange rate, there is an excess demand for yen. To prevent the dollar from depreciating, the United States might:
(a) Raise taxes.
(b) Reduce government spending.
(c) Raise interest rates.
(d) Do all of the above.

_____ 19. A currency bailout:
(a) Occurs when an economy is lent money in order to increase or maintain the value of its currency.
(b) Can help avoid a "domino effect" of depreciating currencies in other economies.
(c) Can be ultimately self-defeating because it saves the country receiving the bailout from implementing politically unpopular domestic policies which could have prevented the problem in the first place.
(d) All of the above are correct.

_____ 20. The capital account includes:
(a) Trade in goods.
(b) Foreign purchases of U.S. assets.
(c) Unilateral transfers.
(d) Trade in services.

Problems and Applications

Exercise 1

This exercise provides practice in determining exchange rates.

1. Table 21.1 depicts the hypothetical demand for and supply of British pounds in terms of U.S. dollars. Use the information in Table 21.1 to plot the demand and supply of British pounds at the exchange rates indicated in Figure 21.1. Then answer questions 2-4.

Table 21.1
Monthly demand for and supply of British pounds in the United States

Dollars per British pound	*Quantity demanded*	*Quantity supplied*
4.50	100	700
4.00	200	600
3.50	300	500
3.00	400	400
2.50	500	300
2.00	600	200
1.50	700	100

Figure 21.1
Demand and supply curves for pounds

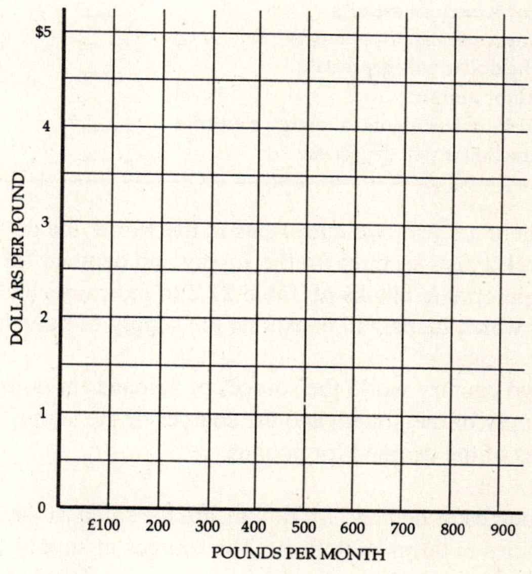

2. What is the equilibrium rate of exchange? __________

3. At a price of $2 per pound there would be excess:
   (a) Demand, and the exchange rate for pounds would rise.
   (b) Demand, and the exchange rate for pounds would fall.
   (c) Supply, and the exchange rate would rise.
   (d) Supply, and the exchange rate would fall.

4. Suppose that Americans suddenly increased their demand for British exports. The dollar price of pounds would (rise, fall).

5. T F Whenever one currency depreciates, another currency must appreciate.

6. As a result of the increased demand for British exports, the pound price of the dollar would (rise, fall).

Exercise 2

This exercise shows why one currency appreciates when another currency depreciates. It also shows why the demand for dollars represents the supply of other currencies, while the supply of dollars represents the demand for other currencies in the foreign-exchange markets. In learning these things, you will get practice in making calculations with exchange rates.

1. Table 21.2 includes the sources of demand and supply of dollars. In the first column, check off the items that are the source of the demand for dollars. In the second column, check off the items that are the source of the supply of dollars. (*Hint*: There are two kinds of speculators—those who think the dollar will rise and those who think it will fall. You must sort the two types of speculators to determine which type will supply dollars and which will demand dollars.)

Table 21.2
Sources of supply and demand for dollars and pounds

	(1) Demand for $	*(2) Supply of $*	*(3) Demand for £*	*(4) Supply of £*
Foreign demand for American exports	___	___	___	___
Foreign demand for American investments	___	___	___	___
Speculation that the dollar will appreciate	___	___	___	___
American demand for imports	___	___	___	___
American demand for investments in foreign countries	___	___	___	___
Speculation that the dollar will depreciate	___	___	___	___

2. If we assume there are just two currencies in the world, the dollar ($) and the pound (£), then the items in Table 21.2 also account for the supply and demand for the pound. Once again place checks in the appropriate blanks of Table 21.2 to indicate which items will constitute the demand for pounds and which items will constitute the supply of pounds.

3. T F In a two country world the sources of demand for dollars are the same as the sources of the supply of the pound, and the sources of the supply of dollars are the same as the sources of the demand for pounds.

4. T F The sources of demand for dollars are the same as the sources of supply for all other currencies in terms of dollars. The sources of supply of dollars are the same as the sources of demand for all other currencies in terms of dollars.

5. Let's return to our assumption that there are only two countries. Use your observations in the previous two questions and your knowledge of converting one currency into another to find the quantities of dollars supplied (column 3) and quantities of dollars demanded (column 6) in Table 21.3. Use the information in Table 21.3, which is the same as the data we used in Exercise 1 above, to compute the supply and demand for pounds.

Table 21.3
Supply and demand for dollars ($) and pounds (£)

(1) *Price of a £ ($ / £)*	(2) *Quantity of £ demanded*	(3) *Quantity of $ supplied*	(4) *Price of a $ (£ / $)*	(5) *Quantity of £ supplied*	(6) *Quantity of $ demanded*
4.50	100	______	______	700	______
4.00	200	______	______	600	______
3.50	300	______	______	500	______
3.00	400	______	______	400	______
2.50	500	______	______	300	______
2.00	600	______	______	200	______
1.50	700	______	______	100	______

6. Complete column 4 of Table 21.3 by converting the price of pounds (£) in terms of dollars ($) in column 1 to the price of dollars in terms of pounds. (*Hint*: They are reciprocals of each other. Remember that to find the price of any good or currency, that good or currency appears in the denominator!)

7. From the data on the demand for the dollar (columns 4 and 6 of Table 21.3), draw the demand curve for the dollar in Figure 21.2. From the data on the supply of the dollar (columns 3 and 4 of Table 21.3), draw the supply curve for the dollar in Figure 21.2.

Figure 21.2
Demand and supply of dollars

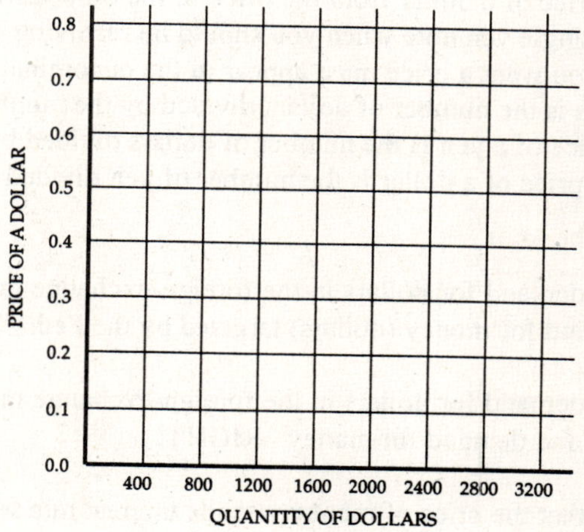

8. The equilibrium value of the dollar is __________ , and the equilibrium quantity of dollars is __________.

9. When you multiply the equilibrium quantity of dollars by the equilibrium exchange rate for the dollar in terms of pounds (£), you find the quantity of pounds is __________. When you find the reciprocal of the equilibrium exchange rate for the dollar, you find the exchange rate for pounds is __________.

10. T F When you multiply the equilibrium quantity of dollars by the equilibrium exchange rate for the dollar in terms of pounds (£), you have calculated the equilibrium quantity of pounds. (Compare your answer to question 9 in this exercise with your answer to question 2, Exercise 1 above.)

11. T F The equilibrium exchange rate for the dollar equals the equilibrium exchange rate for the pound.

Exercise 3

The media often feature articles about international financial issues.

Read the article entitled "Nobel Prize Was Nobler in October." Then answer the following questions.

1. According to the article, what was the dollar value of the Nobel Prize at the time it was announced?______________________________

2. How much was it worth two months later?__________________________

3. Why did the value change so much? ____________________________________

Common Errors

The first statement in each "common error" below is incorrect. Each incorrect statement is followed by a corrected version and an explanation.

1. The price of a dollar in terms of yen is the number of dollars per yen. WRONG!

   The price of a dollar in terms of yen is the number of yen per dollar. RIGHT!

   This mistake can cost a bundle if you are in a foreign country and don't know how to distinguish the price of a dollar from the price of the other currency. In Japan you don't want to give $100 for a single yen note when you should be receiving 100 yen for $1! Remember that the item for which you want a price must appear in the denominator of the price. For example, the price of tomatoes is the number of dollars divided by the number of tomatoes that are purchased. Similarly, the price of a yen is the number of dollars divided by the number of yen that are purchased. The price of a dollar is the number of yen divided by the number of dollars that are purchased.

2. The supply and demand for dollars in the foreign-exchange market is the same thing as the supply and demand for money (dollars) targeted by the Fed. WRONG!

   The supply and demand for dollars in the foreign-exchange market is a totally different concept from the supply and demand for money. RIGHT!

   Remember that the price of money was the interest rate when we were focusing on the supply and demand for money. In the foreign-exchange market the price is the exchange rate, not the interest rate. Furthermore, the supply and demand for money (dollars), which is the focus of the Fed, occurs geographically within the United States. The foreign-exchange market occurs between countries—literally on the phone lines between banks of different countries. We can visualize the foreign-exchange market as an area totally outside of borders in which money temporarily enters for the purpose of being exchanged. While domestic monetary policies may influence the amount of money going into the foreign-exchange market, the link is often indirect. In fact, when the Fed tightens monetary policy to reduce the supply of dollars, the foreign-exchange market may see an *increase* in the supply of dollars as foreigners seek the higher interest rates from a tighter U.S. monetary policy.

3. A country is well off if its currency appreciates steadily over a long period of time. WRONG!

Both appreciating currencies and depreciating currencies create problems. RIGHT!

Be careful! There are problems associated with steadily appreciating currencies *and* with steadily depreciating currencies. People sometimes view a depreciating currency as a source of national shame and dislike the higher cost (and inflation) associated with higher prices of foreign goods. However, depreciation may make a country's exports more competitive, may lead to more jobs, and may help correct a trade deficit. By contrast, a country with an appreciating currency develops employment problems and a loss of competitiveness against other countries, even if it has more buying power as a result of its stronger currency.

4. When countries have trade deficits, money really flows out. When they have surpluses, money really flows in. WRONG!

Money is not physically sent in most transactions, but the claim to ownership is. RIGHT!

Most foreign trade is transacted by check and is just a "flow" of bookkeeping entries. Even when gold is sold, it seldom *physically* flows anywhere. In the case of the United States, under a fixed-exchange-rate system, it stays in Fort Knox even though someone else owns it. Thus, it is the claim to ownership that flows, not the money. When countries run trade deficits, their trading partners add to their claims against them. For countries with a trade surplus, the reverse is true.

5. There are balance-of-payments surpluses and deficits under floating exchange rates. WRONG!

The balance of payments is always zero under floating exchange rates. RIGHT!

Under fixed exchange rates, the government must balance surpluses and deficits on the balance of payments with changes in reserves. With floating exchange rates, there is no reserve currency and any transfers abroad by the government are simply classified as unilateral transfers and are included in the current account. By definition, the current account and the capital account balance each other under a floating exchange-rate system.

•ANSWERS•

Using Key Terms

Across

2. foreign-exchange markets
4. market shortage
6. managed exchange rates
8. gold reserves
9. appreciation
10. exchange rate
11. depreciation
13. gold standard
14. equilibrium price
15. balance-of-payments surplus

Down

1. balance-of-payments deficit
2. foreign exchange reserves
3. flexible exchange rate
5. balance of payments
7. devaluation
12. trade deficit

True or False

1. T
2. F Increased foreign travel by Americans tends to increase the demand for foreign currency, thus increasing the supply of U.S. dollars and reducing the value of the dollar.
3. T
4. T
5. T
6. T
7. F U.S. goods will be relatively more expensive to Japan thus reducing exports.
8. F Fixed exchange rates tend to cause balance-of-payments deficits and surpluses because they cause shortages and surpluses of currencies.
9. T
10. F A country experiencing trade deficits will have higher foreign debt and interest rates because that country will have to borrow to finance the additional goods and services it is consuming over what it is producing.

Multiple Choice

1. a	5. b	9. b	13. a	17. c
2. a	6. d	10. d	14. c	18. d
3. c	7. a	11. a	15. b	19. d
4. d	8. d	12. c	16. a	20. b

Problems and Applications

Exercise 1

1. **Figure 21.1 Answer**

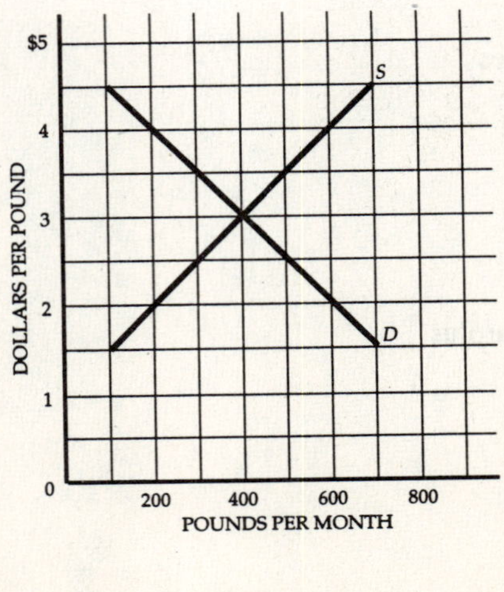

2. $3 per British pound 3. a 4. rise 5. T 6. fall

Exercise 2

1. and 2. **Table 21.2 Answer**

	(1) Demand for $	(2) Supply of $	(3) Demand for £	(4) Supply of £
Foreign demand for American exports	X			X
Foreign demand for American investments	X			X
Speculation that the dollar will appreciate	X			X
American demand for imports		X	X	
American demand for investments in foreign countries		X	X	
Speculation that the dollar will depreciate		X	X	

3. T
4. T

5. and 6. **Table 21.3 Answer**

Price of a £ ($/£) (1)		Quantity of £ demanded (2)		Quantity of $ supplied (3)	Price of a $ (£/$) (4)	Quantity of £ supplied (5)	Quantity of $ demanded (6)
4.50	x	100	=	450	0.222 = 1/4.50	700	3,150
4.00	x	200	=	800	0.25 = 1/4	600	2,400
3.50	x	300	=	1,050	0.29 = 1/3.50	500	1,750
3.00	x	400	=	1,200	0.33 = 1/3	400	1,200
2.50	x	500	=	1,250	0.40 = 1/2.50	300	750
2.00	x	600	=	1,200	0.50 = 1/2	200	400
1.50	x	700	=	1,050	0.67 = 1/1.50	100	150

7. **Figure 21.2 Answer**

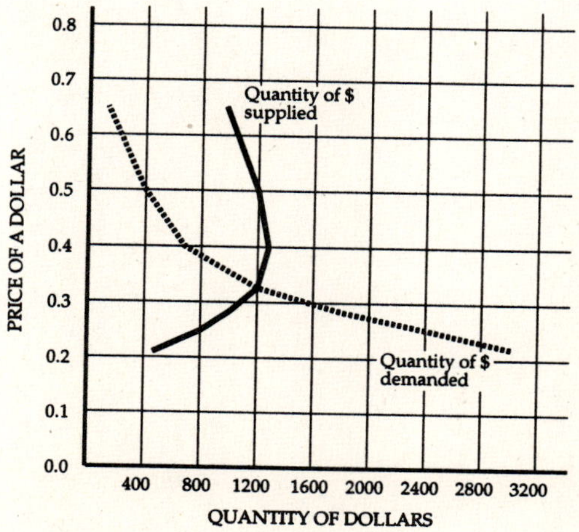

8. 1/3 £ per dollar; $1,200
9. 400 (= 1,200 x 1/3); $3 per pound [= 1/(1/3)]
10. T
11. F The equilibrium exchange rate for the dollar equals the *reciprocal* of the equilibrium exchange rate for the pound.

Exercise 3

1. $1.2 million
2. $958,000
3. The Swedish krona depreciated, which caused the value of the prize to decrease.